YOUR MIDWEST GARDEN

AN OWNER'S MANUAL

JAN RIGGENBACH

UNIVERSITY OF NEBRASKA PRESS • LINCOLN AND LONDON

Library of Congress
Cataloging-in-Publication Data
Riggenbach, Jan.
Your Midwest garden : an owner's
manual / Jan Riggenbach.
p. cm. Includes index.
ISBN 978-0-8032-4009-4
(pbk. : alk. paper)
1. Gardening—Middle West.
2. Plants—Middle West. I. Title.
SB453.2.M53R55 2013
635.0977—dc23 2012037940

Set in Arno and Neutraface
by Laura Wellington.
Designed by Nathan Putens.

CONTENTS

PREFACE

To survive in the Midwest, a plant has to be tough. Tough enough to survive winter's bitter cold, often without the moderating effect of a snow blanket. Tough enough to withstand soaring temperatures in summer as well as the high humidity that encourages foliage diseases. Tough enough to stand up to high winds, severe droughts, even periodic floods.

So, what does it take to make a successful garden in the Midwest, where the prairie soils are rich and the weather is wicked? I've learned by trial and error, first as a curious child in Missouri, then by stuffing plants onto a city yard in Nebraska, and later by planting to my heart's content on an acreage in Iowa.

As a garden writer, I've had a chance to visit hundreds of gardens and research plots throughout the Midwest and enjoy countless hours of "garden talk" with Midwest gardeners.

Experience has gradually taught me which plants can take this climate in their stride and which are better left to other regions. I've learned how to control common Midwest pests and diseases without resorting to chemicals that harm other living things. I continue to search for new tricks to help my plants better cope with the challenges they face.

Since 1975 I've shared my garden successes and failures with readers of my syndicated newspaper column, "Midwest Gardening." This book offers a new look at the best of the information and ideas in those columns, revised and updated, along with charts and an index for easy reference.

Happy gardening!

Author's note: This book is written especially for gardeners in the twelve Midwest states: Illinois, Indiana, Iowa, Kansas, Michigan, Minnesota, Missouri, Nebraska, North Dakota, Ohio, South Dakota, and Wisconsin.

YOUR MIDWEST GARDEN

CHAPTER 1

ANNUALS

SEASONAL SHOWOFFS

Sweltering, sweaty summer days can make the Midwest feel like the Caribbean. So a lot of perennials take a break — from blooming. What's left to make the midsummer garden colorful and exciting? Annuals! They're what give the best Midwest gardens the lush look of the tropics in high summer.

After the first fall frost turns many plants to mush, annuals can fill that void, too, with cold-tolerant varieties sprucing up the landscape until Thanksgiving or even beyond.

With only a single season to live their whole lives, annuals are programmed to bloom their hearts out in all kinds of weather, providing weeks of continuous color.

Dozens of new introductions every year join hundreds of tried-and-true favorites, providing today's gardeners a huge palette of annuals. By selecting some of the newcomers and others from the host of old-fashioned standbys, it's easier than ever to stage your own exciting annual event.

Annuals That Plant Themselves

"Is that plant a perennial or an annual?"

That's one of the most common questions I hear.

If I say the plant is an annual, I often hear a murmured, "Oh, that's too bad," as the eyes of some in the audience glaze over. These are the people who routinely dismiss annuals because of the belief that all annuals require extra time and expense to replant every year.

But that's not true. It's been decades since I've planted many of my favorite annuals in my own garden. These self-seeding annuals return year after year without any effort on my part. Better yet, I never have to dig and divide them, a routine task required to successfully grow most perennials.

All that's necessary for success with self-seeding annuals is to allow some seeds to fall to the ground at the end of the season.

What plants behave this way? One of my favorites is melampodium. These bushy plants, which are covered all season with yellow daisy-like flowers, seem to laugh at heat and drought. And they never require dead-heading, the removal of spent blossoms to encourage new ones.

Another favorite is globe amaranth, also known as gomphrena. I like its cute ball-shaped flowers of lavender, pink, purple, red, or white.

The flower spikes of scarlet sage attract hummingbirds and butterflies all summer. From late summer through fall, volunteer plants of the closely related mealycup sage tint the garden purple.

A low border of volunteer ageratums rings a few shrubs. Towering castor beans and angel's trumpets show off in the back of a border. The daisy-like blossoms of cosmos nod on graceful stems in my cut-flower garden. All of these beauties reappear year after year. What could be easier than that?

SELF-SEEDING ANNUALS AND BIENNIALS

Angel's trumpet (*Datura metel*)
Bachelor buttons (*Centaurea cyanus*)
Black-eyed Susan (*Rudbeckia hirta*)
Castor bean (*Ricinus communis*)
Cosmos (*C. bipinnatus* and *C. sulphureus*)
Dahlberg daisy (*Thymophylla tenuiloba*)
Floss flower (*Ageratum houstonianum*)
Four o'clock (*Mirabilis jalapa*)
Globe amaranth (*Gomphrena globosa*)
Immortelle (*Xeranthemum annuum*)

Kiss-me-over-the-garden-gate (*Persicaria orientalis*, syn. *Polygonum orientale*)

Larkspur (*Consolida ajacis*)

Love-in-a-mist (*Nigella damascena*)

Mealy-cup sage (*Salvia farinacea*)

Melampodium (*M. divaricatum*, syn. *M. paludosum*)

Moss rose (*Portulaca grandiflora*)

Peruvian zinnia (*Z. peruviana*)

Poppy (*Papaver nudicaule*, *P. rhoeas*, and *P. somniferum*)

Pot marigold (*Calendula officinalis*)

Scarlet sage (*Salvia coccinea*)

Spider flower (*Cleome hassleriana*)

Standing cypress (*Ipomopsis rubra*)

Sweet alyssum (*Lobularia maritima*)

Woodland tobacco (*Nicotiana sylvestris*)

Towering Annuals

With the proliferation of bedding plants, many people started to think of annuals as neat but boring little mounds of color. No wonder: tall annuals shoot up so fast they would be a nightmare for a commercial grower to produce in little packs or small pots.

But now, as many gardeners rediscover the joy of growing plants from seed, a kaleidoscope of interesting annuals is showing up in gardens again.

If you have a lot of space to fill, tall annuals are the answer. While perennials take several years to mature, these annuals shoot up to great

BEST BET

If you want to get self-seeding annuals established in your garden, you don't have to wait until spring. In late summer or autumn, just scatter the seeds on the ground where you want the plants to grow. You don't even have to cover the seeds with soil.

heights in just a few weeks. Quick to bloom, most continue flowering until frost.

Here are a few fast-growing annuals that will show off in your Midwest garden:

Castor bean looks like a tropical tree by the end of summer with its huge, palm-shaped leaves towering above other garden plants. Once called "the palm of Christ," castor beans were popular in Victorian gardens.

Choose varieties with purple or red leaves, pink or red flowers, and heights ranging from 3 to 10 feet. Plant them in a sunny spot but, because castor bean seeds are poisonous, avoid planting them where small children play.

Mexican sunflower grows quickly into a dense, shrubby plant 5 or 6 feet tall. The fiery orange or yellow daisy-like flowers that cover the plant from top to bottom are great for cutting, and they attract butterflies, too.

Don't coddle Mexican sunflower; these natives of Mexico like their sun hot and their soil dry.

Hollyhock mallow (*Malva*), a cottage garden favorite, was scorned in Victorian times as too invasive. In my garden, volunteer seedlings are a welcome reminder of the striped pink or purple flowers that will soon bloom.

Although classed as a perennial, hollyhock mallow has always behaved as a self-seeding annual in my garden. Flowering begins in late spring while the plants are only 1 or 2 feet tall. By summer's end, the flower-covered stalks stand an impressive 3 to 5 feet tall. Thriving in sun or partial shade, they are less prone to disease than regular hollyhocks.

Annuals for Summer's Heat

Sooner or later, my perennial garden suffers a summer slump. Somewhere between the riotous blooms of midsummer and the beginning of the fall show of asters and mums, I notice that the prevailing color of perennials is green.

Thank goodness for annual flowers, now full-grown and blooming nonstop. Scattered throughout the perennial beds, annuals get their chance for glory in August.

Many heat-tolerant annuals are surprisingly easy to grow. Cosmos, for example, thrives in poor soil. Silky flowers in crimson, gold, orange, pink, rose, white, or yellow adorn the lacy foliage from midsummer until frost atop plants 2 to 4 feet tall, depending on variety.

Cleome is another great performer that thrives despite heat and drought. Also known as spider flower, cleome always draws plenty of oohs and ahs. The tall, dramatic plants produce masses of large, airy flowers in blends of pink, purple, rose, or white.

Moss rose is a short, heat-loving annual perfect for edging summer flowerbeds. Its fleshy, needle-like leaves help the plants survive dry spells. You can choose varieties with single or double flowers, in any color but true blue. Sundial hybrids offer a wide range of colors, strong performance, and flowers that stay open longer than most other varieties.

A close relative of the persistent weed called purslane, moss rose grows as vigorously as the weed. Go ahead and plant moss rose in poor soil, with minimal water and no fertilizer. That's when it's at its best.

Dahlberg daisy, with its tiny yellow daisies covering 6-inch mounds of fragrant, feathery foliage, is another edging plant that stands up beautifully to summer's heat. From seeds planted many years ago, they persist in my garden, sowing themselves here and there along the garden paths.

Dahlberg daisies look especially nice growing along the brick walk in front of my Zagreb coreopsis, where the pint-sized annuals echo the color, texture, and form of that hardy perennial.

Angelonias, sometimes called summer snapdragons, are adaptable plants that keep right on blooming not only through hot weather but well into autumn, too. With delicate-looking flower spikes filled with two-lipped blossoms that resemble snapdragons, angelonias are available both as upright plants 18 to 30 inches tall and as low, trailing plants that are perfect in baskets. Most named varieties are sold as plants, but, if you prefer, you can grow the Serena series from seed.

Color choices include lavender, orchid, pink, purple, violet, and white, plus some with two-toned flowers. In bouquets, they make beautiful and long-lasting cut flowers.

One reason I like angelonias is because the deer don't.

Cosmos (*Cosmos* species)
Dahlberg daisy (*Thymophylla tenuiloba*)
Euphorbia (*E.* hybrids)
Gazania (*G. rigens*)
Lisianthus (*Eustoma grandiflorum*)
Marigold (*Tagetes* species and hybrids)
Melampodium (*M. divaricatum,* syn. *M. paludosum*)
Moss rose (*Portulaca grandiflora*)
Ornamental pepper (*Capsicum annuum*)
Spider flower (*Cleome hassleriana*)
Summer snapdragon (*Angelonia angustifolia* and hybrids)
Vinca (*Catharanthus roseus*)
Zinnia (all *Zinnia* species and hybrids)

PRETTY PENTAS

I first got to know pentas one particularly brutal summer. Some of my annuals in containers had "cooked" in the blazing sun by August, so I went to a local garden center in search of replacements.

Pentas, also known as Egyptian star-flowers, caught my eye. They were the only plants in the place that still looked springtime fresh, with clusters of star-shaped flowers and handsome dark-green foliage.

The pentas I took home that day staged a continuous show that lasted until frost. Butterflies and hummingbirds, which paid constant visits to the flowers, doubled my admiration for these durable plants.

In recent years plant breeders have been developing pentas that are even more desirable. Compact, early-blooming varieties grow about 12 to 15 inches tall. You can choose pentas in a variety of colors, including lavender, magenta, mauve, pink, red, rose, and white.

Pentas are a perfect choice if your containers tend to get too thirsty before you can get back with more water; they actually prefer to dry out a little between waterings.

Rushing to set pentas out in spring is counterproductive, since night-time temperatures below 50 degrees delay flowering.

If you have a sun-baked container or garden spot where the soil dries out as soon as you turn your back, you can't go wrong with vinca.

Flowering vinca (*Catharanthus*, not to be confused with *Vinca minor*, the ground cover, aka creeping myrtle or periwinkle) is the quintessential low-maintenance annual. As long as you don't pamper vinca with too much food and water, or plant it where an automatic sprinkler keeps the leaves too wet, vinca looks fabulous all summer. No need to spend any time cutting off dying blossoms. Vinca is self-cleaning; spent flowers simply fall off by themselves.

And vinca is adaptable. Although it owes its fame to the ability to withstand sun-baked soil, this annual also puts on a respectable performance in partial shade. I depend on it in a spot with a difficult mix of morning shade and afternoon sun, where impatiens would be doomed.

You'll find a wide selection of vinca varieties in lavender, pink, purple, red, rose, or white wherever bedding plants are sold. I'm particularly fond of a deep violet vinca called First Kiss Blueberry, winner of an All-America Selections award. If you prefer to grow your own transplants, vinca is also easy to grow from seed, although it needs an eight- to ten-week head start indoors.

While vinca is normally trouble free, an unusually cool or wet summer can spell disaster. Disease encouraged by such conditions can turn leaves yellow, stunt plants, and eventually kill vinca. That's why I'm excited about Cora, a vigorous, disease-resistant vinca series that thrives even under adverse conditions. After extensive trials leading up to the Olympics in Beijing, Cora was selected for large display beds after outlasting competing varieties from all over the world.

The series offers unusually big flowers and sturdy, vigorous plants that grow 14 to 16 inches tall and about 2 feet wide.

BEST BET

Don't rush flowering vinca into the ground. If planted before the weather is warm and settled, vinca just sits and sulks. It might even succumb to root rot or other fungus disease.

There's nothing delicate about a zinnia, my husband, Don's, favorite flower. Although Don is a tree man who's more apt to see high tree branches than low flowers, the little patches of zinnias that brighten our vegetable garden never fail to win his admiration. He tells me he just likes the fact that such tough, coarse-textured plants are also so colorful.

So when cool-season peas and spinach vacate their space in the garden, I often scatter seeds of fancy zinnias to fill the empty spots. The big, bold blossoms look like dahlia or cactus flowers.

Zinnias grow quickly and easily from seed planted directly in the garden. In fact, that's the best way to grow them, since they resent transplanting and tall varieties left in plant packs too long seldom recover. Quick to flower, the plants keep blooming until frost.

Natives of Mexico, zinnias thrive in hot, dry weather in full sun. The seeds I sow in midsummer usually escape the powdery mildew and other fungus diseases that often take a heavy toll on zinnias planted in spring in this region.

To keep zinnias healthy as long as possible, avoid overhead watering. Thin tall, fancy-flowered varieties to allow 18 inches between plants so air can circulate freely. Remove flowers as soon as they fade. Or take the easy way out and plant disease-resistant varieties.

Although you won't find disease resistance in zinnias that have giant 4- to 6-inch flowers, there are smaller, mounding zinnias, like the award-winning Profusion series, that are seldom bothered by disease. Not long-stemmed beauties for cutting, they have simple, daisy-like flowers. These foot-tall zinnias are nevertheless perfect for a mixed border. Butterflies seem to prefer the single blossoms, too. And you'll never have to deadhead these zinnias. New leaves cover the fading blossoms as 2- to 3-inch, daisy-like flowers continue to open.

Zahara zinnias, a series with good disease-resistance, offer bigger blossoms on slightly taller plants.

Persian Carpet zinnias, a cultivar of the narrow-leaf species, not only stay healthy but also do a reliable job of reseeding themselves year after year. Their small flowers bloom in a cheerful mix of bright colors.

TOUGH EUPHORBIAS

Once in a while a new plant comes along that zooms to the top of the popularity charts as soon as gardeners realize it is much more than just another pretty face.

An annual euphorbia named Diamond Frost did just that. This no-fail plant thrives in sun or shade. It tolerates exceptional heat and drought and can even quickly revive itself from a near-death experience if you forget to water it. The plants seem to be nearly immune to pests and diseases.

In autumn, the show goes on despite the arrival of cold weather. If you can't bear to give it up for winter, Diamond Frost will even continue to bloom indoors as a houseplant. In winter, it's a hit when paired with holiday poinsettias.

Oh, and did I mention that this tough and durable plant is also gorgeous? Its sprays of tiny white flowers resembling baby's breath contrast with attractive dark-green foliage. The plant looks great whether you give it a pot of its own or combine it with other plants in a container.

Sold already blooming in small pots, Diamond Frost just keeps getting better. Eventually it grows about 18 inches tall and wide.

More recently, Breathless Blush with red-flushed foliage and Breathless White have joined the lineup of annual euphorbias. You can't grow any of these euphorbias from seed. Look for started plants at garden centers.

SHEARING FOR RENEWAL

When the lobelia stops blooming and some of its stems turn brown, I don't panic. That's just the way lobelia registers its displeasure with hot weather.

With a light shearing and enough water to keep the soil moist, I know the lobelia will bounce back in full bloom as soon as cool weather returns.

The sweet alyssum edging the garden path also languishes in the heat of summer. So, looking forward to a new round of its tiny, sweet-scented blossoms when cooler weather arrives in fall, I give my plants a heavy shearing to help them recharge. Rejuvenated, sweet alyssum often blooms until Thanksgiving or beyond.

Moss rose is a different story. The succulent leaves of this low creeper aren't fazed by the dog days of August. Unlike lobelia, moss rose thrives in dry soil where little else will grow. Nevertheless, moss rose plants also benefit from a light summer shearing. Shearing removes the seed capsules, shaves a few inches off the height, and promotes a fresh round of the 1-inch blooms.

Other annuals that benefit from a light midsummer shearing when they start looking ratty include ageratum, China pinks, Swan River daisy, and trailing verbena.

Cold-Weather Annuals

Of all cold-weather showoffs in our region, pansies are the best known. Blooming with large or small blossoms and with plain or fancy "faces," they come in your choice of bright colors or pastels.

To keep pansies blooming longer, snap off faded flowers. When plants get leggy and stop blooming in hot weather, shear them back to about 2 inches and add fertilizer. Healthy plants will rebound in cool weather.

Thanks to work by plant breeders, we can now plant pansies in autumn in our Midwest gardens and enjoy those same pansies again in spring, just like southern gardeners have been doing for ages.

The keys to winter survival for pansies in our region: a spot with good drainage where water doesn't stand, and a mulch such as shredded leaves pulled up snug around plants after the ground freezes.

Varieties with medium-size flowers are more apt to survive winter than giant-flowered pansies. I've had good luck with Inspire, Maxim, Universal Plus, and Cool Wave pansies.

COLD-TOLERANT NEWCOMERS

Choosing annuals for cool-weather containers? Don't stop with pansies. Thanks to some cold-tolerant newcomers, spring and autumn gardening in the Midwest offers many other exciting possibilities.

Diascia, or twinspur, for example. My diascia plants amaze me by producing a continuous show of tubular flowers late in the season, sometimes even lasting until mid-December.

A member of the snapdragon family, diascia comes in apricot, coral, peach, pink, rose, and white. Many varieties have a sprawling form that combines well with other plants and looks nice in a hanging basket.

Plant tags often recommend a site with full sun for diascia. But I've discovered that my plants are more likely to survive the searing heat of a typical Midwest summer if grown in a spot sheltered from the hot afternoon sun.

Nemesia, also a member of the snapdragon family, is another hot new plant for cool-weather containers.

A small plant no more than a foot tall, nemesia takes a break from blooming in hot weather. But once temperatures cool down in fall, it's covered with small, snapdragon-like blossoms of pink, purple, red, white, or yellow. Compact Innocence, a white-flowered variety, emits a powerfully sweet perfume.

Nemesia grows well in sun or partial shade.

Cape daisies (*Osteospermum*) are also great candidates for spring or autumn color: If you wonder all summer why yours aren't blooming, you'll find out in the fall. Like a lot of us, they eagerly wait for some chilly weather.

Wonderful for bouquets, cape daisies have big daisy-like flowers in many bright and muted colors. Choose cream, magenta, mauve, orange, peach, pink, purple, white, or yellow. Many varieties have azure-blue centers.

Also known as African daisies, cape daisies bloom best when grown in full sun and poor but well-drained soil. The more you cut, the more they bloom.

AUTUMN RENAISSANCE

With the arrival of crisp autumn weather, heat-loving annuals like vinca and impatiens decline, then die at the first touch of frost. But the show isn't over yet. Fall temperatures are just the boost some garden flowers need for an end-of-season burst of color.

In autumn, the snapdragons that bloomed admirably in my garden in spring, then languished in the heat, are once again covered with colorful spikes.

Calendulas, or pot marigolds, bloom in yellow and orange, sometimes with a tint of copper or red. The plants can survive repeated frost and often bloom through Thanksgiving.

Annual blue salvias are a special delight in autumn. I love the bright blue spikes of tubular flowers and smooth, soft, gray-green leaves.

Because I allow some seeds to drop to the ground every autumn, I enjoy informal groups of self-sown blue salvias nestled among earlier-blooming perennials.

Cup flowers make pint-size edging plants and are also ideal for draping over the sides of containers. Their blue or white, 1-inch flowers bloom all summer, but they really shine when the weather cools. Flowering often lasts late into the fall.

COLD-WEATHER ANNUALS

Cape daisy (*Osteospermum* hybrids)
China pinks (*Dianthus chinensis*)
Cup flower (*Nierembergia hippomanica*)
Mealy-cup sage (*Salvia farinacea*)
Nemesia (*N. strumosa*)
Ornamental cabbage and kale (*Brassica oleracea*)
Pansy (*Viola × wittrockiana*)
Pot marigold (*Calendula officinalis*)
Snapdragon (*Antirrhinum majus*)
Stock (*Matthiola incana*)
Twinspur diascia (*D.* hybrids)

STOCKS YOU CAN GROW

If you've never heard of garden stocks, ask your grandmother. They're old-fashioned flowers, so named because of their thick stems.

Stocks are beginning to earn a place in modern gardens, too, as more folks discover their sweet cinnamon scent and beautiful flowering spikes filled with double blossoms. Best of all, stocks are a cool-season flower you can enjoy before the weather is warm enough for most bedding plants.

There are many different kinds of stocks, ranging from 8-inch dwarfs to varieties 2 feet tall. One type often grown in today's gardens is called ten-week stocks, because it bursts into bloom about ten weeks after the seeds are planted. The foot-tall plants are very fragrant and come in shades of pink, purple, and white.

It's easy to grow stocks from seed. Just firm the seeds onto the soil without covering them, because the seeds need light to sprout. Give seeds a six-week head start indoors, starting seeds in individual pots. As the popularity of stocks continues to grow, no doubt transplants will become easier to find.

Stocks are perfect for planting in containers near the door, so you can enjoy their early spring color and fragrance, along with pansies, snapdragons, China pinks, and other cold-hardy annuals. During spring's cool weather, all perform best in full sun.

FLOWERING CABBAGES AND KALES

After the first fall frost, flowering cabbages and kales are in their prime. The colorful leaves of these cool-weather plants usually last at least through Thanksgiving, often beyond.

Deciding which ones are cabbages and which are kales depends on whom you ask, since the names are often used interchangeably. Many gardeners settle it by calling a variety that forms a head, an ornamental cabbage; one that grows in a clump of curly or fringed leaves, an ornamental kale.

Both are bicolored with splashes of red, pink, white, green, or purple, their outer leaves usually darker than the contrasting centers.

Some gardeners delight in planting these ornamentals from seed in spring and nurturing them through the season. It's rewarding and inexpensive, but there's a catch: You have to be willing to spray or dust the plants all summer long or the leaves will be riddled by cabbage worms. And there's nothing very ornamental about that! I usually take the easy way out and buy them as bedding plants in early autumn.

BEST BET

Ornamental cabbages and kales are edible, but vegetable varieties taste better. Go ahead and use leaves of one of the ornamental varieties for an attractive garnish, but stick to the vegetable types for your salads.

OLD-FASHIONED PINKS

Thanks to the work of plant breeders, an old-fashioned garden annual is better than ever. China pinks, long appreciated for their cool-weather performance, now come in hybrids that have built-in heat tolerance, too.

I watch in amazement as a hybrid called Corona Cherry Magic blooms again and again in a window box despite periods of hot temperatures.

An All-America Selections winner, Corona Cherry Magic owes its "magic" to the variable coloring of its flowers. Sometimes they're cherry red, sometimes lavender. Other times, you'll see almost a tie-dyed effect or a mosaic of both colors, marked with stripes, flecks, or contrasting centers. Corona Cherry Magic grows about 8 inches tall with flowers that are often twice as big as the 1-inch blossoms of most other varieties of pinks.

The Ideal series offers heat-tolerant pinks in your choice of a full range of colors, including solids and bicolors, on 10-inch-tall plants. If you're looking for more compact plants, the Super Parfait series grows only 6 to 8 inches tall.

As cooler fall temperatures arrive, expect all varieties of pinks to thrive. Unlike more tender annuals, pinks easily survive light frosts. Try them in fall containers as partners for other cold-tolerant annuals such as pansies, twinspurs, and pot marigolds.

With their bright, cheerful colors and a sometimes-spicy fragrance, pinks have low, mounded shapes and charming fringed petals that look like they've been "pinked" with shears. These short plants are a longtime favorite for growing along the paths of a cottage garden.

Pinks thrive in full sun in well-drained soil. Allow room for good air circulation and add mulch to help keep the roots cool.

When most of the flowers fade, give the plants a light shearing to encourage reblooms.

When conditions are just right, annual pinks sometimes behave more like short-lived perennials, surviving for a winter or two. I've even had plants overwinter in a container on occasion. If old flowers aren't sheared before seeds form, pinks may also self-sow, producing a new crop of plants of varying heights and colors.

Annuals for Shade

If you have a garden in the shade, chances are you already love impatiens. As easy to grow as they are beautiful, impatiens bloom profusely in spots too shady for most other annuals.

Choosing which kinds of impatiens to grow is probably more complicated than actually growing them. The choice of colors, sizes, and forms is expanding rapidly, with many exciting new varieties.

You can find impatiens in every color of the rainbow except true blue. Some have bicolored blossoms, with dark-edged petals or white stars. Leaf color may be bright green or dark bronze. Flower form varies, too, from single to semi-double to fully double flowers.

Impatiens are easy to grow from seed but need an early start indoors in late February or early March for good-sized transplants ready to set out in May.

If you prefer to buy plants, you'll find a good selection of impatiens offered as bedding plants in spring.

After danger of spring frost, plant impatiens outdoors in a spot protected from sun. Plants bloom best in filtered shade, such as beneath a tree with high branches. Add compost to the soil but hold off on nitrogen fertilizers, which produce more height and less flowers.

Impatiens love the Midwest's humid summer weather and thrive in a moist but well-drained soil. Pests and diseases are seldom a problem. The continuously blooming plants always look neat and clean, since dead blossoms simply drop off on their own.

If you want to plant impatiens under a mature tree, plant the flowers in containers sunk into the ground. That way, the impatiens won't have to compete with the tree's roots for water and nutrients.

The height of impatiens plants is affected primarily by variety, but distance between plants affects height, too; plants grow taller the closer together you put them. Generally, spacing plants 8 to 10 inches apart will produce a nice display.

For containers that get morning sun and afternoon shade, New Guinea hybrid impatiens are ideal. Robust plants with large flowers and colorful foliage, they are quite showy.

I count on the Fusion series of impatiens for spectacular plants that are always hummingbird favorites. Not your average impatiens, they have exotic, almost tropical-looking, cup-shaped flowers in your choice of apricot, coral, peach, or yellow. Growing up to 16 inches tall and wide, the plants are quite a bit larger than ordinary impatiens.

What other annuals thrive in the shade? Torenia, also called the wishbone flower, is one of my favorites. Its snapdragon-like blossoms come in pink, purple, and yellow. Today's varieties are vastly improved over the old seed-grown varieties I used to grow.

Bush violet has delicate, trumpet-shaped flowers of blue-purple or white.

Wax begonias, which come in many colorful choices, tolerate the heat and humidity of a Midwest summer exceptionally well.

Veranda helmet flower has bicolored blue-purple flower spikes reminiscent of its sun-loving relatives, the salvias. The glossy, dark-green foliage is attractive, too.

Maracas Brazilian fireworks is a delightfully unique tropical plant from South America. Each exotic bloom stalk has a striking and long-lasting hot-pink central core punctuated by small lavender-purple flowers. The plants have fantastic foliage, too, with silver markings on the long, angular, deep-green leaves. Only about 8 inches tall, they bloom beautifully even in deep shade.

BEST BET

To thwart the fungus disease known as impatiens downy mildew, select only plants that have healthy, dark-green leaves. Immediately remove and bag any impatiens plant that shows early signs of the disease: pale green foliage with subtle mottling, leaves turned downward, and white downy growth on the underside of the leaves. Rotate impatiens with other shade-loving annuals such as wax begonias and coleus. In beds with partial sun, plant New Guinea impatiens and SunPatiens; both appear to be immune to impatiens downy mildew.

Brazilian fireworks (*Porphyrocoma pohliana*)

Bush violet (*Browallia speciosa*)

Coleus (*Solenostemon scutellariodes*)

Dragon Wing begonia (*Begonia* hybrid)

Helmet flower (*Scutellaria javanica*)

Impatiens (*I. walleriana*)

New Guinea impatiens (*I. hawkeri*)

Wax begonia (*B. semperflorens-cultorum*)

Wishbone flower (*Torenia* hybrids)

......

Favorites for Sun

Compared to the list of shade-loving annuals, the list of plants that will thrive in full sun is long. It includes most of the region's longtime favorites like petunias, marigolds, sunflowers, verbenas, and geraniums. Many newer annuals, such as fan flower and calibrachoa, also love the sun.

PRETTY PETUNIAS

Amidst all the jokes about Midwest weather, petunias get the last laugh.

These colorful annuals can take the heat. Once established, they stand up well to drought. Petunias tolerate cold, too, blooming continuously until the first hard frost. And though they look bedraggled after a heavy rain, most kinds of petunias recover their good looks quickly once they dry.

Petunias' trumpet-shaped blossoms come in a wider range of colors than any other flower. You also have the choice of plain or ruffled, single or double, solid or bicolored. Some varieties have contrasting veins, fringed edges, or white-tipped petals.

Along with their colorful flowers all summer long, many petunias — especially older varieties — add a sweet fragrance to the evening air. Butterflies and hummingbirds adore the flowers.

Today's gardeners can choose from trailing varieties ideal for hanging baskets and window boxes, spreading types that quickly carpet the ground with color, and petite plants just the right size to grow in a bowl. Closely related calibrachoas, often called miniature petunias, offer dainty petunia-like blossoms that are perfect for planting in pots.

No matter what type of petunias you choose, they all prefer plenty of sun. All day sun is best; half day is acceptable. They like moist soil but also require good drainage. While many kinds tolerate poor soil, the vigorous spreading petunias, like the popular Wave series, have big appetites. If you're growing them in a container, add fertilizer to the water every two weeks. If you plant your petunias in a garden bed, add compost plus a light sprinkle of a slow-release organic fertilizer at planting time.

What can go wrong with petunias? The most common problem is the plants' tendency to get "leggy." Pinch back a few of the longest stems every couple of weeks to keep the plants looking their best. If you're leaving for a vacation, pinch back all the stems to new, vigorous growth. By the time you get home, the petunias will be lush and beautiful again.

Like tomatoes and potatoes, petunias belong to the nightshade family. To lessen problems with disease, choose a spot for your petunias where no members of the family have grown recently.

Petunias, like people, are more apt to suffer from disease if stressed. Reducing stress for petunias means making sure they have enough food and water. Don't overdo, though; soggy soil encourages root rot.

If a petunia develops leaf spots or mottled foliage, remove the plant before your other petunias are infected.

If flowering suddenly stops, tobacco budworms may be to blame.

BEST BET

If the foliage of petunias or calibrachoas turns light green, the plants are probably announcing their need for fertilizer. Add a few drops of acid fertilizer each time you water. Besides providing nutrients, an acid fertilizer also helps counter the effect of frequent additions of tap water, which is alkaline. Better yet, install an attractive rain barrel to collect rainwater from the roof and use that to water your container plants.

Handpicking the worms at dusk, when the caterpillars are most active, is one of the best options available to the home gardener.

Plant breeders have been hard at work, bringing us a wide choice of colors, sizes, and habits in verbenas. Some varieties are grown from seed, others from cuttings. Some have fine, feathery foliage, others broader leaves.

Small upright verbenas, such as the 'Quartz' series, grow 8 to 10 inches tall, ideal for window boxes. Others have a trailing form, ideal for cascading over the sides of a container or wall, or covering the ground with a carpet of color. But all have large, showy clusters of tiny flowers that add color to the garden for months on end.

Verbenas respond well to mulch, which preserves moisture and helps keep the roots cool. Remove spent flowers on upright types to promote continued blooming. If trailing types stop blooming in hot weather, shear them lightly.

In 1993, a verbena named Imagination won an All-America Selections award. One of the first of the trailing types, it has violet-blue flowers and fine, lacy foliage on branches that sprawl 2 feet in all directions. Easy to grow from seed, it's generally free of disease and inexpensive enough to use lavishly in the garden as a ground cover or in hanging baskets and other containers.

In recent years, many other new trailing types have joined Imagination. The ever-increasing choice of colors in trailing verbenas now includes lilac, light or dark pink, rose, purple, and light blue.

BEST BET

Stressed verbenas are prone to powdery mildew. Pale-colored leaves are often the first sign of this fungus disease. Soon white powdery patches develop, then the leaves turn yellow and die. To help prevent mildew, allow plenty of room for good air circulation. Don't let the soil dry out. Remove any infected stems and destroy severely infected plants.

Geraniums are survivors. They're the only annuals I've ever seen that can withstand the horror of growing in a pot filled with clay soil and left to bake in the sun.

Of course, geraniums perform best when treated to more loving care. But there's no question that geraniums are one of the easiest and most adaptable annuals.

The only thing geraniums absolutely won't tolerate is "wet feet." The plants always rebel if their soil stays soggy.

If geraniums could have their pick of growing conditions, what else would they choose? Full sun for at least half a day. Rich, well-drained soil. And water when the soil surface feels dry to the touch, with half-strength fertilizer added every second or third watering.

Technically, these favorite bedding plants belong to the genus *Pelargonium*; the scientific name *Geranium* belongs to a group of closely related perennials. By the time the scientists who name plants figured out they had made a mistake in grouping the plants together, the name had already stuck.

There are many types of tender geraniums. Zonal geraniums, named for the horseshoe-shaped band of color on their leaves, are the type we all know best. Red is still the most popular color, but pink, lavender, lilac, salmon, rose, and white are gaining. These pastel-colored blossoms seem to glow in the evening light, welcoming you outdoors at the end of the day.

Fancy-leaf varieties offer chartreuse or multicolored foliage, sometimes ruffled or shiny, sometimes with glorious scent. They combine beautifully with other plants in large containers.

Regal, or Martha Washington, geraniums are much admired for their huge, showy blossoms. But they're finicky to grow in the Midwest, where summer nights are too hot for their liking.

The beautiful trailing ivy geraniums, with leaves that resemble true ivy, are finicky, too. When hot weather arrives, they often stop blooming. A better bet for hanging baskets in our region: alpine ivies, floribundas, or cascade geraniums. All bloom better than ivy geraniums when our summers turn hot.

To keep all types of geraniums looking their best and also help prevent disease and pest problems, regularly pick off and destroy any yellow leaves and dead flowers.

If flowering temporarily ceases during a summer heat wave, it's often because geraniums don't like the hot temperature. You might be able to help by moving potted plants into the shade on hot afternoons.

Tobacco budworms are a more troubling cause for lack of flowers. Early signs of trouble: buds with tiny holes surrounded by a substance that resembles sawdust, and flowers with ragged-looking petals.

To control budworms, handpicking is one of the best options for the home gardener. Check plants at dusk, when the caterpillars are most active. While young caterpillars are likely to be busy tunneling through small buds and stems, larger caterpillars should be easy to spot chewing holes in petals, buds, and leaves. Look for striped caterpillars of almost any color, including red, dark brown, and green.

If buds dry up before they open, the problem is sometimes blamed on low humidity in western regions of this country. Here in the Midwest, though, low humidity is not usually a problem unless, of course, you're trying to grow a potted geranium in an air-conditioned house. Instead, the more likely culprits are tiny insects called thrips. To check, pull open a bud and inspect the base of the petals for the pests.

To control thrips, pick off and destroy any dried-up buds, then spray the plants with insecticidal soap.

If the leaves have water-soaked spots that eventually turn brown and corky, you're probably overwatering.

Sunken brown or tan spots on the leaves are a sign of a bacterial disease.

BEST BET

It goes without saying that you should choose only geraniums with healthy foliage to bring in for winter or to use for taking cuttings. If you've had a budworm problem outdoors, it would be well worth the time to repot that prized geranium in fresh soil before bringing it in for winter.

It's often spread by splashing water, or whiteflies. Keep geranium foliage dry whenever possible and control whiteflies with insecticidal soap.

If large angular patches on the leaves die and stems shrivel and turn black, destroy the infected plant.

WEAVE MAGIC WITH MARIGOLDS

You don't have to have a green thumb to succeed with marigolds. As long as you plant them in a sunny garden spot, marigolds are some of the easiest flowers to grow.

Many folks buy marigolds in plant packs, but you can also plant marigold seeds right in your garden. The big seeds are easy to handle and quick to sprout. Gardeners who are willing to start with seeds can choose from a much bigger selection of varieties.

When I think of marigolds, I usually picture yellow or orange flowers. But marigolds also come in burgundy, red, and creamy white, with many variations in between.

Most trouble-free of all marigolds are the French varieties, which grow only 6 to 12 inches tall. I'm partial to one called 'Golden Gates', an All-America Selections winner that features gold and maroon bicolored blooms twice the size of most other French marigolds.

African marigolds such as the 'Inca' series grow into big shrubby plants, with carnation-like blossoms.

A third type, called signet marigold, doesn't even look like a marigold. The lacy foliage doesn't smell like one, either; the delightful fragrance is more like that of a lemon. The plants, only about 8 inches tall, produce masses of dainty, single flowers. Lemon Gem is one of the best.

Marigolds don't generally suffer from problems, but if the weather turns hot and dry, look out for spider mites. These tiny pests suck sap

BEST BET

Gray mold, or botrytis, may cover marigolds' decaying leaves, stems, and spent flowers with spots and mold, especially in cool, wet weather. To help control gray mold, regularly remove old flowers from the plants.

out of the leaves, leaving the plants looking pale and lifeless and covered with tiny webs. Discouraging spider mites is easy; just hose the plants off with water every day or two.

If leaves wilt, then yellow and die, a fungus that attacks the roots and spreads into the stems is the likely culprit. This problem is most common when tall varieties of marigolds grow in waterlogged soil. Remove any plants that show such symptoms, and don't plant marigolds in the same place again, since the fungus remains in the soil indefinitely.

Aster yellows can turn marigold leaves yellow and stunt the plants. If you see a plant showing such symptoms, pull it out and dispose of it before leafhoppers can spread the infection to healthy plants.

More often than not, marigolds perform perfectly, brightening Midwest gardens for months with their bright blossoms.

SUNFLOWERS

When I picture a sunflower, it's gigantic and golden-yellow, perched atop a tall stalk. But as I look around at the variety of sunflowers blooming in gardens, I realize it's time to update my mental image.

These days, sunflowers are also red, bronze, orange, white, or pale yellow, with centers of green, black, brown, or yellow.

Compared to most other flowers, all sunflowers are big. But by sunflower standards, the flowers of some varieties are downright small, measuring only 4 inches across. Some of the plants still tower over my head, but now you can also choose from a full range of smaller sizes, including 16-inch dwarfs that are small enough to grow in pots.

Besides the traditional single-stalk sunflowers that produce one flower per plant, there are also bushy varieties with many side branches that have several dozen blooms on a single plant.

Perhaps the most startling change in sunflowers is the introduction of plants that produce no pollen and therefore no seed. This type was bred primarily for the cut-flower industry. The advantages are that the flowers are long lasting, and there's no pollen to stain the tablecloth or other indoor surfaces. Pollen-free sunflowers are also good garden performers, blooming over a long period. And without the weight of developing seeds, the flowers don't droop.

Most sunflowers, however, still produce seed, no matter how small, and that's a plus if you love birds. It's a treat to watch goldfinches flock to the plants as soon as the seeds begin to ripen.

If you hope to eat the seeds yourself, though, the best variety is still Mammoth Russian. Its giant flowers produce lots of big seeds. As soon as the seeds start to ripen, clip off the seed heads, leaving a foot-long stem attached to each flower head. Then, hang the flowers by their stems in a protected place, such as a garage, where the birds can't get to them.

Better yet, lay the flowers face down on a sheet of screen wire suspended from the garage ceiling. As the sunflowers dry, any seeds that drop will be caught by the screen.

After several weeks, rub your hand over each head to remove the remaining seeds.

LISIANTHUS

In the southern Great Plains, Texas bluebells were once a common sight. Now this American native is turning heads in Midwest gardens.

Known in our region as lisianthus, the blossoms are prized both for their exquisite beauty and their long life as cut flowers. Buds shaped like rosebuds open to silky flowers that look something like poppies.

In recent years, lisianthus has attracted the attention of hybridizers. Now, besides the original purple-blue, you can choose from more than a dozen colors and bicolors. Heights vary greatly, too, from dwarf plants ideal for growing in window boxes to long-stemmed beauties with sprays of blossoms that stand 3 feet tall.

My favorite for a steady supply of beautiful blue flowers to fill my

BEST BET

Insects sometimes eat the insides of stored sunflower kernels. There are two easy ways to prevent this damage. Bake the loose seeds for ten minutes in a 250-degree oven, or put the seeds in a plastic bag in the freezer for several days. Then store the seeds in a closed container. To roast sunflower seeds for a snack, spread them on a cookie sheet and bake at 350 degrees until the seeds swell and the hulls crack.

vases is a lisianthus called Forever Blue. This compact, 12-inch-tall variety earned an All-America Selections award for its dense branching that produces bountiful blooms all summer.

Lisianthus grows best in full sun but also tolerates partial shade. If the summer turns out to be hot and dry, so much the better. Flowers cut for bouquets will last a week or two. If you prefer to enjoy the flowers in the garden, snip off spent flowers to keep the plants looking their best and promote continued blooming.

You can grow lisianthus from seed, but you have to start them indoors by mid-February at the latest. These seeds need warmth and light to sprout. Transplants are also readily available in spring to plant after danger of frost.

For best results, plant lisianthus in soil that is rich, moist, and well drained. The plants grow very slowly in spring, but you needn't worry: once hot summer weather arrives, lisianthus speeds up.

Pests and diseases are seldom a problem. If aphids congregate on the leaves or buds, spray with insecticidal soap.

To make tall types of lisianthus grow bushier, pinch off growing tips several times early in the season. Otherwise, these varieties may require staking.

DEPENDABLE POPPIES

If you start itching to get into the garden in early spring, grab a packet of poppy seeds and get going. March is perfect for planting poppies. You don't even have to wait for the soil to be dry enough to rake. Just scatter the seeds on bare soil or even on top of the snow, allowing the seeds to settle into the soil as the snow melts.

Poppies thrive with little care, performing best in dry soil with no extra fertilizer. Sowing seeds where you want poppies to grow works best, because poppies don't take readily to transplanting.

Just ninety days after sowing seeds of most kinds of annual poppies, expect the first nodding flower buds to open into silky flowers, held high on their wiry stems.

Corn poppies, the beloved scarlet flowers from the famous World War I poem, "In Flanders Fields," are still popular today in informal cottage gardens. Shirley poppies, another longtime favorite, often have double flowers with extra petals and come in various blends of pink, red, rose, salmon, and white. There are also frilly, peony-flowered poppies that bloom in pink, purple, red, or white.

Iceland poppies are usually described as perennial, but here in the Midwest I think it's more accurate to call them annuals. Our summer heat, not winter's cold, is what stands in the way of their long life. Fortunately, they make fine annuals; seeds sown in early spring will bloom the first summer. If the plants survive to bloom another year, consider it a bonus.

Usually about a foot tall, Iceland poppies are shorter than most other poppies. Their fragrant flowers come in a full range of colors that includes cream and yellow, as well as more common poppy colors.

Poppies are prolific self-seeders. I used to let all the seeds drop to the ground. The result: a beautiful cut-flower garden in June, followed by lots of empty space after the poppies gave up in the heat of summer.

Nowadays, I clip off most of the pods before they dump their seeds, while allowing the pods on my prettiest plants to mature. The result: my own strain of beautiful poppies, in my favorite colors, in just the right number.

ANNUALS FOR SUN

Angel's trumpet (*Datura metel*)
Bachelor buttons (*Centaurea cyanus*)
Calibrachoa (*C.* × *hybrida*)
Castor bean (*Ricinus communis*)
Celosia (*C. argentea*)
Cosmos (*Cosmos* species)

BEST BET

All poppies make wonderful cut flowers, provided you stop the flow of milky sap that seeps from their stems after cutting. Searing the cut stem over a flame or dipping the end in boiling water should do the trick. The more often you cut, the longer poppies bloom, with the show often lasting six to eight weeks.

Cup flower (*Nierembergia hippomanica*)

Dahlberg daisy (*Thymophylla tenuiloba*)

Egyptian star-flower (*Pentas lanceolata*)

Fan flower (*Scaevola aemula*)

Floss flower (*Ageratum houstonianum*)

Four o'clock (*Mirabilis jalapa*)

Gazania (*G. rigens*)

Globe amaranth (*Gomphrena globosa*)

Immortelle (*Xeranthemum annuum*)

Kiss-me-over-the-garden-gate (*Persicaria orientalis*, syn. *Polygonum orientale*)

Lantana (*L. camara*)

Larkspur (*Consolida ajacis*)

Love-in-a-mist (*Nigella damascena*)

Lisianthus (*Eustoma grandiflorum*)

Marigold (*Tagetes* species)

Mealy-cup sage (*Salvia farinacea*)

Melampodium (*M. divaricatum*, syn. *M. paludosum*)

Mexican sunflower (*Tithonia rotundifolia*)

Moss rose (*Portulaca grandiflora*)

Ornamental pepper (*Capsicum annuum*)

Petunia (*P.* × *hybrida*)

Poppy (*Papaver nudicaule*, *P. rhoeas*, and *P. somniferum*)

Pot marigold (*Calendula officinalis*)

Scarlet sage (*Salvia coccinea*)

Spider flower (*Cleome hassleriana*)

Sunflower (*Helianthus annuus*)

Summer cypress (*Bassia scoparia*, syn. *Kochia scoparia*)

Sweet alyssum (*Lobularia maritima*)

Verbena (*V.* × *hybrida*)

Vinca (*Catharanthus roseus*)

Zinnia (*Zinnia* species and hybrids)

Easy-Care Candidates for Containers

Growing flowers in containers doesn't have to be difficult. Some plants are so fail-proof, they threaten to turn all brown thumbs green.

Dragon Wing begonia, for example. Whether I plant it in sun or shade, I know this heat-lover will sail through the summer without any problems. It's ideal for large containers, hanging baskets, or window boxes where the sturdy, foot-tall plant can show off its huge, shiny leaves and dangling clusters of red or pink flowers.

My appreciation for lantana as an easy container plant goes back many years, soon after our move to the country. That dry summer, hordes of grasshoppers ate just about every plant in sight and even nibbled some holes in our new nylon window screens. But they didn't touch the lantanas.

I'm guessing it's the citrus scent of lantana's bright-green leaves that puts off insects but, whatever it is, I've yet to see a lantana leaf serve as lunch for any pest. The big clusters of tiny flowers, on the other hand, serve as a magnet for butterflies. To make the most of the butterfly show, it's fun to grow a lantana in a container you can easily see from the house.

Flower colors include orange, pink, red, white, and yellow as well as wild combinations of mixed colors.

Where it never freezes, lantanas grow like a shrub. In the Midwest they make great heat-tolerant container plants, available in your choice of trailing or upright habit. I save my lantanas year after year, growing them under a fluorescent light in the basement in winter. Because I have limited indoor space, I downsize plants to be overwintered indoors: I whack off a large portion of the roots so the remaining root system will fit in a 6-inch pot, then remove an equal portion of the stems and leaves.

Hot peppers are happiest when the summer weather turns brutal. Some of my other plants look droopy, but not the handsome ornamental peppers growing in full sun in a planter on my hot concrete driveway. My favorite: Black Pearl, an All-America Selections winner that has pure-black foliage and dense clusters of shiny black peppers.

With flower breeders coming up with so many wonderful new cascading plants, it's no wonder that the popularity of hanging baskets is soaring.

Besides the usual upright types of flowering vinca, we now also have varieties with a spreading habit, perfect in hanging baskets or for softening the edge of a large container. The Mediterranean series and Cora Cascade hybrids offer trailing types in your choice of many colors, including apricot, lilac, magenta, and rose.

Like other varieties of vinca, these spreading varieties offer maintenance-free plants that are perfect for planting in a hot, sunny spot.

Bacopa, a relative newcomer, has already worked its way to the top of my list of favorites to use in baskets on my deck. With the deck's eastern exposure, the plants thrive with morning sun followed by shade in the heat of the afternoon. Bacopa is easy to grow, provided the soil doesn't dry out.

Fan flower is a real beauty, with dozens of blue-violet, fan-shaped flowers on dark green stems tumbling over the sides of a hanging basket. I've had good luck planting it in either full sun or partial shade. A native of the hot, dry climate of Australia, fan flower has no trouble thriving in the heat of a Midwest summer.

Calibrachoa produces masses of flowers that look like little petunias. The plants do well in full sun or partial shade and seem to be able to take whatever the weather dishes out, from searing summer heat to frosty fall temperatures. Some varieties are upright, but trailing types work best in baskets.

Even snapdragons now come in trailing forms that are perfect for hanging baskets. Look for baskets of cascading snapdragon varieties such as Luminaire at garden centers. Cascadia and Lampion are two color mixes you can grow from seed, but they'll require an extra-early start indoors.

Trailing types of torenia, the wishbone flower, are ideal for baskets in the shade. Summer Wave Blue is my favorite.

Fanfare impatiens offer another great choice for shady baskets. With spreading stems covered with bright blooms from their centers to their tips, these colorful cascading plants come in blush, fuchsia, lavender, and orange.

Focus on Foliage

Purple. Chartreuse. Silver. Red. Yellow. Pink. White. You can have them all in the garden, without a single flower.

Plants with colorful foliage are in style, just like they were in Victorian times, only now we have a larger selection. I especially enjoy pairing a couple of plants with contrasting foliage colors in containers. Then the pots look great even if nothing in them is blooming.

Persian shield is one of my favorites. Who could resist its deep purple leaves with a beautiful metallic silver sheen?

An old-fashioned plant recently rediscovered by gardeners, Persian shield will grow 3 feet tall if you let it. Frequent pinching of the growing tips not only produces a more compact plant but also encourages new leaves that show off with the brightest purple.

In the Midwest, Persian shield performs best with morning sun and afternoon shade, and enough water to keep the soil moist.

Few gardeners had ever heard of licorice plant (*Helichrysum*) until recent years, but now its felt-like foliage is frequently seen weaving its way through container plantings. It comes in your choice of large or small leaves that are silver, chartreuse, or variegated. Plant licorice in sun or partial shade.

Numerous varieties of plectranthus, all cousins of the once-popular Swedish ivy, come in an array of colors. Like Swedish ivy, all are easy to grow in sun or partial shade.

One is called simply Golden, though it actually looks more chartreuse than gold. It combines beautifully with dark colors in a mixed container.

BEST BET

When the weather turns hot, tropical plants thrive. Chances are you already have some houseplants that will add to the scene when moved outdoors with other tropical specimens. For bold, seasonal ground covers, take cuttings of any of your vining houseplants with colorful foliage, such as purple heart, wandering Jew, or pothos. They're also ideal candidates for mixing together with flowering plants in containers.

Silver Shield is a sturdy, 2-foot-tall upright plant with big silver leaves that glow in the moonlight.

The leaves of Mona Lavender are purplish green on top, dark purple on the underside. While most kinds of plectranthus are grown primarily for their foliage, Mona Lavender also delights me with abundant dark-lavender flower spikes in late summer and early fall.

This is just a sampling of the many varieties of plectranthus available. Watch for them when you're plant shopping, and you'll be amazed at the possibilities. All are easy, even for beginners. And thanks to their scented foliage, they are usually ignored by rabbits and deer.

COLORFUL COLEUS

Beloved by Victorians but then nearly forgotten, coleus is now coming back strong.

No wonder! Newer coleus varieties thrive in sun as well as shade. And this tropical plant boasts colorful leaves as showy as any flower . . . without any wait or worry. Equally good in the garden or in containers, coleus is easy to grow and seldom bothered by pests or diseases.

Some of the old coleus favorites are back in garden centers along with some spectacular new ones. The leaves may be smooth or frilly, big or little, plain or deeply cut. And the colors are gorgeous: plum with splashes of pink, burgundy with yellow centers, yellow with red flecks, and dark red with a yellow outline, to name a few.

Some, such as the giant-leaf Kong series and the dramatic red-and-purple Black Dragon, are easy to grow from seed started indoors about two months before the last spring frost. Most kinds of modern varieties, though, are offered only as started plants, not seeds. These are the varieties most likely to grow well in full sun. Coleus plants with thick leaves and dark colors also tend to be good candidates for growing in full sun.

> ### BEST BET
>
> To keep coleus at its best, pinch out any seed heads that form. Feel free to also pinch off the growing tips to keep your coleus any size and shape you desire.

You can plant coleus outside any time after the danger of frost has passed. The plants love heat and look great all summer long until fall frost.

If you can't bear to lose your favorite varieties to winter cold, bring in plants or take cuttings to grow indoors.

Easy, Old-Fashioned Annuals

Old-fashioned annuals are not only interesting plants, they have intriguing names, too.

Take painted tongue (*Salpiglossis sinuata*), for example. A South American native, painted tongue has been grown in our country since pioneer days.

I love painted tongue's rich and varied color combinations of blue, purple, rose, red, violet, and yellow, with contrasting veins and centers or exquisite stained-glass patterns. The 2-inch, funnel-shaped flowers bloom from midsummer to frost on 2-foot-tall plants. In bouquets, the blossoms are long lasting and easily admired at close range.

You can plant seeds of painted tongue in the garden, but — for earlier blooms — I prefer to give them a head start indoors. In March, I sow the seeds on the surface of damp potting soil in containers. After the last spring frost, I space the seedlings 12 inches apart in a sunny site, then stick a small, twiggy branch into the ground beside each plant for support.

Looking for other unusual annuals that can spice up your flower beds? The dangling, reddish-purple tassels of love-lies-bleeding (*Amaranthus caudatus*) never fail to make me smile.

Because the plants reach a height of 4 feet or more, I delegate them to a spot by the garden fence. Dangling over the fence, the pendulous flowers are real show-offs. And, although the stems are quite thick and usually self-supporting, the fence sometimes comes in handy for tying up plants downed by a storm.

A sun-lover, love-lies-bleeding is one of those undemanding annuals that actually performs best if the soil isn't too rich.

Another plant with a softer look but an equally fascinating old-fashioned name is love-in-a-mist (*Nigella damascena*). Pretty, 1-inch flowers of blue or white (and, less commonly, pink) nestle in ferny foliage about a foot tall. Just as nice, I think, are the rounded, decorative seed pods that are both interesting to see in the garden and long lasting in dried arrangements.

Love-in-a-mist is easy to grow in full sun and is a dependable self-seeder.

Sweet scabious (*Scabiosa atropurpurea*) has rounded pincushion flowers on plants that grow 2 or 3 feet tall. Besides the original, almost-black flower once called "mourning bride," today's colors include blue, lavender, pink, and rose.

Like the closely related perennial pincushion flower, sweet scabious is excellent for cutting and attractive to butterflies. The plants grow 2 or 3 feet tall and do best in full sun. Start seeds indoors four to six weeks before the last expected spring frost.

Mignonette (*Reseda odorata*) is grown not for its beauty but for its strong, sweet fragrance. It's the "little darling" that Napoleon brought from Egypt for Josephine.

In early spring and again in late summer, scatter some of the seeds in the garden and in containers. Also add some showier flowers as cover for mignonette's lackluster white or yellow spikes. The plants grow about a foot tall and, in the Midwest, do best with morning sun and afternoon shade.

CHAPTER 2

PERENNIALS

REPEAT PERFORMERS

Perennials are the gardener's savings account. They keep generating interest even when you're busy doing other things. With a little planning, perennials can provide a year-round show.

Showers of flowers are special anytime, but especially in spring. That's why spring-blooming perennials like columbine, bleeding heart, iris, and peony are so popular. They provide the early garden color that winter-weary Midwest gardeners crave.

The show goes on throughout the summer, with a continuous parade of colors, textures, shapes, and sizes.

Other perennials color the fall garden and enliven the dead of winter.

Stretching the Season

The autumn blossoms of Japanese toad lily remind me of miniature orchids. It's the perfect plant for lining a woodland path, so you can enjoy its small blossoms at close range. Even when not blooming, toad lilies make handsome plants, thanks to arching stems lined with lance-shaped leaves.

Most toad lilies grow 2 or 3 feet tall. Many have white or lilac flowers spotted or streaked with purple. Some have gold-edged leaves to brighten the woodland garden throughout the growing season.

Tube clematis, another late-season beauty, is covered with blue flowers in early fall. Not a vine like most other kinds of clematis, it's instead a shrub-like plant you can grow as a perennial. Fluffy white seedheads extend the ornamental value through late fall.

The charm of azure monkshood's dark-blue, helmet-shaped flowers is irresistible. Growing on sturdy stems 3 or 4 feet tall, they bloom in September and October.

My monkshoods thrive in morning sun and afternoon shade. To my delight, they've slowly spread over the years and now weave their late-season color through spring-blooming shrubs.

Some of the best surprises in the autumn garden come in tiny packages. One such delight is a small sedum called October daphne, which grows no more than 10 inches tall.

Throughout the summer, the scalloped blue-green foliage of this low-growing sedum plays a supporting role. Then, just when most other plants in the garden are winding down, October daphne begins to bloom, its deep-pink flower clusters contrasting beautifully with its handsome foliage.

Cold weather only serves to enhance the color of the leaves, which may develop a pinkish cast or, more often, pink margins.

Delicate looking but tough as nails, October daphne thrives in sun or partial shade. It requires only a well-drained soil. Butterflies adore it.

....

BLOOMS FOR ALL SEASONS
....

SPRING

Barrenwort (*Epimedium* species and hybrids)
Hardy to USDA zone 4
Bleeding heart (*Lamprocapnos spectabilis*, syn. *Dicentra spectabilis*)
Hardy to USDA zone 3
Columbine (*Aquilegia canadensis*)
Hardy to USDA zone 3
Foamflower (*Tiarella wherryi* and hybrids)
Hardy to USDA zone 3
Iris (Bearded iris hybrids and *Iris siberica*)
Hardy to USDA zone 4
Lenten rose (*Helleborus* × *hybridus*)
Hardy to USDA zone 4

Lungwort (*Pulmonaria saccharata*)
Hardy to USDA zone 3
Pasque flower (*Pulsatilla patens*)
Hardy to USDA zone 3
Peony (*Paeonia* hybrids)
Hardy to USDA zone 3

SUMMER

Astilbe (*A.* × *arendsii*)
Hardy to USDA zone 3
Bellflower (*Campanula* species)
Hardy to USDA zone 3
Catmint (*Nepeta faassenii*)
Hardy to USDA zone 3
Coreopsis (*C.* species and hybrids)
Hardy to USDA zone 3
Cushion spurge (*Euphorbia polychroma*)
Hardy to USDA zone 4
Daylily (*Hemerocallis* hybrids)
Hardy to USDA zone 3
Geranium (*G.* hybrids)
Hardy to USDA zone 3, depending on cultivar
Goatsbeard (*Aruncus dioicus*)
Hardy to USDA zone 3
Phlox (*P. paniculata*)
Hardy to USDA zone 3
Veronica (*V. spicata* and hybrids)
Hardy to USDA zone 4
Yarrow (*Achillea* hybrids)
Hardy to USDA zone 3

AUTUMN

Aster, New England (*Symphyotrichum novae-angliae*, syn. *A. novae-angliae*)
Hardy to USDA zone 3
Aster, white wood (*Eurybia divaricata*, syn. *A. divaricatus*)

Hardy to USDA zone 4

Azure monkshood (*Aconitum carmichaelii* 'Arendsii')

Hardy to USDA zone 3

Boltonia (*B. asteroides*)

Hardy to USDA zone 3

Bottle gentian (*Gentiana andrewsii*)

Hardy to USDA zone 3

Japanese anemone (*A.* × *hybrida*)

Hardy to USDA zone 5

Japanese toad lily (*Tricyrtis hirta*)

Hardy to USDA zone 4

Helen's flower (*Helenium* hybrids)

Hardy to USDA zone 4

October daphne (*Sedum sieboldii*)

Hardy to USDA zone 3

Tube clematis (*Clematis heracleifolia*)

Hardy to USDA zone 4

In winter, a few strong-stemmed perennials that remain upright hold the "bloom" of snow. Good candidates: Russian sage, Autumn Joy sedum, and Goldsturm rudbeckia.

Even plain green is a welcome sight when I walk through my garden in February. Lenten rose hybrids fill that bill with their handsome dark-green leaves held out like fingers on a hand. In March, their long-lasting, nodding blossoms of cream, pink, purple, or white emerge, an early show that coincides with the blooming of the Ruby Giant crocuses if I'm lucky.

For a splashy statement in the winter garden, ornamental grasses and dwarf conifers are bigger and bolder. But all the tiny treasures that add a splash of color are like icing on the cake.

While most garden perennials are nothing more than a little pile of dead leaves in winter, the foliage of a few low-growing plants adds a bit of color whenever not completely covered by snow.

Foamflower foliage is even more colorful in winter than during the growing season. The finely cut leaves of a cultivar named Iron Butterfly, for example, are dark purple, edged with green in summer. In winter, they have rosy-pink edges that shine in the morning sun.

Many kinds of coralbells, foamy bells, and barrenworts also hold their attractive foliage color into winter.

Some creeping sedums retain their good looks during the winter. I'm particularly fond of Angelina. Chartreuse in summer, it turns reddish orange in winter.

Perennials for Special Places

PLANTS FOR ROCK WALLS

After my husband, Don, built a retaining wall in late fall, I spent the winter making a list of perennials I could use to hide the new wall.

Not that there's anything wrong with the retaining wall. Actually it's quite attractive, as retaining walls go. Each stone is a blend of black and gray concrete, with flecks of limestone that give the appearance of granite. And every landscape needs structure, or bones. But who wants to look at bare bones?

Fortunately, there are many wonderful plants that can cascade over a wall, softening the edges and turning cold concrete into a work of art. Here are some good choices:

Rock soapwort *(Saponaria ocymoides)* creeps and trails over rocks, hugging the ground. Pink flowers cover the plants in early summer. There's also a white-flowered variety called Snow Tips. You can encourage repeat bloom by shearing the plants after the first round of blooms, or stretch your bloom season by planting Max Frei, a long-blooming hybrid that takes off when other soapworts fade.

Rock soapwort is winter hardy throughout the Midwest and grows best in full sun. Plants demand well-drained soil, which they're sure to find at the top of a retaining wall.

Rockcress *(Arabis caucasica)* blooms in early spring, with masses of white flowers covering the hairy, gray-green leaves. If you cut this foot-tall, spreading plant back by half after flowers fade, it not only looks better but sometimes reblooms, too. Hardy to zone 4, rockcress performs best in full sun and in well-drained soil.

Serbian bellflower *(Campanula poscharskyana)* boasts 18-inch-long stems that drape beautifully over a wall, with blue, star-shaped flowers in spring. A good choice for a spot that offers afternoon shade, Serbian bellflower is hardy to zone 3 and tolerant of dry soil.

Purple poppy mallow *(Callirhoe involucrata)*, an attractive and durable wildflower, sprawls too much to fit in a tidy garden bed. It's perfect, though, when planted where it can cascade over a wall. The magenta, cup-shaped flowers keep coming all summer. This native is hardy to zone 4 and performs best in full sun and well-drained soil.

PERENNIALS FOR POOR SOIL

Perennial flax (*Linum perenne*) is perfectly satisfied to grow on the gravelly mound of poor soil at the edge of my garden.

The simple, sky-blue flowers bloom on delicate-looking, almost ferny foliage that belies the plant's tough nature.

Although technically a perennial, flax is not long lived. It doesn't matter, though, because the plants readily reseed, providing a constant supply of plants in various stages of maturity. I like to let them weave themselves in and out among other drought-tolerant perennials on my sunny slope, visually tying the bed together with blue.

Whenever a flax plant starts to look straggly, I shear it back by half or more. Meanwhile, other flax volunteer plants stand ready to fill the void, so the garden is never without the welcome blue. Flax grows about 18 inches tall.

If you like to coddle your plants, flax is not for you. Too much feeding or watering will kill it.

MORE PERENNIALS FOR POOR, DRY SOIL AND HOT SUN

Butterfly milkweed (*Asclepias tuberosa*)
Catmint (*Nepeta faassenii*)
Lamb's ear (*Stachys byzantina*)
Leadplant (*Amorpha canescens*)
Missouri primrose (*Oenothera macrocarpa*)

Prairie smoke (*Geum triflorum*)

Pussytoes (*Antennaria* species)

Russian sage (*Perovskia atriplicifolia*)

Yarrow (*Achillea* hybrids)

PLANNING FOR WIND

A little wind in the garden is a good thing, providing a cooling breeze in summer and good air circulation to help thwart plant diseases like mildew and small insect pests like aphids.

A lot of wind, on the other hand, is a nightmare. It breaks brittle stems, strips off tender new leaves and shoots, and dries out the soil in record time.

The best long-term solution is to block most of the wind with a mixed hedge of wind-worthy shrubs, such as cotoneaster, lilac, ninebark, spirea, and viburnum.

It takes a few years to grow a good windbreak, but you can have a beautiful garden while you wait. Instead of plants with large or soft leaves, choose resilient plants with flexible stems that can bend and sway with the wind. Tough-as-nails daylilies, for example, make a good alternative to true lilies, which have tall stems that can snap in the wind.

Wind won't hurt rock garden plants. Many are true alpines, native to mountain areas above the timberline where the winds really howl. These plants do, however, require good drainage. In that respect, the wind actually helps by drying out the soil faster. A few of my favorite rock garden plants include mountain-lover, hens and chicks, moss campion, sea thrift, dianthus, and alpine gentian.

Prairie natives such as butterfly milkweed, boltonia, purple cone-flower, and leadplant are also ideal candidates for a windswept site in the Midwest.

Other perennials that stand up to wind include threadleaf coreopsis, flax, sedum, yarrow, cushion spurge, and artemisia. Ornamental grasses also do well and add the pleasure of hearing the wind whisper through their narrow leaves.

You can easily force many kinds of tall perennials to grow shorter and stronger simply by cutting the plants back by about half in late spring. A few that respond well to this treatment include balloon flower, helenium, Joe-Pye weed, monkshood, Russian sage, and veronica.

Sometimes great things come in small packages. That's certainly true in the case of some outstanding perennials. In the midst of the garden, these diminutive plants might get lost. But edging a walk or in the front of a border, they really shine.

One tiny treasure is a prostrate veronica named Goldwell, which grows only about 4 inches tall. It has tiny blue-purple flowers that bloom in May and June. But it's the foliage that's truly special. Each tiny green leaf is edged in gold, making a showy plant for the front of the border throughout the growing season.

Goldwell spreads into a low, tight mat, with a single plant spreading about 18 inches wide. Useful as a ground cover as well as an edging, it also looks great spilling over the side of a container filled with mixed plants. A good candidate for well-drained soil, it performs well in sun or partial shade.

A closely related creeping veronica called blue wooly speedwell (*V. pectinata*) makes a handsome gray-green carpet only about 2 inches tall. It owes its name to the long white hairs that cover the leaves and produce a wooly appearance. Mine thrives in a dry spot that is difficult to water, where many plants had previously perished.

In spring, blue wooly speedwell is covered with tiny white-eyed, true-blue flowers. Thriving in sun or partial shade, it creeps by sending out roots wherever a leaf meets the soil.

Dwarf goatsbeard (*Aruncus aethusifolius*), a tiny version of its big sister, stands only about 8 inches tall. It's a good choice for edging a path in a woodland garden. Feathery, creamy-white, 3- to 4-inch flower spikes bloom in midsummer, but the ferny foliage remains attractive throughout the season.

PLANTING UNDER A TREE

A friend gave me a tall order: Recommend an easy-care perennial that will thrive in the mostly shaded spot under a tree. This perennial must smother weeds, grow no more than a foot tall, resist rabbit browsing, and bloom all summer.

There are many wonderful plants that thrive beneath trees, but a trouble-free perennial that blooms all summer? In the shade? Rare indeed! I told him I'd think about it and get back to him.

As I scanned my own landscape, I spied one kind of plant that would meet all of my friend's criteria. It's lamium, a plant often stuck with the unappealing common name of spotted dead nettle. Others call it false salvia.

Lamium has silver-mottled foliage that lights up the shade. Whorls of pink or white flowers continue blooming throughout the summer. Sometimes I see hummingbirds visiting the blossoms.

The plants, which grow 6 to 12 inches tall, spread slowly to make a dense ground cover that will keep weeds from sprouting. Scented foliage discourages browsing by animals. These adaptable plants grow best in moist soil, but they also tolerate drought once they're established.

There are many different varieties of lamium, with varying degrees of variegation. The foliage of Chequers, for example, has more green. White Nancy has more silver. Ghost is almost pure silver. Not surprisingly, varieties with mostly silver foliage tend to be somewhat less vigorous than those with a good amount of green in their leaves.

While lamium is great for planting under trees, it isn't perfect. In the heat of summer, the plants may start to look floppy or ratty. Fortunately, lamium can be quickly renewed by shearing the plants back to fresh leaves. If you have a lot of plants, a string trimmer will do the job in a jiffy.

Where lamium seeds fall, new plants will sprout. This is actually a plus if you're trying to cover an area quickly and inexpensively. The shallow-rooted plants are easy to pull if they sprout where you don't

BEST BET

If the tree you're planting under happens to be a walnut, choose perennials that won't suffer from the toxic effect of the juglone produced by the walnut's roots. Good choices include astilbe, ajuga, barrenwort, beebalm, bleeding heart, bloodroot, coralbells, fern, foamflower, geranium, goatsbeard, hosta, lady's mantle, lungwort, Siberian bugloss, and Solomon's seal.

want them. The disadvantage of volunteer seedlings is that the foliage coloring may vary from the variety you originally selected.

Another favorite perennial for planting under trees is barrenwort (*Epi-medium*). While its tiny, columbine-like flowers bloom only for a short time in spring, the heart-shaped leaves are handsome throughout the growing season and offer fall color as well. The plants grow 8 to 12 inches tall. You can choose varieties with red, violet, white, or yellow blooms.

ADAPTABLE PERENNIALS: FROM MUD TO DUST

Some perennials demand well-drained soil. Others thrive in a bog. But what can you plant in a spot that routinely goes from mud to dust?

Fortunately there are a few adaptable perennials that tolerate either extreme. Hardy hibiscus, for one. Native to marshes, it can take standing water. But marshes sometimes dry up, and hibiscus is programmed to survive that, too. No matter the weather, you can count on its huge, saucer-shaped flowers in red, pink, or white to bloom from July to frost.

Depending on variety, the plants grow 3 to 6 feet tall. Despite their tropical appearance, many kinds are hardy in the Midwest through zone 4, thriving in full sun or partial shade.

Adaptable perennials such as hibiscus are ideal for a low-lying landscape where rainwater drains from surrounding hills. They're also good candidates for a rain garden, which is muddy after a rain but dries out when the rains stop.

OTHER ADAPTABLE PERENNIALS

Boltonia (*B. asteroides*)
Cup plant (*Silphium perfoliatum*)
Golden Alexander (*Zizia aurea*)
Helen's flower (*Helenium autumnale*)
New England aster (*A. novae-angliae*, syn.
　Symphyotrichum novae-angliae)
Turtlehead (*Chelone glabra*)
Culver's root (*Veronicastrum virginicum*)
Purple coneflower (*Echinacea purpurea*)

Stiff goldenrod (*Solidago rigida*)
Sweet Joe-Pye weed (*Eupatorium purpureum*)
Wild bergamot (*Monarda fistulosa*)

Sun-Loving Perennials

COREOPSIS

Year in and year out, coreopsis remains a garden favorite.

What's not to love? In sunny gardens, coreopsis is one of the easiest perennials to grow. It produces cheerful yellow daisy-like flowers most of the summer. The flowers attract butterflies and make excellent bouquets. And the plants are generally ignored by deer.

Don't take this genus for granted just because it's been common in gardens for decades. These days, coreopsis flowers come in interesting new colors and shapes. And some new varieties have increased vigor and disease-resistance.

A coreopsis named Full Moon has proved to be a pure delight in my garden. A hybrid between the threadleaf type, like Moonbeam, and tickseeds (*Coreopsis grandiflora*) such as Early Sunrise, it seems to have the best qualities of both parents. Strong and healthy, it's covered from early summer to early fall with big canary-yellow blossoms.

The golden-yellow flowers of Jethro Tull coreopsis add an interesting twist, with unusual fluted petals.

Another new hybrid called Redshift adds some fun color variation. In summer, its creamy-yellow flowers with red eyes blend with other garden flowers. But once the nights cool down in the fall, the flowers shout for attention with their deep red streaks.

Lightning Flash, a variety of the super-hardy tall tickseed (*Coreopsis tripteris*), is fun to grow because of its striking gold foliage. Definitely a candidate for the back of the border, this plant grows 4 or 5 feet tall. You'll have to wait until summer's end to see any of the yellow flowers.

Pink varieties such as Sweet Dreams, on the other hand, are short lived in my garden. Nevertheless, they bloom so prolifically that I think they're worth growing even if they only live a single season.

Moonbeam, 1992 Perennial Plant of the Year winner with lemon-yellow flowers, continues to be a popular threadleaf type. In wet weather, though, it sometimes rots off at the ground or develops mildew. Although winter hardy throughout the Midwest, it may fizzle out after a few years. Zagreb, a sister variety with golden-yellow flowers and the same ferny foliage, has proved to be more dependable than Moonbeam in my garden.

After the first flush of coreopsis blooms fades, use shears to clean off all the dead blossoms in a flash. In late fall, remove all the foliage to help control disease. Dig and divide plants in the spring if they are crowded and had few blooms.

SALVIAS

Salvias bloom best in full sun and require well-drained soil. They're tough, easy-to-grow plants but will grow weak and floppy in too much shade or overly rich soil.

While many perennial salvias bloom heavily in early summer, I have three kinds that bloom for an extended time *if* I remember to clip off their fading flowers. Caradonna is a particularly strong grower about 2 feet tall with blue-purple flowers on unusual dark-purple stems. Marcus is a dwarf only half as tall, perfect for small spaces. Its flowers are violet-purple. Purple Rain has smoky-purple flowers and fuzzy leaves. The 18-inch-tall plants bloom continuously from July through September.

YARROW

A good choice for a lazy gardener, yarrow is not recommended for gardeners who like to coddle their plants. The plants tend to grow lanky and spread aggressively if grown in rich soil with ample water. Top-dressing plants with a 1-inch layer of compost once a year supplies ample nutrients. Watering is seldom necessary once plants are established.

And what flowers! Packed into distinctive, large, flat clusters that measure up to 5 inches across, they come in your choice of lavender, pink, red, salmon, white, or yellow. All attract butterflies and make great cut flowers, fresh or dried.

The ferny, gray-green foliage is another plus, contrasting nicely with other garden plants. Deer and rabbits seldom show any interest in eating the fragrant leaves.

Thanks to the work of plant breeders, yarrow just keeps getting better. Many new varieties stand up to summer's heat and humidity without melting down.

The flowers of Apricot Delight, a yarrow in the Tutti Frutti series, evolve through a range of pink shades, from palest apricot to near red.

Angelique, Paprika, Pomegranate, and Strawberry Seduction are good red cultivars. Moonshine, an old favorite, and Sunny Seduction have yellow flowers. Wonderful Wampee is a rich pink, and Walter Funcke flowers are reddish orange.

These varieties are all sold as plants, but growing yarrow from seed is another option. If you start with seed, expect the colors and sizes of the plants to vary. A good seed mix is Summer Pastels, winner of an All-America Selections award. The colors include cream, lemon, lilac, orange, red, salmon, white, and yellow.

Cut off and remove dead flowers to improve the plant's appearance, encourage more blooms, and prevent reseeding.

To keep yarrows growing vigorously, dig and divide the plants in spring every two or three years.

Although yarrows are extremely cold hardy, sometimes winter throws them a curve. One year I lost most of my yarrows when an early storm locked them in a block of ice for several months. It wasn't the cold that killed them; they just couldn't breathe.

DAYLILIES

All daylilies are delightful, but my current favorite is so beautiful that I have to brew a cup of tea and sit awhile to admire its blossoms.

The object of my affection is a daylily called Kindly Light. A spider type daylily with huge, pure-yellow flowers and thin, strappy petals, its blossoms stand in marked contrast to the trumpet-shaped flowers of my other daylilies.

There are thousands of different kinds of daylilies. They come in every color except blue, often with contrasting bands, eye-zones, or halos. Although the typical daylily flower is shaped like a trumpet, you can also find daylilies with blossoms that are shaped more like stars, pinwheels, or circles. Double flowers with extra petals look more like peony blossoms.

Visiting a daylily farm during peak bloom season is one of the best ways to discover your own favorites.

For the longest season of blooms, it's fun to include some rebloomers such as red Pardon Me, lemon-yellow Bitsy, and creamy-yellow Stella Supreme. Night bloomers like Prairie Moonlight are wonderful in the evening garden.

Daylilies are easy to grow in full sun or partial shade. Afternoon shade helps red and purple varieties maintain their vibrant colors longer.

When the number of blooms begins to decline, usually after three to five years, it's time to dig and divide daylilies. One of the best times for dividing is as soon as the weather cools down after bloom time. But daylilies are so resilient the job is usually successful when tackled any time during the growing season.

Once established, daylilies tend to be drought resistant and long lived.

In late summer, it's normal for lower leaves to turn yellow. To spiff up the appearance, pull the yellowed leaves from the plants. Also pull out dead flower stalks.

PEONIES

If you haven't looked at peony choices recently, you're in for a pleasant surprise. Flower form ranges from those with simple petals, called singles, to those with extra petals and fancy ruffles, called doubles. Some resemble a dahlia, others a lotus or cactus flower, and there are even peonies with long, narrow, twisted petals that look like a spider.

Color choices, once limited to coral, pink, red, or white, now include exotic lime-green and creamy-yellow, with many two-toned varieties also available.

You can choose a big and sturdy 3-foot-tall peony or a small, fine-textured peony only 14 or 15 inches tall, ideal for growing in a rock garden or any place where space is limited.

Most varieties are fragrant and all are great for cutting.

Best of all, breeders have produced many strong-stemmed varieties that do a better job of supporting heavy flowers.

As long as you have a sunny spot and well-drained soil, garden peonies are long lived and dependable. Take time to enrich the soil before you plant by digging several bucketsful of compost or other organic materials into a 3-foot-square spot for each plant.

Place the root so that the pink buds, or "eyes," that are on top of the root are 1 to 2 inches below the soil surface.

Stories abound about farm dads who used to mow down garden peonies with the tractor as soon as the last bloom died in late spring. In spite of such harsh treatment, the stalwart peonies survived.

If you love your peonies, though, that's not the way to treat them. The recommended time to cut and remove peony foliage is at the end of the growing season, not near the beginning. That's because peonies, like other plants, need their leaves in order to manufacture food and grow stronger.

Your reward for waiting until fall to cut back peonies often includes not only a stronger plant but also pretty autumn foliage that may be tinged with red or purple.

If your peonies are infected with a common fungal disease called leaf blotch, though, you are no doubt itching to get rid of the ugly leaves covered with purplish-brown spots.

Since the worst of the spots are usually on the outside leaves, you can improve the plant's looks simply by giving your peony bush a small trim. By allowing the rest of the foliage to remain, you won't be left with an empty space for fall.

After fall frost, cut and remove the remaining foliage to reduce future problems with diseases such as leaf blotch and gray mold.

September is the traditional time to dig and divide crowded clumps or to plant new peonies.

TALL SEDUMS

I never met a sedum I didn't like. No matter what the weather, these adaptable perennials always look great. Almost indestructible, the plants live long lives. That's how sedum earned its common name: live-forever.

Autumn Joy long ago built its reputation as a workhorse in the garden. Now, thanks to new hybrids, the choices are mind boggling.

Matrona's pink flowers look a lot like Autumn Joy, but the reddish-purple stems and thick gray-green leaves with rosy-pink edges are an extra treat.

Vera Jameson looks beautiful in the garden long before the dusty-pink flowers open in early autumn, thanks to its beautiful foot-tall purple foliage.

Purple Emperor is favored for its dark-purple leaves.

Mr. Goodbud, Neon, T Rex, and Xenox are prized for extra-strong stems that aren't as apt to flop as those of Autumn Joy.

Sedums' thick, fleshy leaves store water and help the plants survive periods of drought. The plants don't balk when the weather is wet, either, provided the soil is well drained. They'll sail right through both hot summers and cold winters with no trouble at all. They need little fertilizer.

Divide tall sedums in spring if the stems were weak and floppy the previous autumn.

Favorites for Partial Shade

BELLFLOWERS

A diverse group of hardy perennials in sizes ranging from tiny creepers to tall background plants, bellflowers provide bell-shaped blossoms of blue, lavender, or white for weeks in summer.

Most bellflowers are welcome in my garden, but I've banished the species known as spotted bellflower (*Campanula punctata*).

Though once delighted by the prolific flowers of spotted bellflower cultivars such as Cherry Bells, I soon learned this species doesn't play well with others. Before long, their rhizomes wormed their way into the crowns of neighboring roses, baby's breath, and other perennials, threatening to choke them to death.

While I don't usually mind the work of taming aggressive plants, spotted bellflower is in a class of its own. Even a single tiny white thread of a rhizome left behind sprouts a new plant. After years of trying to dig them all out, I still find a few more sprouting every spring.

Nevertheless, I still consider spotted bellflowers a fine candidate for growing in a container, where their roots are contained by the pot. This species would also make a fine ground cover. Just don't mix it with less-vigorous plants.

For the garden, I use better-behaved bellflowers like Blue Clips Carpathian harebell. Only about 8 inches tall, it has masses of up-facing violet-blue flowers.

Some hybrids have proven particularly useful. In a six-year trial at the Chicago Botanic Garden, Plant Evaluation Manager Richard Hawke found a bellflower named Sarastro to be the shining star. From June until late July, it covers itself with long, violet-blue, bell-shaped flowers on 20-inch-tall plants.

Ironically, one of Sarastro's parents is the unruly spotted bellflower that spreads like wild. Thankfully, Sarastro didn't inherit that aggressive tendency.

Kent Belle, the offspring of great bellflower (*Campanula latifolia*) and a Korean species (*C. takesimana*), didn't fare as well in the Chicago trials, where it was floppy enough to require staking. In my garden, though, Kent Belle has performed very well, with reblooming purple bells on sturdy 2-foot-tall plants.

I also like Birch Hybrid, a heavy bloomer that grows only 6 inches tall. It's a cross between Serbian and Dalmatian bellflowers.

Bellflowers require well-drained soil, which is particularly important for their winter survival. Although they grow well in full sun, they're more tolerant of drought if shaded from the hot afternoon sun. Deadheading spent blossoms encourages many kinds of bellflower to keep blooming.

CORALBELLS

When I was new to gardening, I planted coralbells for their dainty bell-shaped flowers of pink, red, or white that float above the low, mounding foliage. I loved watching hummingbirds visit the blossoms and sometimes I even cut some of the wiry stems for a bouquet. But I never paid much attention to the foliage.

That all changed in the early '90s with the introduction of Palace Purple, which has foot-tall, bronze-purple leaves. Since then, plant breeders have been hard at work producing coralbells with increasingly gorgeous leaves. Flowers, no longer the main event, play second fiddle to the colorful foliage that lasts all season.

Some of the new varieties have foliage that is such a dark purple it is almost black. The leaves of others are lime-green or peachy-orange. Some have ruffled leaves. All are great fun to mix and match with other plants, both in the garden and in containers.

Some coralbells are proving to be stronger growers than others. For tolerance to the Midwest's heat and humidity, the focus is on hybrids that include in their parentage hairy alumroot (*Heuchera villosa*), native to the southeastern United States. Examples include Caramel, which has stunning yellow-orange leaves with purple-red undersides, and Pinot Noir, which has deep-purple leaves with a silver overlay. Chartreuse Citronelle and dark-purple Mocha also have hairy alumroot in their heritage.

Coralbells are generally easy to grow. Pests and diseases are not usually severe, although protection from rabbits may be necessary.

Because coralbells have shallow roots and tend to push up as they grow, the plants are subject to frost-heaving in winter. It helps to plant them an inch deeper in the soil than they were growing in their pots. Well-drained soil is required for winter survival and also helps prevent stem rot.

Black vine weevils and the closely related strawberry root weevils occasionally cause serious damage. Adults feed at night, notching the leaves. The larvae feed underground on the roots. Suspect these insects if a plant wilts when the soil isn't dry or if part of the crown breaks off at the soil level. Beneficial nematodes, although not an instant cure, provide long-term control.

MEADOW RUE

Perfect candidates for a woodland garden, meadow rues (*Thalictrum*) thrive in dappled shade.

This large group of plants in the buttercup family is diverse. Some are giants that grow 6 feet tall, while others are tiny creepers only a few inches high. By growing several different kinds, you can have a parade of blossoms in lavender, pink, yellow, cream, lilac, or pale green from spring through early fall.

A hybrid called Black Stockings is a spring bloomer, with large, fluffy, lavender flowers nodding on almost-black stems. This meadow rue grows about 4 feet tall.

Yellow meadow rue blooms in June, with sprays of fuzzy, sulfur-yellow flowers on 5-foot-tall stems.

Kyushu meadow rue is tiny enough to fit into the smallest garden. Only about 4 inches tall in bloom, the plants are covered with small pinkish-lavender flowers most of the summer. To protect this tiny plant from being swallowed up by bigger perennials, I planted it right beside my front walkway. Through the years, it has slowly intermingled with a miniature hosta, producing a delightful effect.

Lavender mist meadow rue blooms from mid- to late summer, with misty lavender-purple flowers highlighted with yellow centers. The bluish-green foliage, often compared to that of the maidenhair fern, is equally attractive. The sturdy stems grow at least 5 feet tall.

Problems with meadow rues are few. Leaf miners and powdery mildew occasionally attack, but ragged-looking foliage can be cut to the ground after flowering to encourage a new flush of healthy leaves.

GOATSBEARD

Goatsbeard is a summer standout. At 4 to 6 feet tall and 3 to 4 feet wide, it looks more like a shrub than a perennial. In June and July, it's topped with huge feathery plumes of creamy-white flowers that resemble giant astilbes. Even after the blooms fade, the ferny foliage makes a fine backdrop for smaller shade-loving flowers.

The ideal spot to plant goatsbeard is in rich, moist soil in partial shade. But goatsbeard is a very adaptable plant that will tolerate dry soil once established. You can even grow it in full sun, as long as you give it extra moisture. Goatsbeard thrives in deep shade, too, although it won't flower as much if it gets no sunlight at all.

My own plants grow under trees where they receive sunlight for only a very brief time each day, but they still manage to put on a respectable flower show every summer. Deer, rabbits, insects, and disease have never been a problem.

Goatsbeard is long lived and doesn't require dividing. Although tall, the plants don't need staking. The only drawback is the patience required while you wait for the plant to mature.

Goatsbeard flower plumes are great for cutting. Male and female flowers are borne on separate plants. Male goatsbeard flowers are considered somewhat more attractive, while the female plants produce attractive seed heads. It would be hard to choose but, since nurseries don't differentiate between male and female plants, you don't have to decide anyway. If you happen to have both male and female plants, though, you might be lucky enough to get a few volunteer seedlings.

The seed heads are attractive in fall, contrasting nicely with the gold-colored autumn foliage of goatsbeard. You can allow the seed heads to remain for winter interest, or cut them for dried arrangements.

COLUMBINES

One of the best-known and most loved perennials, columbine is a springtime delight. Of the dozens of different species, my own favorite is the same one our hummingbirds prefer: the native red and yellow Canadian columbine.

The hummingbirds are one reason I love Canadian columbine. The other reason? I know I can count on it in my garden. Other columbines, typically short-lived plants, come and go. But the Canadian columbine remains, thanks to prolific volunteer plants always waiting in the wings to replace plants that die.

Rocky Mountain columbine, Colorado's state flower, is another well-known favorite. Its sky-blue and white blossoms are always welcome in the garden. Alpine columbine, a native of Switzerland, has deep-blue blossoms. And I adore the yellow blossoms of golden columbine, native to the southern Rockies.

Hybrid columbines offer an expanded range of colors.

In the Midwest, columbines perform best — and blooms last longer — when the plants are protected from the hot afternoon sun. They like moist soil, but good drainage is also a must. Winter hardiness is not a problem. On the other hand, keeping wet leaves or other soggy mulch pulled closely around plants in winter can be fatal.

Successfully dividing a columbine plant would be difficult, but it also isn't necessary. Individual plants seldom live long enough to require division.

Removing spent flowers may help prolong the life of prized varieties.

If leaf miners make wavy tracks through the leaves of my columbines, I simply pick off and destroy the affected leaves. Mildew is normally a problem only if plants are crowded too close together for the air to circulate freely.

Notably promiscuous, columbines cross readily when grown in close proximity in the garden.

JAPANESE ANEMONES

Silky pink or white flowers on long, wiry stems nod gracefully in the wind above lush maple-like leaves. That's what you get if you have a patch of fall-blooming anemones.

Also known as windflowers, anemones don't really like the wind. In the Midwest, they do much better when tucked into a protected site that has morning sun and afternoon shade. They're perfect for a woodland garden and wonderful for cutting.

Some tried and true varieties of Japanese anemones include Honorine Jobert, pure white with yellow centers, and rose-colored September Charm. In bloom, these varieties stand 30 inches tall or more.

The pink flowers of Robusstissima grape-leaf anemone may not stand quite as tall, but the plants are the most vigorous growers and also the hardiest. If they're happy where you plant them, they will spread and may even become invasive.

Japanese anemones grow best in moist, well-drained soil to which lots of organic matter has been added. Pests and diseases aren't usually a concern, although blister beetles attack the plants in some areas. Handpick these large insects into a bucket of soapy water as soon as they're noticed.

After frost turns the leaves black, cut the plants back to the ground. When the soil freezes, add some evergreen boughs or other loose mulch for winter protection.

Division is seldom needed. If you want to attempt it, or move your plants to another spot, do it only in the spring.

BLUESTAR AMSONIA

I've long believed that bluestars deserve to be better known and more widely planted. They're hardy, carefree plants. North American natives, they owe the common name of bluestar to their late-spring, pale-blue flowers. Showier yet, I think, is the bright yellow color of their foliage in autumn.

The first amsonia I planted was willow bluestar (*Amsonia*

BEST BET

Fall-blooming anemones are often late to appear in spring. Mark their location so you don't accidentally slice into their crowns when doing your spring planting.

tabernaemontana). It grows in 3-foot-tall clumps with narrow, glossy leaves that blow in the wind.

The tall, willowy foliage makes this bluestar a handsome backdrop for short, summer-flowering perennials planted in front.

Shining bluestar (*Amsonia illustris*) is similar, only its leaves are both shinier and more leathery.

Arkansas bluestar (*Amsonia hubrichtii*), the Perennial Plant Association's 2011 Perennial Plant of the Year, is sometimes called threadleaf bluestar. The association describes the 3-inch, needle-shaped leaves as "finer than a feather duster." That makes for interesting contrast of textures when Arkansas bluestar is paired with perennials or shrubs that have big, bold leaves.

Arkansas bluestar grows into a bushy plant 3 feet tall and wide.

Downy bluestar (*Amsonia ciliata*) is similar to threadleaf but smaller, growing only about half as tall. Its golden foliage glows like a beacon, taking center stage in my rock garden every autumn.

All these amsonias grow best in rich, moist, well-drained soil, although they seem to be very tolerant of less-than-ideal conditions. In my garden, none have been feasted on by either deer or rabbits. Insects and diseases have never been a problem, either.

Perennial guru Allan Armitage says bluestar is always on his list of no-brainers: "Plant it and get out of the way."

If your amsonias grow taller than you prefer, you can simply shear them back by as much as half as soon as the flowers fade.

My willow amsonia sometimes reseeds itself more than I'd like, but removing seed pods offers an easy solution to the problem.

Choice Perennials for Shade

ASTILBES

For summer color in a shady garden, you can't beat astilbes. The feathery plumes of lavender, mahogany, pink, red, violet, or white are real showoffs. The ferny foliage, which often has tints of bronze or purple, is beautiful, too.

By planting some early, late, and midseason varieties, you can enjoy many weeks of color.

Astilbe flowers are great for cutting. Or you can allow the dried flower spikes to stand in the garden to add their subtle beauty to the winter landscape.

If astilbes have a fault, it's that they like to grow in soil that is well drained but also stays constantly moist. If the soil dries out, the leaves will turn crispy brown and the flowers may stop coming.

Nevertheless, there's hope for gardeners like me who would rather grow plants that aren't so finicky about getting watered on time. Some kinds of astilbe — most notably Chinese astilbes — tolerate growing in dry soil.

While Chinese astilbes will grow a little taller and more vigorously in soil that stays constantly moist, they still put on a respectable show in dry soil.

Dependable growers in my garden include raspberry-red Visions and its cousins, Visions in Pink and Visions in Red. These compact Chinese varieties grow 15 to 20 inches tall.

Purple Candles blooms later in the season, with 3-foot-tall, candle-like plumes of reddish purple.

For a difficult and often neglected site, I've been impressed with a Chinese astilbe called Pumila. It spreads slowly to make a great ground cover only 10 or 12 inches tall. One of the last astilbes to bloom, its narrow, lilac-rose plumes rise above a low carpet of foliage.

Digging compost or other organic matter into the soil before you plant will go a long way toward keeping astilbes happy. Also use a mulch to help preserve soil moisture.

Astilbes tend to be heavy feeders. Gardeners serious about coaxing maximum performance out of astilbes often add a liquid fertilizer once a month during the growing season.

Insect pests seldom bother Midwest astilbes but mildew can mar the foliage. The best cure for mildew is to thin plants for better air circulation. You can dig and divide crowded plants in spring or fall. If your astilbes suffer from mildew, also be sure to clean up dead foliage in the fall.

MORE FLOWERING PERENNIALS FOR SHADE

Aster, white wood (*Eurybia divaricata*, syn. *A. divaricatus*)
Barrenwort (*Epimedium* species and hybrids)

Bleeding heart (*Lamprocapnos spectabilis*, syn. *Dicentra spectabilis*)
Bloodroot (*Sanguinaria canadensis*)
Foamflower (*Tiarella wherryi* and hybrids)
Jack-in-the-pulpit (*Arisaema triphyllum*)
Lungwort (*Pulmonaria saccharata*)
Rue anemone (*Anemonella thalictroides*)
Snakeroot (*Actaea racemosa*, syn. *Cimicifuga racemosa*)
Timber phlox (*Phlox divaricata*)
Virginia bluebells (*Mertensia virginica*)
White baneberry (*Actaea pachypoda*)

I count on plants with variegated foliage for constant contrast in the shade garden, even when nothing is blooming. Variegated Solomon's seal, which I grow not so much for its tiny white, bell-shaped flowers but primarily for the attractive arching stems with white-edged leaves, fills the bill.

HOSTAS

When it comes to foliage favorites, hostas are the undisputed queen. You can choose from hundreds of different kinds in shades of green, blue, or gold, often with yellow or white markings. They may be dwarfs only a few inches tall, or big clumps that stand 2 feet tall or more.

The leaves also have varied shapes, including oval, teardrop, and oblong. The lavender, purple, or white lily-like blossoms are sometimes fragrant, depending on variety. And hostas are long lived and easy to grow.

No wonder some folks get hooked and become hosta collectors!

Midsummer weather can do a number on hostas. To survive hot, dry weather, they need extra water. A mulch such as shredded bark helps conserve soil moisture and slowly decays to add the extra organic matter hostas like.

Just like people, hostas can sunburn. If a tree that provided the plants' shade dies, you'll need to move the hostas to a spot where they'll be protected from the sun. The best time for the move is spring or fall. In the meantime, you can spread a piece of shade-cloth across plants to protect them from burning.

Longing for a place that is cool and green and shady? A nook filled with ferns can be mighty inviting on a hot day.

Although ferns have a reputation for being finicky growers that demand moist soil, many are surprisingly adaptable, long lived, and easy to grow in Midwest shade gardens.

Many gardeners know and love the Japanese painted fern (*Athyrium*) called Pictum. The Perennial Plant Association's Plant of the Year in 2004, Pictum has fronds that look like they're painted with gray, green, and purple, with silver accents and wine-red stems and veins.

Another one of my favorites is Ghost. It has Japanese painted fern for one parent, lady fern for the other.

While Japanese painted ferns usually grow about 12 to 18 inches tall, Ghost is taller, with a strong, upright shape it gets from the lady fern. Its name, as you might suspect, comes from its ghostly pale fronds.

Many wood ferns (*Dryopteris*) are also well suited to growing in Midwest gardens. One called male fern has erect fronds that often grow 3 feet tall.

The native maidenhair fern (*Adiantum*) is one of the most graceful and well adapted for Midwest gardens. Its fan-shaped fronds look almost lacy. Shiny black stems and golden fall color add to its appeal.

You can plant container-grown ferns in a shady garden bed any time during the growing season. Be sure to dig compost, shredded leaves, or other organic matter into the planting hole first. After planting, water thoroughly and mulch to conserve moisture.

By December, most outdoor ferns have shriveled in the cold. Not so with Christmas fern (*Polystichum*), a native of the eastern North American woodlands. Its sturdy, evergreen fronds are a winter delight in shady Midwest gardens.

This robust and cold-tolerant fern is easy and adaptable, though it grows best in light shade and moist but well-drained soil. Its arching, leathery fronds stand 1 to 2 feet tall.

My Christmas fern has survived without coddling for years, gradually expanding its crown.

Maintaining Perennials

When new gardeners hear about "pinching" plants, they're understandably puzzled.

Just where do you pinch them? And why?

The "where" is the growing tip of each stem. You can literally pinch off the tip between your thumb and forefinger, or — if you have a lot of plants — you can speed up the job by using scissors or grass shears to remove many growing tips with one cut.

The "why" is that cut stems branch out, resulting in a more compact plant with many more blossoms.

Chrysanthemums are one of the classic plants that gardeners pinch, often several times during the spring and early summer. Mums that aren't pinched back tend to topple in autumn under the weight of their blossoms. (Some of the new varieties, which have been bred for compact shape and better branching, are an exception. Pinch only your mums that grow tall and straggly.)

Sometimes, perennials need more than a mere pinch. Cutting shoots back by half is not too drastic for those that routinely grow too big for their space. If Russian sage, for example, crowds its neighbors, cut it back in late spring. Do the same to control the ultimate size of boltonia. Without pruning, both of these perennials may grow 4 feet tall and wide, and that's a big bite in a small garden.

Late spring is also the time to take preventive measures to keep some types of perennials from flopping over as the season wears on. If your tall sedums are growing in too much shade or in crowded clumps you haven't had time to thin, cut the shoots back by half to help the plants stay upright. Cutting back by half also curbs the tendency of balloon flower and tall varieties of asters and yarrows to sag.

While pinching and shearing are great gardening techniques for producing more flowers, compact shapes, and stronger stems, these procedures are not for every plant. If astilbe is cut back, it may not bloom at all. The same goes for goatsbeard, foxglove, gas plant, and queen-of-the-prairie.

When some of my garden plants start to look shabby in midsummer, a pair of garden scissors works wonders.

By the time the old leaves are yellowed, spotted, or damaged by insects, many kinds of perennials have already produced fresh new growth at the base. All that is needed is to clip the old stems near the base to reveal a beautiful plant that looks springtime fresh. Although it takes some time, this grooming work is easy and greatly rewarding.

Perennial types of salvia are particularly good for working this magic. Not only does removing the old stems improve the plants' appearance, but the vigorous new stems often put out another round of flowers that extend the bloom season many weeks.

Many of the taller varieties of veronica also have fresh new growth waiting to be revealed by the time their old foliage starts to brown. So do many kinds of perennial geraniums.

Cutting back delphiniums after the bloom season will remove mildewed foliage and reveal fresh new growth. Often the delphiniums will even bloom again. Although these late-bloom stalks tend to be shorter and smaller, they're always welcome.

It's easy to tell by looking which perennials will respond well to this type of grooming. Just look for new growth at the base.

For some other perennials, shearing tired-looking plants back about halfway works better. That's how I renew catmint, for example. Its stems tend to fall down, particularly after heavy rains, leaving open centers that aren't very attractive. By cutting the stems halfway back, they stand up straight again, improving the plants' appearance. New leaves and a fresh round of blooms often follow.

Silvermound artemisia, which makes a beautiful mound earlier in the season, is also prone to opening up in the center in midsummer. Cutting back halfway restores its good looks.

DIG AND DIVIDE

When I'm sitting in my office at the computer, it's easy to write that it's time to dig and divide your overgrown perennials. When I'm standing in my garden looking at my own crowded perennials, I sometimes feel overwhelmed.

Small perennials like chrysanthemums aren't the problem. Although they need division every year or two, that job is relatively easy.

The trouble is with plants that have extensive root systems that require a lot of time and energy to dig up and divide. Large ornamental grasses are some of the most difficult plants to dig up. Yet they tend to die out in the middle of the clumps if allowed to grow unabated.

Dividing daylilies also feels like heavy labor, but without it vigorous varieties soon grow so crowded that blooming stops.

One spring when I was especially short on time and energy, I cheated on the traditional method of digging and dividing perennials. Instead of digging up the whole plant, I used a sharp spade to slice off a few sections of each plant that needed dividing. Then I filled the empty space left in the ground with compost, which helps rebuild the soil.

This method worked so well that I've been using it ever since. It solves the crowding problem without uprooting the part of the plant I want to keep. I also like the opportunity to replenish the soil by filling the holes with compost. Leftover clumps of perennials are usually easy to give away.

PESTS AND DISEASES

If you see some plants that look like they were sprinkled with baby powder, blame powdery mildew.

This fungus disease is both easy to spot and very common. The list of susceptible plants is long.

Some ornamental plants that are frequent targets of the disease include bee balm and garden phlox. Powdery mildew infections tend to be worst when the soil is dry but the humidity is high. A good strategy is to water the soil as soon as it dries out but refrain from using an overhead sprinkler.

You can save yourself a lot of grief if you begin with disease-resistant

> **BEST BET**
>
> Limit the time and effort required to maintain a perennial garden by choosing some perennials that will thrive for years without division: bugbane, Lenten rose, monkshood for shade or partial shade; baby's breath, blue false indigo, gas plant, balloon flower, lupine, and statice for sun.

varieties whenever possible. Among bee balms, for example, Gardenview Scarlet and Marshalls Delight have good track records for resistance. Shortwood and Katherine are two cultivars of garden phlox that demonstrate good resistance to mildew.

Other preventive measures include planting susceptible plants where they'll get morning sun to quickly dry the overnight dew, and giving each plant enough space for good air circulation.

Thin out plants. For example, pull out all but five shoots of each garden phlox plant to help preserve its health. If bee balm becomes infected, don't be afraid to cut plants back to the ground after flowering. You'll be surprised how quickly fresh new foliage fills the void.

Sulfur sprays and powders are a time-honored solution for mildew and other fungus diseases, but there's something even better. Believe it or not, it's baking soda.

Some gardeners concoct their own solution of baking soda and summer horticultural oil mixed together in water. I prefer to use GreenCure, a thoroughly tested baking soda product developed at Cornell University. An effective and economical alternative to chemical fungicides, it also stops other fungus diseases such as gray mold, downy mildew, anthracnose, and leaf spot, and continues to act as a preventive for about two weeks.

If yarrow suffers from stem rot or mildewed foliage, simply cut the affected stalks to the ground. New shoots will soon appear. Allow enough room for good air circulation to help keep your yarrows healthy.

Daylilies sometimes suffer from fungus diseases such as leaf streak and daylily rust. If you see leaves with spots or streaks, gather and dispose of the affected foliage and disinfect your pruners in alcohol or a chlorine bleach solution.

For an easy way to control problems in the iris patch, remove all old iris foliage and bloom stalks before new spring growth appears.

Cleaning up the patch removes iris borer eggs — laid in autumn on the leaves and stalks — before they have a chance to hatch and tunnel into the rhizomes. An early spring cleanup also removes spores that could cause leaf-spot diseases.

In summer, if you see iris leaves with chewed, jagged edges along with streaks and spots, an iris borer is the likely culprit. Clip such leaves right down to the rhizome, then peel the leaf apart and destroy any caterpillar feeding there. Fresh new leaves will soon sprout.

People who grow many kinds of hostas made an interesting discovery: Snails and slugs like some hostas a lot better than others.

The slimy mollusks, it seems, prefer hostas with thin, tender leaves but ignore those with thick, tough, or puckered foliage. While you can't expect hosta selection to provide foolproof protection if there's a heavy infestation of pests, there's no question that choosing slug-resistant varieties offers a good start toward damage control.

Some hostas that aren't likely to be bothered include many blue varieties such as Blue Mammoth and Krossa Regal. Sum and Substance, the huge gold-leaf hosta, and Golden Bullion offer good resistance, too. Another good bet is a hosta with puckered leaves, such as Black Hills or Midas Touch. Even the well-known Frances Williams has leaves thick enough to resist slugs.

But how do you protect hostas that have tender leaves? Fortunately, the war against slugs and snails recently got easier, thanks to the introduction of Sluggo and other products that contain iron phosphate. Appealing to the mollusks but harmless to other creatures, it spoils the appetite of snails and slugs as soon as they have a taste.

Just scatter the granules on the ground around any plants you want to protect, then repeat the application in two weeks.

A fungus disease called crown rot can cause hosta leaves to yellow, wilt, and then collapse. If you pull off the affected leaves, you'll see what looks like white threads.

Once thought to be a problem only in southern states, crown rot flourishes in warm, moist weather. In recent years, it has plagued some gardens in the upper Midwest.

If it happens in your garden, remove and dispose of affected hostas. Don't transplant any plants from the affected area into another part of the garden. Wash your tools and be careful about tracking soil out of the affected area. Fill the void with perennials resistant to the disease, such as barrenworts, foamflowers, hellebores, and coralbells.

The disease is fairly easy to contain because it is not windborne and spreads slowly only through the soil or plants.

When my daughter moved to an older home, she couldn't wait to start taming the large, overgrown yard and add some of her favorite plants.

One growing season later, after watching rabbits nibble her new Japanese painted ferns, coralbells, and roses to the ground, she was near despair.

Her solution? Find some new favorites, plants the rabbits wouldn't find so tasty. Now she's enjoying plenty of garden color without the frustration.

Before I share a list of bunny-resistant perennials, I must add a caveat. There is really no such thing as a completely rabbit-proof plant. When hungry enough, rabbits have been known to nibble on almost anything. If you have a large population of rabbits in your yard, the only guaranteed protection for a prized perennial, shrub, or young tree is something that excludes the bunnies, such as a circle of chicken wire.

Nevertheless, my daughter and I find that rabbits normally leave untouched many plants that have scented foliage such as catmint and lavender.

Gas plant, which has lemon-scented foliage and white or purple flowers, is somewhat slow to establish but worth the wait.

Rabbits also tend to avoid irises, both bearded and Siberian types.

While my coralbells are often devastated by rabbits, the bunnies tend to avoid a related plant, foamflower (*Tiarella*). I'm willing to enjoy foamflower's variegated leaves and showy flower spikes in my woodland garden and confine my coralbells to containers or to garden beds by the house, where rabbits have been less of a problem.

BEST BET

The plants on the rabbit-resistant list are usually also ignored by deer. Some additional deer-resistant perennials include black-eyed Susan, butterfly milkweed, cheddar pinks, coreopsis, goldenrod, Missouri primrose, rattlesnake master, and sun-loving ornamental grasses.

Ornamental Grasses

Remember the little boy who said the moon was more important than the sun? "Because the moon shines at night," he said, "when we really need it."

That's the way I feel about ornamental grasses. They give the garden color and form in the fall and winter, when we really need them.

When summer's bright colors are gone, the wine-red color of Shenandoah switch grass is especially welcome. At a height of only 3 to 4 feet, Shenandoah is shorter than most kinds of switch grass and makes a good partner for perennials. In my garden, Husker Red penstemon and Shenandoah make a good-looking pair.

Blue oatgrass grows into a stiff and spiky 2-foot ball, adding interesting structure to the garden any time of year. Its silver-blue foliage fades a little in cold weather but still looks colorful in the winter landscape.

Karl Foerster feather reed grass stands 5 feet tall with a vertical shape that makes it easy to integrate with perennials and shrubs in the garden. You can count on it to remain attractive and upright throughout the winter.

Less well known is a close relative, fall-blooming feather reed grass, sometimes called Korean feather reed grass. Unlike Karl Foerster, which blooms in early summer, the fall-blooming species waits until September to send up its fine-textured, purple-red flowers that gradually fade to silver gray.

Fall-blooming feather reed grass is shorter than Karl Foerster and has a more relaxed, arching form.

Tufted hair grass has long-lasting flower panicles that age to a light golden color in autumn, shining in the morning dew. The 2-foot-tall clumps combine well with perennials.

Ornamental grasses are the ultimate easy-care plants. Once established, they survive without fertilizer or supplemental water. Pests and diseases are rarely a problem.

In return for gracing the garden with good looks from late spring through winter, ornamental grasses require only one annual maintenance chore: cut the plants back almost to the ground in late winter or early spring, before new growth begins.

This annual grass cleanup is more for appearance than necessity. Without brown leaves mixed in with fresh green leaves, grasses look better. Another plus: new shoots emerge earlier than they would otherwise.

Depending on how big each clump is, I usually use either pruning shears or hedge shears for cutting off grass tops. For really large clumps of established grasses, an electric hedge trimmer or a string trimmer with a brush-blade attachment comes in handy. Tying the tops of big grass clumps together with twine or bungee cords before cutting helps make cleanup a snap.

Most grasses thrive for years when left undisturbed. When the center of a clump starts to die, though, it's time to dig and divide.

Some grasses, including feather reed grass and blue fescue, are cool-season grasses that are best divided in early spring. Others, such as switch grass and purple moor grass, are warm-season grasses that are apt to rot if you divide them before mid-May. If in doubt, wait until you see the first sign of new growth to dig and divide any of your ornamental grasses.

GRASSES FOR SHADE

Now that ornamental grasses are a staple of sunny gardens, gardeners are also seeking grasses that will thrive in the shade.

There are a few. Two native grasses — northern sea oats and bottle brush grass — grow well in open shade. In truth, many gardeners find these two grow a little too well, reseeding themselves with abandon unless their seed heads are removed before the seeds fall to the soil.

Another, golden Japanese forest grass (*Hakonechloa macra* 'Aureola'), is most at home in the Midwest in shade where the temperature is cooler and the soil isn't so quick to dry out. Its graceful stems resemble bamboo.

But the biggest selection of "grasses" for shade doesn't come from true grasses at all, but from sedges (*Carex*).

Anyone who has battled with nutsedge spreading throughout the yard and garden might tremble at the thought of purposely planting any kind of sedge. But trust me: Among the hundreds of different kinds of sedges, you can find many that are well-behaved, beautiful, and useful in shady gardens. Another plus: deer rarely bother sedges.

Beatlemania spring sedge makes a 6-inch-tall mound of gracefully arching dark-green leaves edged with gold. It performs best in moist soil.

Oehme variegated palm sedge is a native that grows up to 2 feet tall. The leaves, which have yellow margins, radiate around the stems like a palm tree. A natural for use at water's edge, this sedge requires moist soil.

Blue Zinger sedge can tolerate some drought. Its broad leaves are frosty blue and grow in clumps about a foot tall.

Ice Dance sedge is one of my favorites. I like the way its narrow green-and-white-striped leaves light up the shade. This sedge grows about a foot tall and spreads very slowly by rhizomes.

Much to my surprise, I've developed a real fondness for bronze New Zealand hair sedge. I used to think brown leaves meant a plant was dead or dying, but I've discovered this unusual color adds attractive contrast to the plentiful greens in the landscape.

Ground Covers

Ground covers have a reputation as boring plants. Useful, for sure, particularly as easy-care foliage for carpeting a large area of ground you'd rather not mow. But still boring.

There's nothing boring, though, about the beautiful purple-bronze leaves of Bronze Beauty ajuga blanketing the ground around a bright-green conifer. Or Burgundy Glow ajuga, with its foliage of burgundy, pink, green, and creamy white, weaving its way around a hydrangea.

After the flamboyant annuals fade away in cold weather, the more subtle colors of these ground-cover plants are especially pleasing.

By allowing several different kinds of ground-cover plants to weave themselves together, you can create an interesting kaleidoscope of colors, textures, and shapes. I think creeping sedums make particularly fine partners for ajuga. The dark-green, needle-like leaves of a small sedum called Green Spruce, for example, look beautiful paired with Burgundy Glow ajuga. Tricolor sedum, with its leaves of pink, green and white, is another pretty partner.

Both ajuga and sedum require well-drained soil. If either fails to survive the winter, the culprit is more likely to be poor drainage than a lack of hardiness.

When people think of ground covers, aggressive-spreading plants often come to mind. While these are very useful in large areas, there are also many wonderful slow-growing ground-cover plants that make a great backdrop for perennials and annuals in garden beds.

PERENNIALS AS LIVING MULCH

Mulch is practical but not particularly ornamental. I'm okay with mulched rows in the vegetable garden, but in my flower gardens I'd rather look at plants than a sea of mulch.

Increasingly, I'm using low, creeping plants as a living mulch around taller ornamentals. I still have a long way to go, but I'm having fun experimenting. And I can't help noticing that my plants seem particularly happy with this arrangement.

Noted plantsman Roy Diblik agrees that a plant prefers to live in a close-knit community rather than be grown as a specimen surrounded by mulch. What a plant wants, he says, is buddies.

A friend in Missouri uses all kinds of creeping sedums as a living mulch around her perennials. Since these low sedums are generally recommended for hot, sunny spots, I was surprised how well they were doing in the partial shade of her taller plants. But it looked good, and it was working, so I've been copying her idea and I love the results.

For the shadiest spots, I've found that the native white-blooming wild sedum (*S. ternatum*) works particularly well.

The best plants for a living mulch are perennials that will grow in peace with their neighbors, without overwhelming them.

OTHER EASILY MANAGED GROUND COVERS

Allegheny pachysandra (*Pachysandra procombens*)
Barrenwort (*Epimedium* species and hybrids)
Blue comfrey (*Symphytum grandiflorum*)
Coralbells (*Heuchera* hybrids)
Geranium (*G.* species and hybrids)
Foamflower (Tiarella *wherryi* and hybrids)
Foamy bells (× *Heucherella*)
Herman's Pride yellow archangel (*Lamiastrum galeobdolon* 'Herman's Pride')
Lady's mantle (*Alchemilla vulgaris*)
Lungwort (*Pulmonaria saccharata*)
Plumbago (*Ceratostigma plumbaginoides*)
Wild ginger (*Asarum canadense*)
Yellow corydalis (*C. lutea*)

USEFUL GROUND COVERS FOR LARGE AREAS

Allegheny foamflower (*Tiarella cordifolia*)
Japanese pachysandra (*P. terminalis*)
Periwinkle (*Vinca minor*)
Variegated Solomon's seal (*Polygonatum odoratum* 'Variegatum')

CHAPTER 3

WILDFLOWERS

A LITTLE PRAIRIE BY THE HOUSE

Once upon a time the prairie served as pharmacy, general store, and grocery store. The prairie plants that grew here then are beautiful, adaptable choices for our gardens today. They also have intriguing stories to tell.

Take rattlesnake master (*Eryngium yuccifolium*), for example. This 4-foot-tall statuesque plant is interesting enough, with yucca-type foliage topped by spiky white balls. As for its story, some say the root was brewed as a tea to treat victims of rattlesnake bites. Others say if you chewed on the root and blew on your hands, you could pick up a rattler without injury.

Rattlesnake master also served a variety of other medicinal uses and was credited for good luck in gambling. I don't know about the gambling part, but I can vouch for the plant's good fortune in avoiding munching by deer. Drought-tolerant, it's happiest in full sun.

Compass plant (*Silphium laciniatum*) has unique, dark-green, divided leaves that orient themselves north and south and helped early travelers find their way. Like many enduring prairie plants, compass plant needs time to grow a sturdy taproot before using energy to produce flowers. Once established it will last just about forever.

A good candidate for the back of a sunny flower border, compass plant can shoot up to 8 feet tall, with dozens of yellow, daisy-like flowers June to September.

Joe-Pye weed (*Eupatorium purpureum*) makes an unforgettable impression in late summer with showy, flat-topped clusters of rose-purple flowers often surrounded by butterflies. These sturdy plants grow 4 to 6 feet tall.

Who was Joe Pye? My dictionary says the origin of the name Joe-Pye weed is unknown, but many plant historians think the name comes not from a man but from *jopi*, the American Indian word for typhoid fever. There is no doubt that the bitter tea made from this showy meadow plant was used to treat a variety of ills.

Native to low meadows and woodland edges, Joe-Pye weed adapts to either full sun or partial shade. The less light it gets, the taller the plant grows and the more likely it is to require staking. A low spot in the garden where the soil tends to stay moist is ideal. Allow 3 feet between plants for good air circulation to prevent mildew. For a shorter plant, just shear plants back by half in early June.

Most gardeners are familiar with the reddish-purple daisies and bristly orange cones of the much-loved purple coneflower (*Echinacea purpurea*). But it's another species, the pale purple coneflower (*E. pallida*), which was frequently used by Native Americans to treat pain and a variety of ills. This coneflower has a subtle beauty I adore, with drooping, pale-rose petals and narrow leaves.

I've heard that its chopped roots were added to vodka for medicinal use, and I wonder how anyone knew whether it was the plant or the vodka that did the trick. At any rate, I value the beauty of these 3-foot-tall plants in a sunny border.

Natives come in shapes and sizes to fit any garden, with some just the right size to fill a tiny niche and others that grow so tall they tower over people's heads. Here are some more prairie natives that thrive in a sunny space:

Wild petunia *(Ruellia humilis)* hugs the ground, covering itself with lilac-blue, tubular flowers that attract hummingbirds. A small plant you can use to weave around other perennials, it makes a pretty ground cover. This adaptable plant grows in any soil but is particularly valuable in dry, rocky soils where few plants thrive. But watch out: If happy where it's planted, it can be a rambunctious self-seeder.

Cup plant *(Silphium perfoliatum)*, a close relative of compass plant, is a giant perennial like its kin. Hummingbirds and butterflies come to sip the rainwater and dew that collect in its little cups, formed where large leaves encircle the stems. After the yellow flowers fade, goldfinches and other birds flock to both cup plant and compass plant to feast on the ripening seeds.

Butterfly milkweed *(Asclepias tuberosa)* is a must for attracting monarch butterflies. Its orange-red flower clusters bloom on 2-foot-tall plants from July to September. The plants thrive in any well-drained soil.

Prairie smoke *(Geum triflorum)* blooms in spring, with nodding pink flowers that are followed by long-lasting seed heads that are pink and feathery. Less than a foot tall, the fuzzy plants are easy to grow as long as the soil is well drained and will thrive even in poor, dry soil.

Mexican hat *(Ratibida columnifera)* flowers resemble sombreros, with prominent central cones and drooping yellow petals. The plants grow up to 3 feet tall. A close relative, yellow coneflower (*Ratibida pinnata*) grows even taller. Easy to grow from seed, these adaptable plants often self-sow if seeds are allowed to fall to the ground.

Purple prairie clover *(Dalea purpurea)*, a legume with a 10-foot taproot, can outlast any drought. Each plant produces a 2-foot-tall, fountain-like clump of stems, each topped with a tightly packed cluster of purple flowers.

A Sure Sign of Spring

In early spring, I eagerly anticipate the opening of the first pasque flower (*Pulsatilla patens*), with blossoms often pushing up through the season's last snow. I can only imagine the joy that pioneers and Native Americans must have felt when greeted by a whole field in bloom at the end of a long winter.

The state flower of South Dakota, pasque flower stands only about

BEST BET

Native plants are the secret to attracting more of this region's birds and butterflies to your garden. Plan for a succession of blooms from spring through fall.

6 inches tall and has big flowers somewhat reminiscent of large crocus blossoms.

Petal-like lavender, purple, or blue sepals are covered with silky hairs and surround yellow centers. After the sepals fall, finely divided foliage emerges. It, too, is covered with silky hairs.

Pasque flower blossoms don't last long, but the show doesn't end when they fade. If you don't rush to pinch off dead flowers, you'll be rewarded with attractive, long-lasting, glossy seed heads and maybe some volunteer seedlings, too.

For the longest-lived plants, choose a spot with good drainage. I grow mine in the rock garden, which suits the plants just fine. They grow well in full sun or in the partial shade provided by somewhat taller plants.

Once hot weather arrives, pasque flowers often disappear for the rest of the growing season. Fortunately, there are many native plants that can fill the void. One of my favorites is purple poppy mallow (*Callirhoe involucrata*), also known as wine cups.

A creeping plant with wine-red, cup-shaped flowers that keep on coming for months, this native wonder weaves in and out among other plants, knitting the garden together. Its finely dissected leaves are also attractive. A deep taproot sees the plant through hard times.

Tough Plants

Tough places call for tough plants. One of the toughest spots for plants to thrive is a sun-baked garden surrounded by asphalt or concrete.

I admire a particularly pretty garden that's in just such a place, a hot and sunny island surrounded by a circular driveway. The plants must also survive dry spells without benefit of a sprinkler system. Nevertheless, the little garden produces a constant parade of color from native plants. Flowers mostly in shades of blue and purple, with a touch of pink, bloom from spring through fall. They intermingle with tough prairie grasses, which retain their good looks all winter.

In early spring when the grasses are cut back and the perennials are just beginning to emerge, flowering bulbs such as daffodils and grape hyacinths fill the void. Since the bulbs go dormant after blooming, they're perfectly satisfied to spend their summer in the hot, dry island.

What kinds of perennials thrive in this hostile site? One of the first to bloom is blue false indigo (*Baptisia australis*). A tall, bushy plant 3 or 4 feet high and wide, it boasts spikes of indigo-blue flowers that resemble those of sweet peas.

Blue false indigo retains its unblemished blue-green foliage through autumn, thanks to deep roots that carry the plant through dry spells. Persistent black seed pods add to its attractiveness.

Around the edges of the island garden, bushy skullcap (*Scutellaria resinosa*) blooms all summer with purplish-blue blossoms on small plants no more than a foot tall. Although not long lived, there are always enough seedlings to carry on the show year after year.

From July through October, the showy rose-purple blossoms of purple coneflowers (*Echinacea purpurea*) appear, weaving in and out among the grasses and other perennials.

Emerald-green fountains of prairie dropseed and the arching leaves of little bluestem sway in the wind and add winter interest even after the wildflowers fade.

If you have a similar hot, dry, sunny spot but blues and purples aren't your favorites, don't worry. There are plenty of tough prairie plants in yellows, oranges, and reds you can substitute. Some good candidates include black-eyed Susan, blanket flower, Mexican hat, butterfly milkweed, Missouri primrose, and lance-leaf coreopsis.

EASY SUSANS

Virtually unstoppable, black-eyed Susans (*Rudbeckia hirta*) keep right on blooming all summer whether rains come or not. Their familiar yellow daisies attract butterflies and produce armloads of flowers for bouquets.

Although often behaving as biennials with two-year life spans, the plants will self-sow indefinitely, producing charming variations in height and color.

If I water my garden with an overhead sprinkler or fail to allow my black-eyed Susans enough space for good air circulation, my plants sometimes fall victim to diseases such as mildew, gray mold, or stem rot. No matter. When I pull out the ailing plants, there are usually new volunteers waiting to take their places.

The Rudbeckia group also includes a number of hardy perennials.

Best known is Goldsturm, the 1999 Perennial Plant of the Year. Handsome and easy to grow, this sturdy, 2-foot-tall plant produces loads of golden-yellow flowers with prominent dark cones and dark green leaves.

Missouri black-eyed Susan (*Rudbeckia missouriensis*) grows about a foot tall, topped with bright-yellow, long-stemmed flowers ideal for bouquets.

PURPLE CONEFLOWERS

A favorite of butterflies, coneflowers also make great cut flowers for bouquets. If the season's last flowers are left standing, the cones add winter beauty and attract finches to the winter garden.

Regardless of whether you grow the native purple coneflower or some of the fancy new hybrids, all tolerate partial shade. But you'll get more blooms if you choose a spot that that gets at least six hours of sunlight per day.

Purple coneflowers thrive in lean, well-drained soil. If grown in too much shade or overly rich soil, they may require staking. Once established, they're drought tolerant and carefree.

If volunteer seedlings are a nuisance, remove the flowers as they fade. This deadheading also promotes continued blooms and improves the plants' appearance. You might want to stop deadheading in autumn, to save the long-lasting cones for winter interest.

Plan to dig and divide coneflowers every three or four years in spring to keep them vigorous.

BEST BET

Few pests or diseases attack coneflowers, but once in a while a plant will be distorted and have light-green leaves, a branching top, and few flowers. If you see such a plant, pull it out and discard it before insects spread this virus-like disease to healthy plants.

Penstemons' spires of tubular flowers are much more than another pretty face in the garden. They make great cut flowers and attract hummingbirds, too.

Penstemons tolerate poor soil and drought. What they don't tolerate is coddling. In fact, the only gardeners who seem to have trouble growing penstemons are people who are constantly fussing over their plants, providing generous doses of fertilizer and water.

The best-known penstemon in Midwest gardens is Husker Red, a University of Nebraska introduction that gained fame as the Perennial Plant Association's 1996 Perennial Plant of the Year. This big, husky plant, a selection of foxglove beardtongue (*Penstemon digitalis*), has reddish-colored foliage and white flowers in June and July on 3-foot-tall plants.

Large-flowered beardtongue (*Penstemon grandiflorus*) tends to fizzle out after four or five years. Nevertheless, the showy spikes of large pink, purple, or white flowers in May and June make this native worth including in your garden. If conditions are right, it may even self-sow to keep the show going. Large-flowered beardtongue grows 2 to 4 feet tall.

Penstemons do fine in full sun and also tolerate partial shade, but they demand well-drained soil. Winter sogginess is the biggest enemy of most penstemons.

If you're not cutting penstemon flowers for bouquets, you might want to cut them after blooms fade, just to improve the plant's appearance.

BLANKET FLOWER

If you have a hot, dry, sunny spot you'd like to blanket with color, you can't go wrong with flamboyant blanket flowers (*Gaillardia*).

Native to Midwest plains and meadows, these easy-to-grow flowers aren't fazed by our periodic droughts or hot sun. They thrive in poor soil and are seldom bothered by pests. Even deer usually pass by blanket flowers, thanks to the plants' hairy leaves.

The daisy-like flowers blaze in a mix of hot oranges, reds, and yellows with their multicolored petals arranged around globe-shaped centers. Prolific flowers keep coming from June to September, with plenty of extras to enjoy indoors in bouquets.

Blanket flowers tend to be short lived. Dividing plants every two or three years when they emerge in early spring can help them retain their vigor. Be sure to select a spot with well-drained soil and slope the soil away from the plants' centers; blanket flowers won't tolerate wet feet.

Cutting off faded blanket flowers before they set seed is an easy cure if you don't want them to reseed.

Drought-tolerant and long-blooming, blanket flowers are also ideal candidates for growing in sunny containers.

BAPTISIA

Blue false indigo (*Baptisia australis*) shows off in late spring with 12-inch spikes of purple lupine-like blossoms that attract butterflies. The flowers are followed by large black seed pods that are attractive in dried arrangements.

Members of the Perennial Plant Association selected this easy-to-grow wildflower as Plant of the Year for 2010. It's one of those rare perennials that inspires admiration even when the plant is not in bloom. Plants grow up to 4 feet tall and wide, large enough to double as shrubs, with handsome blue-green foliage that persists throughout the growing season.

If your garden is too small to make room for such a large plant, there is also a smaller version of blue false indigo (*Baptisia minor*). This baptisia has all the same virtues but grows less than half as big.

If you can be patient for several years while your baptisia puts down its deep roots, you'll be rewarded with a dependable, long-lived plant. Once established, it will tolerate drought. Deer rarely are a problem, but rabbits sometimes nibble on my plants.

Baptisia plants grow best in well-drained soil of average fertility. They thrive in full sun and also tolerate light shade.

Because of the deep taproot, the plants are best left undisturbed. That's why you'll find a seemingly misplaced specimen growing inside my fenced vegetable garden. It's a remnant of a wildflower patch I once had in that area, but I enjoy it too much to risk losing it by moving it.

There are more than a dozen different species of baptisia, plus natural hybrids created by bees buzzing from blossom to blossom of different species. At the Chicago Botanic Garden, Jim Ault has been taking advantage of this rich gene pool to produce new varieties with flowers in unique colors.

If you'd love to see a constant parade of butterflies, try cultivating several different kinds of blazing stars (*Liatris*). Butterfly magnets, these hardy perennials will bloom from July until the first fall frost.

Some kinds of blazing stars reach their peak of bloom in September, perfect timing to attract migrating monarchs.

Most kinds have grass-like foliage and flower spikes that resemble a bottlebrush. These showy flowers bloom in various shades of pink and purple and look spectacular in the garden. If you can bear to cut any, the flowers are exceptionally long lasting in bouquets.

If you'd rather leave the stalks in the garden after the blooms fade, though, you'll be rewarded with an even longer-lasting show: a parade of goldfinches and other birds that come to dine on the seeds in winter.

Some blazing stars grow only about a foot tall, ideal for small gardens. Others can shoot up 5 feet or more. When tall varieties are flowering, I sometimes have to stake the bloom stalks to keep them upright. You could also pair them with prairie grasses and let them lean on the grasses for support.

Dense blazing star (*Liatris spicata*), also known as spike blazing star, is the type most widely available at garden centers, perhaps because it's so adaptable and easy to grow. This mauve-purple native grows 3 to 4 feet tall. A compact cultivar named 'Kobold' stands only 2 feet tall.

If you prefer, you can grow dense blazing star from fall-planted corms, often sold by bulb specialists.

Prairie blazing star (*Liatris pycnostachya*) is the most spectacular species in my garden. It grows 5 feet tall with gorgeous spikes of tightly packed, pinkish-purple flowers.

For a different look, I love rough blazing star (*Liatris aspera*). Also called button blazing star, its flowers look more like clusters of buttons than bottle brushes. While prairie and dense blazing stars grow well in moist clay soil, rough blazing star is a good choice for dry or rocky soil. In bloom, it stands about 3 feet tall.

If you're looking for something smaller, the 15- to 18-inch tall dotted blazing star (*Liatris punctata*) or foot-tall dwarf blazing star (*Liatris cylindracea*) are good bets. Both are good choices for dry, well-drained soil.

CULVER'S ROOT

The tall, candelabra-like flower spikes of a native wildflower called Culver's root (*Veronicastrum virginicum*) dress up prairies and meadows from midsummer to early fall.

One of my favorite flowers for the back of a flower border, Culver's root stands an impressive 4 to 6 feet tall. The blooms are sometimes creamy white, sometimes lavender, but always spectacular. The flower spikes are as outstanding in flower arrangements as they are in the garden.

Culver's root is closely related to veronica, which the flower spikes resemble. The plants are narrow, distinguished by whorls of deep green leaves lined up along the stems in groups of five.

You can grow Culver's root in full sun or partial shade, but with too much shade the plants may require staking. To avoid staking, you can cut the plants back by about half in mid- to late spring. Pruned plants will grow only about half as tall, but they will stand up straight.

Culver's root grows best in rich, moist soil but will tolerate somewhat dry soil once the plants are established.

Pest and disease problems are generally few, but sometimes four-lined plant bugs attack many of my perennials, including Culver's root. The damage is mostly cosmetic, with small tan spots on the leaves. Since it's too late to do anything by the time the spots are noticeable, I simply pinch off the leaves that look the worst.

The Wet Set

Native to floodplains and wet meadows, these Midwest wildflowers are ideally suited for planting in a soggy spot or rain garden:

White turtlehead *(Chelone glabra)* gets its name from its unique flower shape, resembling a turtle head with an open mouth. The upright, 2- to 4-foot-tall plants thrive in full sun or partial shade, blooming in August and September. (*Chelone lyonii*, a bushy turtlehead native to the mountains of Appalachia, has pink flowers and thrives in similar conditions.)

Cardinal flower *(Lobelia cardinalis)* puts on a spectacular show of bright red flower spikes from midsummer to early fall. A favorite with hummingbirds, the 3-foot-tall plants prefer afternoon shade.

Swamp milkweed *(Asclepias incarnata)* has large, dusky-pink flower clusters that are magnets for butterflies from early to midsummer. Growing about 4 feet tall, the plants bloom best in full sun.

Queen-of-the-prairie *(Filipendula rubra)* is another big plant that grows up to 5 feet tall, with large and showy pink flower clusters that look like cotton candy.

Late Bloomers

While most perennials are pooping out by early fall, new buds of Helen's flower (*Helenium autumnale*) keep popping out, creating an end-of-the-season splash of bold, hot colors.

A native of wet, sunny meadows, this wildflower is often overlooked by Midwest gardeners. That's too bad. The gorgeous red, yellow, and orange daisy-like flowers bloom from August to frost on sturdy plants 3 or 4 feet tall. Diseases and pests are seldom a problem. Winter kill isn't a problem, either; Helen's flower is hardy throughout the Midwest.

In fact, as near as I can tell, Helen's flower has only one flaw. The plant is usually stuck with an unappealing and undeserved common name: sneezeweed.

Because of its height, Helen's flower makes an ideal plant for the middle or back of a border, where it makes an impressive autumn display when combined with ornamental grasses and tall varieties of asters. The flowers make long-lasting bouquets.

BEST BET

In place of purple loosestrife, the widely banned wetland invader, choose spectacular and easy-to-grow native substitutes that like the same garden conditions, stand up tall, bloom for a long time, and pose no threat to the environment. Queen-of-the-prairie, prairie blazing star, and swamp milkweed all make good substitutes for purple loosestrife.

Helen's flower performs best when divided every two or three years.

Asters also show off in fall, attracting butterflies to their flowers. Sun-loving plants with daisy-type blossoms, they come in heights ranging from 1 to 6 feet and a wide choice of colors that includes blue, purple, lavender, white, pink, and crimson.

One native species called silky aster (*Symphyotrichum sericeum*, syn. *Aster sericeus*) has silky leaves and tons of light blue flowers. Very tolerant of drought and neglect, silky aster tends to be floppy only if you try to grow it in rich, moist soil. It grows 1 to 2 feet tall.

For a taller aster, I'm partial to smooth aster (*Symphyotrichum laeve*, syn. *Aster laevis*). I love its large, cone-shaped clusters of pale, sky-blue flowers on sturdy stems. The plants grow about 4 feet tall, but you can encourage shorter plants by cutting them back by half in late spring. Tall aster seeds itself around a bit, but any unwanted volunteers are easy to pull.

To help control mildew, allow asters room for good air circulation and water the soil in dry weather. Also clean up infected plant debris at the end of the season and divide plants every two years.

While nothing says autumn quite like an aster, you might fool someone with boltonia, a mildew-resistant aster look-alike.

A solid cloud of white flowers covers the Snowbank boltonia plants in my garden every fall. Looking at the 4-foot-tall drift of white blossoms, I can easily imagine how Snowbank got its name.

Boltonias are a miracle plant for lazy gardeners. The plants are tall but strong-stemmed, so they seldom require staking if grown in full sun. They thrive in any soil and seldom suffer from pests or diseases.

Like asters, boltonia multiplies faster than many other perennials, so plan to dig and divide plants every two years.

One of the last of the prairie flowers to show off is bottle gentian (*Gentiana andrewsii*). Its unique clusters of bright-blue, bottle-shaped blossoms and deep-green leaves are all the more eye-catching when surrounding plants are taking on the subdued, golden tints of autumn.

Why do the buds stay closed like bottles instead of opening like other flowers? The answer depends on whom you ask. Some think it's to limit cross-pollination, since only bumblebees are strong enough to force their way inside. Another guess: the closed flowers provide a safe haven for bumblebees at night.

A native of open woods and wet meadows, bottle gentian grows about 2 feet tall and thrives in full sun or partial shade.

Wildflowers for Shade

If, as Emerson wrote, "earth laughs in flowers," then spring is a mirthful riot in Midwest woodlands. Beginning in early April, a continuous parade of spring-blooming wildflowers marches across the forest floor.

By duplicating nature's handiwork in shady places in your own yard, you can easily enjoy the flowers' beauty even on days too busy for a walk in the woods.

Bloodroot (*Sanguinaria canadensis*), one of the first to bloom in spring, produces exquisite, waxy, pure-white, 2-inch blossoms that have golden centers. A single leaf emerges wrapped around each flower stalk, then gradually unfurls.

When bloodroot blossoms open, whoever sees them first at our place spreads the word. Bloodroot's bloom period is relatively short, and we don't want to miss the show. Fortunately, the handsome, lobed, blue-green leaves expand to fill the void after the flowers are gone.

A member of the poppy family, bloodroot plants grow 6 to 14 inches tall and spread very slowly into a small colony. If the weather turns dry, the plants protect themselves by going dormant, only to reappear unscathed the following spring.

Here are some other ephemeral beauties:

Virginia bluebells *(Mertensia virginica)* create an early splash of color, with pink buds opening to clusters of sky-blue bells on plants 1 or 2 feet tall.

Snow trillium *(T. nivale)* is the first of the trilliums to appear, followed by a parade of dainty three-petaled trilliums in red, purple, white, or greenish-yellow.

Mayapple *(Podophyllum peltatum)* grows as much as 18 inches tall, with creamy-white saucer-shaped blossoms nodding beneath a lush umbrella of foliage. After the poisonous, greenish-yellow "apples" ripen and summer temperatures soar, plants usually disappear for the rest of the season.

Dutchman's breeches *(Dicentra cucullaria)*, a relative of bleeding heart, produces blossoms that look like tiny upside-down pantaloons adorning small plants 6 or 8 inches tall. Blooming in April or May, the flowers are white or pink.

Rue anemone (*Anemonella thalictroides*), a member of the buttercup family, tops out at no more than 10 inches tall. Simple 1-inch white or pale pink blossoms are held above the dainty, blue-green foliage on wiry stems. Flowering continues over many weeks in spring.

While many shade-loving perennials are programmed to bloom early and then disappear as the canopy of leaves closes in overhead, rue anemone seems to last longer than most. If the soil doesn't dry out, the plants often persist until midsummer.

Because the beauty of most spring ephemerals is fleeting, the shady summer garden requires some perennials that have persistent foliage. Solomon's plume (*Smilacina racemosa*) is one native that is up to the job. Its clusters of fuzzy, creamy-white plumes bloom in late spring, but the 2- to 3-foot-tall gracefully arching stems and shiny leaves remain until frost. Cream-colored berries ripen to bright red in late summer.

The tiny spring flowers of wild ginger (*Asarum canadense*) may escape notice, but the handsome heart-shaped leaves persist. So do the graceful fan-shaped fronds of maidenhair fern, adding their delicate, lacy texture until late fall.

These additional shade-loving natives also persist throughout the growing season:

White baneberry (*Actaea pachypoda*) is a bushy plant 2 feet tall. White flowers in spring are followed by glossy white berries on red stalks in autumn. Each berry has a purple spot, giving the plant the common name of "doll's eyes."

Snakeroot (*Actaea racemosa,* syn. *Cimicifuga racemosa*) grows 5 feet tall, topped in July and August with showy white candelabras. The broad leaves are handsome, too. Like white baneberry, it makes a strong vertical accent in a garden of mostly low, mounding plants. Slow to get established, it rewards patience by being dependable and long lived.

Golden Alexander (*Zizia aurea*) grows 1 to 2 feet tall, with clusters of yellow flowers in spring and early summer.

Timber phlox (*Phlox divaricata*), sometimes called wild blue phlox or wild sweet William, grows about a foot tall. The lavender or white flowers appear in May. Seldom dense enough to crowd neighboring plants, they spread slowly into small colonies.

Jack-in-the-pulpit *(Arisaema triphyllum)* produces unique flowers with a hooded "pulpit" surrounding a column-like "jack." If the 12- to 18-inch-tall plants are watered in dry weather, their foliage will persist and the plants will brighten the autumn shade garden with clusters of bright red berries.

Wild geranium *(Geranium maculatum)* covers itself with rose-purple flowers in spring and early summer on plants 1 to 2 feet tall. The handsome foliage remains, often turning burgundy in autumn.

Celandine poppy *(Stylophorum diphyllum)* blooms for weeks in early to late spring, with waxy, golden-yellow, 2-inch flowers. Plants grow 18 inches tall, with handsome and persistent oak-like leaves.

Foamflower *(Tiarella)* has bottlebrush flowers in spring that are white or pale pink, plus handsome foliage that remains attractive throughout the growing season. For pairing with other perennials, choose a clumping cultivar like Sugar and Spice or a creeper such as Jeepers Creepers. Reserve aggressive varieties for use as ground covers.

Wildflowers from Seed

Late winter forecast: snowy, with a chance of wildflowers.

Sowing seeds of native flowers atop the snow has always worked in nature, and it can work for you, too.

Snow, ice, and rain provide the weeks of moist, cold treatment that most wildflower seeds require before they are able to sprout. Sunshine

BEST BET

To mimic the conditions found in the forest, prepare a garden for shade-loving wildflowers by digging organic materials such as shredded leaves or compost into the soil before you plant. To protect our natural heritage, buy nursery-grown specimens rather than digging up native plants in the wild.

"burns" dark seeds into the snow, even on bitter-cold days. As the snow melts, the seeds work their way down to the soil.

At Prairie Moon Nursery in Winona, Minnesota, experience has convinced Bob Copeland that the optimal time for dormant seeding of native plants extends through February. While sowing seeds right before a gentle snowfall might be ideal, he says the true ideal timing is whenever you can get the job done effectively. Just avoid planting seeds when the snow is glazed with ice, or if the wind is gusting over 30 miles an hour.

Won't birds eat all the seeds? Copeland says he gets asked that question a lot. His answer: After you tromp around the planting site, the seeds will no longer lie temptingly on a pristine white blanket. The odds of birds or small mammals consuming enough seeds to spoil your planting are remote.

If you prefer to keep a closer watch on your seeds, you can get them started indoors in pots by using your refrigerator to provide the cold, moist treatment many seeds need. Although admittedly a lot more time consuming than dormant outdoor seeding, I often depend on this method to increase the plant diversity in my small prairie patch.

Different kinds of wildflower seeds need different treatments. To grow Mexican hat or milkweed, for example, I put the little pots of planted seeds in a plastic bag in the refrigerator for thirty days. Seeds of rattlesnake master and bottle gentian require sixty days in the refrigerator.

A few hard-to-sprout native plants, such as Solomon's plume, need cool, moist treatment, followed by warm, moist conditions, followed by a second stint in the refrigerator.

Gentians, some of the most demanding of the perennials I've grown from seed, need eight weeks in the refrigerator, followed by warm temperatures and complete darkness until the seeds sprout.

Baptisia seeds don't require cold treatment but do need a twenty-four-hour soak in warm water.

There are also some easy-to-grow native plants that sprout readily without any pretreatment. Blanket flower, penstemon, bee balm, and purple prairie clover are as easy to grow from seed as tomatoes and marigolds.

While it's both fun and economical to start wildflowers from seed, it makes sense to buy plants if you need only a few natives for a small garden. Either way, you'll be rewarded with well-adapted plants that attract birds and butterflies.

Prairie Grasses

The perfect accent for fall-blooming prairie flowers is prairie grasses.

These native grasses are also a brown-thumber's delight, thriving in lean soils with little or no fertilizer and easily tolerating drought. To stay at their best, these grasses require just one routine chore: Before new growth begins each spring, cut off last year's growth close to the ground.

For a garden setting, I especially like prairie dropseed (*Sporobolus heterolepis*), switch grass (*Panicum virgatum*), and little bluestem (*Schizachyrium scoparium*). All three are well-behaved, fine-textured grasses that won't overwhelm their neighbors.

Prairie dropseed grows in a graceful fountain shape, 2 to 3 feet tall. Without any pampering, it sails through summer's challenging weather, maintaining springtime beauty with emerald-green foliage. In autumn, airy and fragrant seed heads appear and the leaves turn golden-orange.

Switchgrass has a more upright shape and narrow deep-green or blue-green leaves that turn burgundy, gold, or bronze in autumn. Their dainty flower spikes turn golden brown, topping plants that grow 3 to 6 feet tall. I particularly like North Wind, which stands up straighter than other varieties.

Most ornamental grasses fade to the color of wheat in winter, but not little bluestem. The beloved "red grass" of Willa Cather's prairie stories, it maintains its attractive russet red during the dreary months when the garden is desperately in need of a little color. Gently arching leaves grow about 3 feet tall, with attractive silvery seed heads in autumn. If little bluestem gets floppy later on, I simply pull out the seed heads.

Prairie dropseed, switch grass, and little bluestem are all warm-season grasses. If you want to plant a little prairie, sow seeds anytime from May through August. If you have room for just a few grasses, buy started plants and transplant after the last spring frost.

CHAPTER 4

BULBS

COLOR IN A CAPSULE

When autumn leaves begin to fall, it's time to grab your sacks of spring-flowering bulbs and head to the garden.

Never mind that bulbs appeared in garden centers weeks earlier. Or that your neighbors smugly reported that they got all their bulbs in the ground in September. If you procrastinated a bit, your bulbs will be better off for it.

Why? Because bulbs are easily stressed if they're planted in warm soil. Falling autumn leaves are nature's signal that the soil is cool enough to suit bulbs. October and November are prime time for bulb planting in the Midwest, but even December will do if the ground's not frozen.

While you wait for the proper planting time, store bulbs in a sack in a cool place. The hard protective covering of hardy bulbs such as tulips and daffodils will protect them from drying out for several months in autumn.

Dig compost or other organic material into the soil before planting bulbs. In future years, a sprinkle of a slow-release fertilizer on the soil surface in autumn or when the plants first emerge in spring will keep the plants well nourished.

After you finish planting, water the soil. Bulbs need water to put down their roots. Place a piece of welded wire fence fabric or poultry netting over the soil to keep squirrels from digging up the bulbs.

Where to Plant Bulbs

Bulbs are a great choice for a small garden because they don't require a place of their own. The best bulb displays are in layered flower beds, with perennials or ground covers planted right over the top of the bulbs.

Most bulbs require excellent soil drainage. If you have a soggy clay soil, plant your bulbs in a raised bed or berm.

Bulbs also need sunshine, but you can still have a beautiful display of flowering bulbs beneath a tree. Most bulbs — especially early bloomers such as crocuses and miniature daffodils — bloom before the tree sprouts its canopy of leaves.

Avoid planting bulbs in flower beds that you water regularly in summer because bulbs are apt to rot in wet soil when they're dormant. Moisture-loving plants such as astilbe and ligularia, for example, make poor partners for bulbs because they require lots of supplemental water in summer.

Planting bulbs near trees works especially well, since the tree roots quickly take up any excess water that might otherwise rot the bulbs. Another good choice: plant bulbs in beds filled with drought-tolerant perennials that can fend for themselves, such as beardtongue (*Penstemon*), catmint, and yarrow.

Some of the very best spots for spring-flowering bulbs are hidden in autumn, just when you need to find them.

No doubt that's why it took me years to think of crawling under the branches of a large butterfly bush to plant daffodils. Although this sprawling shrub dominates my garden summer through winter, it always left an ugly gap after I cut its branches to the ground in spring. Now I

BEST BET

Before you plant bulbs, consider a trip to the feed store to buy chicken grit. Tossing a handful of chicken grit under and over tulips and other vulnerable bulbs will deter voles. Alternate deterrents include sharp gravel or crushed oyster shell. You can also make your bulbs less appetizing to critters by dipping them in Bulb Guard or spraying them with Ro-pel.

enjoy the early bulb show and, when it fades, the shrubs' new shoots quickly hide the bulbs' withering foliage.

Other good spots for bulbs include at the base of ornamental grasses and under sub-shrubs such as Russian sage and bush clematis. All should be cut back in early spring, about the time bulbs emerge.

What to Do When the Bulb Show Ends

Once the blossoms of spring-flowering bulbs begin to fade, tidy gardeners have a terrible time. Snapping off the old blossoms isn't difficult. But waiting up to ten weeks for the bulbs' foliage to die a natural death? That's what drives tidy gardeners crazy!

For the sake of future flowers, horticulturists frown on most of the plans concocted by fastidious gardeners to disguise their bulbs' yellowing leaves. The experts nix the idea of braiding daffodil leaves or tying tulip foliage into neat little packages. But the "plant police" won't object a bit if you use other plants to hide your bulbs' foliage.

For a quick fix, try planting annuals between the bulbs. Look for easy-care plants like geranium or lantana that won't require frequent watering.

Better yet, depend on self-seeding annuals to do the job. Larkspur and melampodium are two of my favorites. After planting them once, years ago, I know they'll come up every year in the bulb bed, ready to mask the bulbs' yellowing foliage.

The dying leaves of short plants such as grape hyacinth, species tulips, or small alliums are easy to disguise. Simply plant these bulbs under a ground cover such as ajuga or lamium. But a ground cover doesn't do much for hiding the foliage of daffodils, most tulips, or giant alliums. They need taller plants to hide behind.

I once made the mistake of planting daylilies over daffodil bulbs. It looked great — until the daylilies grew crowded. As I dug and divided the daylilies, I couldn't avoid slicing into many of the bulbs beneath. Far better, I realized, to plant bulbs with perennials that prefer to grow undisturbed.

Some of my favorite perennial partners that bloom in spring along with the bulbs include willow bluestar (*Amsonia tabernaemontana*), with starry pale blue flowers and willow-like foliage, and cushion spurge (*Euphorbia polychroma*), which offers bright yellow bracts in spring.

Summer-blooming partners I often use to continue the flower show after the bulbs fade include violet-blue Walker's Low catmint and yellow-flowered Zagreb threadleaf coreopsis.

Prairie natives such as false indigo and butterfly milkweed are perfect because, once established, they seldom require supplemental watering and never need to be dug up and divided.

PLANTING DEPTH FOR SPRING-BLOOMING BULBS

Camass: 4 to 5 inches

Colchicum: 3 to 4 inches

Crocus: 2 to 3 inches

Daffodil, standard: 6 to 8 inches

Daffodil, wild or species: 4 inches

Dog-tooth violet: 3 inches

Fritillaria: 5 inches

Grape hyacinth: 3 inches

Glory-of-the-snow: 3 inches

Grecian windflower: 1 to 2 inches

Hyacinth: 4 to 5 inches

Puschkinia: 3 inches

Siberian squill: 3 to 5 inches

Snowdrop: 3 inches

Snowflake: 3 inches

Star-of-Bethlehem: 3 inches

Tulip, standard: 8 inches

Tulip, wild or species: 4 to 6 inches

Winter aconite: 3 inches

Daffodils

I'm partial to the bright yellow blossoms of daffodils that lift my spirits in spring. I also love daffodils because deer, squirrels, and voles don't.

Another plus: Instead of fizzling out after a few years, daffodils tend to multiply. Hillsides on long-abandoned homesteads where these charming flowers are thriving testify to the bulbs' endurance.

Besides the traditional yellow, daffodils come in orange, pink, white, and bicolors. Some have large, trumpet-shaped flowers. Others have double blossoms with frilly petals, or charming cup-shaped blooms. There are also wild, or species, daffodils that grow from bulbs no larger than the tip of your little finger. They produce miniature blooms atop plants only 5 or 6 inches tall.

When viewed from a distance, daffodils' side-facing, trumpet-shaped blossoms are a delight. Along a walkway or other place where the flowers are viewed at close range, though, I enjoy one of the less common, up-facing varieties, such as Las Vegas or Marieke.

Tulips

In kindergarten, my flower pictures were always tulips: two large, pointy leaves and a single stem topped with a big red flower.

And that's how I continued to picture tulips for many years, despite my growing appreciation for their varied colors and flower forms.

Then I discovered multi-flowered varieties such as Antoinette, Orange Bouquet, and Happy Family, and the way I picture tulips changed forever. Instead of one blossom per stem, these marvelous bulbs produce a whole bouquet, often with five or six flowers on a single stem.

Multi-flowered tulips provide "more bang for the buck," as a friend who runs a public garden often reminds me.

Tulip bulbs need protection from voles and other animal pests. If deer frequent your garden, be prepared in spring to protect emerging tulips with regular sprayings of a deer repellent.

BEST BET

Wild, or species, tulips are small but persistent. Unlike fancy tulip hybrids which often fizzle after a year or two, wild tulips are tough little bulbs that bloom and multiply for years. Most kinds grow less than 8 inches tall. Darwin hybrids are another good choice for long-lasting tulips.

Alliums

Also known as ornamental onions, alliums smell enough like their cousins to discourage would-be pests. They come in a wide variety of flower colors (blue, pink, purple, white, or yellow) and heights (6 to 40 inches), with bloom times that range from spring through fall.

Some alliums have clusters of small flowers arranged in a dense sphere, like a ball, while others are arranged in a loose collection. The clusters vary in size from only an inch to huge balls that measure nearly a foot in diameter.

The range of choices allows for creative pairing with any perennials that grow in sun or partial shade. The showy flower clusters of the alliums bloom on slender stems and appear to be floating in air, hovering above the perennials. You could, for example, enjoy the giant balls of Purple Sensation alliums hovering over a bed of white daisies, or the amethyst-colored flowers of star of Persia (*Allium christophii*) floating above a dark-leaved sedum such as Purple Emperor.

A petite, late-season treasure is the Japanese flowering onion (*Allium thunbergii* 'Ozawa'). Growing less than a foot tall, it produces showy clusters of rosy-purple flowers that last throughout the autumn. The grass-like leaves dress for fall, too, turning from green to a handsome reddish-bronze.

Even in winter, after the blossoms have dried and faded to pink, I welcome the splash of color they provide until the tiny plants are covered by snow.

OTHER PEST-RESISTANT BULBS

Camass

Colchicum

Daffodil

Fritillaria

Glory-of-the-snow

Grape hyacinth

Hyacinth

Scilla

Snowdrop
Spanish bluebell
Winter aconite

....

Hardy Minor Bulbs

For a special delight, try planting a mass of tiny, early-blooming bulbs in the lawn. Blooming in late winter and often appearing as soon as the snow melts, they provide an early splash of color.

After their blooms fade, the plants wither and disappear long before it's time to start mowing. And don't worry that digging holes for bulbs will damage the lawn; minor bulbs require only very small holes, 3 inches deep. A dandelion digger makes the perfect planting tool.

Here are three bulbs you can count on for an early show:

- **Snowdrops** *(Galanthus)* have white nodding flowers shaped like small bells.
- **Winter aconites** *(Eranthis)* produce inch-wide flowers that resemble yellow-gold buttercups.
- **Snow crocuses** *(C. chrysanthus)* boast brightly colored, cup-shaped flowers in blue, purple, white, and yellow.

SMALL BULBS FOR PARTIAL SHADE

In mid-spring, white stars light the walk to my front door. Unlike the heavenly stars, though, my stars shine from the ground and show up better by day than by night.

The fragrant blossoms of hardy bulbs planted in fall, they are stars-of-Bethlehem (*Ornithogalum umbellatum*). The bulbs quickly made themselves at home in the partial shade beneath some shrubs. Carefree and hardy, the 6-inch-tall plants continue to spread themselves through the ground covers in my front yard.

Mention spring bulbs, and most people think first of tulips and daffodils. But there are dozens of other, lesser-known bulbs that, like star-of-Bethlehem, thrive in Midwest gardens. Another is dog-tooth violet (*Erythronium*). Also called trout lily, it has graceful, nodding flowers and colorful leaves. Dog-tooth violets hail from several different continents, including North America.

In a shady garden near the house, I planted a few bulbs of Pagoda, a yellow-flowering dog-tooth violet hybrid. Because dog-tooth violets are slow to settle in, I didn't expect flowers that first spring. Meanwhile, nature was one giant step ahead of me. When my husband, Don, cut a new trail through the woods the following spring, we discovered a whole slope already covered with native white dog-tooth violets.

If you prefer pink or purple, species of dog-tooth violets that are native to Europe and Japan will fill the bill. Like our own dog-tooth violet, they do best in rich, well-drained soil and partial shade.

Here are a few more bulbs that grow exceptionally well in the partial shade beneath trees and shrubs:

- **Grape hyacinths** come in purple, blue, white, and bicolors. Their sweetly scented flowers look like upside-down grape clusters and bloom for three weeks or more in spring. Most kinds grow about 6 inches tall. These bulbs excel at multiplication and quickly form a carpet of spring-blooming flowers.
- **Siberian squill** *(Scilla siberica)* spreads into a 6-inch-tall carpet of intense blue in April, with nodding, star-shaped flowers. A good candidate for naturalizing, the plants spread rapidly by seeds and offsets in moist soil. If you prefer a softer gentian-blue, plant twin-leaf squill (*Scilla bifolia*).
- **Striped squill** *(Puschkinia)* isn't something you'll find in every display of garden bulbs, but it's worth looking for. They'll charm you in early spring with their spikes of bell-shaped blossoms that are bluish white, accented with darker blue stripes. If you prefer, there is also a pure white variety. The plants grow only 5 or 6 inches tall. Extremely easy to grow and cold hardy throughout the Midwest, these natives of Asia Minor thrive in full sun or partial shade in any well-drained soil.
- **Guinea-hen flower** *(Fritillaria meleagris)* is the hardiest of the fritillarias. The purple-and-white flowers have an unusual checkered pattern that earns the plants another common name, checkered lily. Attractive, bell-shaped flowers hang from foot-tall stems. The plants prefer a cool spot and well-drained soil.
- **Grecian windflower** *(Anemone blanda)* produces charming, many-petaled flowers, usually white or a shade of pink. Despite their

common name, they actually dislike wind and prefer to grow in a protected spot. Soak the rhizomes overnight before planting.

Fall-Blooming Bulbs

It's fun to watch the face of someone who has just discovered crocuses blooming in autumn. Anyone who knows crocuses only as spring's first flowers is always quite startled to learn that there are some that bloom at the opposite end of the growing season.

The brightly colored flowers and short, grass-like foliage of fall-flowering crocuses look a lot like the spring-flowering types. They're just programmed for different timing.

While fall-flowering crocuses are not a familiar sight in our region, they've been around a long time. Many are heirlooms dating back to the 1800s. The history of the fall-flowering saffron crocus goes back to ancient Rome, where the lilac-colored flowers were grown for medicine and dye.

Although the saffron crocus is winter hardy only to zone 5 or 6, there are many other fall crocuses that will survive zone 4 winters.

Growing flowers from bulbs usually requires patience, but fall crocuses are a happy exception. Plant some in August and you'll be enjoying their flowers in just a few weeks.

The same goes for colchicums, another kind of fall-flowering bulb. Colchicums are so eager to bloom that gardeners laugh about unplanted bulbs they find blooming in the sack.

Most kinds of colchicum flowers look a lot like crocuses. In fact, they're sometimes called autumn crocus since they produce blooms that look like a super-sized version of the spring-flowering crocus. You can choose colchicums in white or various shades of pink and purple. Some are bicolored. One named Waterlily has large, frilly, double blooms that resemble the flowers of their namesake. Many kinds are cold hardy throughout the Midwest.

Colchicums have one big advantage over crocuses: Critters don't bother colchicums because they're poisonous to animals.

Unlike fall crocuses, colchicums produce flowers on leafless stems. Their leaves grow not in fall but in spring, then gradually wither and die in summer.

These 8-inch-tall strap-like leaves are something of an eyesore in the garden when they begin to yellow in summer. For the sake of the bulbs, you must allow this foliage to remain until completely dead. To help hide it from view, you can plant the bulbs in a ground cover like pachysandra or lamium. Summer-blooming annuals such as impatiens or marigolds also make good companions to screen the yellowing foliage of the bulbs from view.

Bulbs for Wet Sites

If you're longing to grow some spring-blooming bulbs in a low spot that often stays wet, forget daffodils and tulips. A better bet is to plant some camass bulbs. Soggy soil won't faze these bulbs, which grow naturally in wet meadows.

Native to the northwest United States, camass bulbs were cooked and eaten to satisfy the hunger of American Indians, who then taught Lewis and Clark to do the same. I'm not interested in eating these bulbs, but I love to look at the 2-foot-tall plants with narrow, blue-green leaves and amethyst-blue, spiky plumes in late spring. Depending on the variety you choose, you could have blooms not only of blue but also of violet or white, with plant heights ranging from 1 to 3 feet tall.

In the Midwest, camass bulbs are completely winter hardy and thrive in either sun or light shade. Unlike many other bulbs, they adapt readily to growing in clay soil.

Lilies

Not to be confused with daylilies (*Hemerocallis*), which are sometimes called "lilies" for short, true lilies (*Lilium*) grow from fleshy bulbs. Unlike tulips and daffodils, these fleshy bulbs lack a protective cover to keep them from drying out. That means prompt planting is important.

Autumn is prime time to plant lily bulbs. Buy plump bulbs that show no signs of shriveling, and plant them as soon as you get them. The North American Lily Society recommends buying lily bulbs that are packed in plastic bags of peat moss or cedar shavings to help keep the bulbs fresh.

If you already have lilies, autumn is also the best time to dig and divide crowded plants. Many kinds of lilies, especially the Asiatic type, can multiply so fast that the beds are crowded with short, spindly stalks after just two or three years. Crowding also encourages fungus diseases.

When lilies aren't yet crowded, I simply cut the dead stalks at ground level. Removing the stalks every autumn is an easy but important way to discourage diseases.

Lilies demand good drainage. If your soil is often soggy, plant lily bulbs in a raised bed or on a berm.

A simple rule of thumb makes it easy to gauge how deep to plant lilies: Plant each bulb in a hole that is two to three times as deep as the bulb is tall. Water immediately after planting to settle air pockets and start new growth.

Lilies tend to grow tall but not very wide. They prefer to have their "heads" in the sun but their "feet" in the shade. These characteristics combine to make lilies ideal for tucking between lower-growing perennials like mums and daisies.

While you can plant lilies anytime in autumn before the ground freezes, you should wait a while before spreading a blanket of loose mulch such as pine needles or straw over newly planted bulbs. Otherwise, mice or voles might settle into the cozy quarters for the winter, using your lily bulbs for a ready food supply. Wait until the soil surface freezes before adding mulch.

Deer, rabbits, and gophers like lilies, so be prepared to protect your plants with a repellent or wire-mesh enclosure.

Fertilize lilies every spring when the plants emerge, using a complete, slow-release bulb fertilizer. When blossoms fade, clip off the entire seed head but leave the stalk and leaves to help build a bigger bulb for next year.

BEST BET

Old-fashioned orange tiger lilies often harbor virus disease. If you have them in your garden, bulb experts recommend you separate new lily plantings by at least 100 feet.

To postpone the job of digging and dividing lily bulbs as long as possible, wait until each lily stalk is completely dead in fall. Then put your feet on either side and jerk the stalk up. Lots of tiny bulblets usually come up along with the stalk, leaving room for the mother bulb to grow without competition. Share the bulblets with friends, plant them in another bed, or simply dispose of the extras.

Lilies make great cut flowers. To avoid staining your clothing or tablecloth, though, it's a good idea to snip and remove the pollen-bearing anthers in the center of each blossom.

ORIENTAL-TRUMPET HYBRIDS

When plant breeders hit the jackpot, the plant offspring inherits only the best characteristics of both its parents.

Such is the case with the lilies that result from a cross between Oriental and trumpet lilies, sometimes called Orienpets or OT hybrids.

These lilies get their exotic beauty and sweet perfume from their Oriental parent, their stature and vigor from the other. They also seem to be blessed with more resistance to disease than either parent.

Orienpets are tall and showy, with many varieties growing 5 feet tall or more. Each bulb produces numerous blooms in July or August, often producing its show after most other lily flowers have faded. Thanks to the many varieties recently introduced, you can choose from a wide range of colors.

Magic Lilies

After the leaves of magic lilies (*Lycoris squamigera*) wither and disappear in late spring, it's easy to forget the bulbs buried in the garden. So in August it's a happy surprise when the sturdy, leafless stalks suddenly shoot 2 feet up from the ground, topped with a cluster of showy trumpet-shaped, lavender-pink flowers.

The strange behavior has earned magic lilies a variety of common names. You may know them as resurrection lilies, surprise lilies, or naked ladies. Members of the amaryllis family, they're also sometimes called hardy or autumn amaryllis.

Magic lilies are easy to grow. I've yet to see them attacked by any critter, large or small, or by any disease. They're not picky about soil, either, and they bloom well in both full sun and light shade.

Magic lily bulbs multiply with abandon and eventually become too crowded to perform up to par. You can dig and divide them anytime during the growing season, but it's easiest to find the bulbs in early summer, after the foliage yellows but before it disappears. If you postpone the job until after the flowers fade, it won't hurt the bulbs but there's a chance you'll sacrifice next summer's blooms. Be sure to mark the spot where you plant them so you won't inadvertently slice into the bulbs.

If you're not already enjoying magic lilies in your garden, don't be dissuaded by what you might have read about their hardiness. They're more cold tolerant than frequently reported and thrive in gardens throughout the Midwest, provided they're planted 5 inches deep in colder areas.

Tender Bulbs

October is a peculiar month. While we're busy planting hardy bulbs, we have to remember to dig up the tender ones . . . at least if we ever hope to see them alive again.

Technically, most of these tender bulbs — such as dahlias, cannas, and gladioli — aren't really bulbs at all. Most of them are rhizomes, corms, tubers, or tuberous roots. But gardeners conspire to call them all bulbs, just the same.

DAHLIAS

Dahlias appeal to two types of gardeners: those who enjoy the challenge of growing perfect specimens for show, and those willing to tolerate a few imperfections to grow a bounty of colorful flowers without a lot of coddling.

While I greatly admire those who grow flawless dahlias the size of dinner plates, I belong to the group more easily satisfied. Luckily, dahlias don't require Herculean efforts to produce a wonderful flower show from late summer to frost.

The most difficult part of growing dahlias may turn out to be choosing which ones to grow. No other flower comes in so many different colors, shapes, and sizes. Dahlia specialists offer hundreds of named varieties in your choice of bronze, lavender, maroon, orange, pink, purple, red, and white, as well as some with two-tone blooms. You can choose dwarf dahlias only a foot high, or giants that stand 6 feet tall. Some have flowers that are round like pompons, while others look more like the flowers of a cactus or anemone. There are some with simple flowers that have only a single outer ring of petals, and so-called decorative types that have rows of extra petals.

I'm particularly fond of dahlias that have dark foliage. My favorite, called Ellen Houston, has gorgeous leaves that are almost black as well as decorative reddish-orange flowers.

To avoid the chore of staking dahlias, I prefer shorter varieties that grow only 1 or 2 feet tall. Ellen Houston, for example, usually tops out at about 18 inches.

Dahlias bloom best in full sun but also tolerate partial shade. To prevent mildew, allow plenty of space around each plant for good air circulation.

Dahlias prefer moist soil. Mulching the plants not only helps conserve moisture but also helps keep the roots cool for better growth. Frequent shower baths from the garden hose in hot weather go a long way toward keeping spider mites at bay.

The more dahlias you cut for bouquets, the more they bloom. When cool fall temperatures arrive, dahlias are at their best.

Although dahlias aren't winter hardy in the Midwest, their tuberous roots are easy to save. Check stored dahlia roots periodically, discarding any that show signs of rotting. But moisten the packing a little if it seems excessively dry.

HOW TO STORE TENDER BULBS

CALADIUM

When to dig: Before first fall frost.

How to store: Cut off tops after they dry. Store in container filled with perlite, sand, or vermiculite or in their pots at about 60 degrees F.

CALLA LILY

When to dig: After first fall frost.

How to store: Allow rhizomes to dry, then store in perlite, sand, or vermiculite or in their pots in a cool, frost-free place.

CANNA

When to dig: After first fall frost.

How to store: Clip off foliage. Let rhizomes dry a day or two. Allow a little soil to remain on each clump. Pack upside down in boxes or sacks and store in a cool, frost-free place.

DAHLIA

When to dig: After first fall frost.

How to store: Clip foliage back to 4 inches. Leave each clump upside down two hours for excess moisture to drain from stem. Shake off loose soil. Sandwich clumps upside down in a cardboard box between layers of sand, vermiculite, perlite, or dry leaves. Store in a cool, frost-free place.

ELEPHANT'S EAR

When to dig: Before first fall frost.

How to store: Cut back tops after they dry. Store tubers in a sack or in their pots at 60 degrees.

GLADIOLUS

When to dig: After first fall frost.

How to store: Cut the foliage 1 or 2 inches above the corm. Spread corms in a single layer to dry for several weeks indoors. Separate new corms from old, withered corms. Discard the old and store the new in a sack in a cool, frost-free place.

PERUVIAN DAFFODIL

When to dig: Before first fall frost.

How to store: Best to leave in soil in containers and move pots indoors to a cool, frost-free place.

PINEAPPLE LILY

When to dig: Before first fall frost.

How to store: Best to leave in soil in containers and move pots indoors to a cool, frost-free place.

TIGER FLOWER

When to dig: After first fall frost.

Hot to store: Allow to air dry, then store in sack at a cool, frost-free temperature.

TUBEROSE

When to dig: After first fall frost.

How to store: Allow clumps to air dry, then store in sack at about 60 degrees.

TUBEROUS BEGONIA

When to dig: Before first fall frost.

How to store: Allow to dry, then cut off tops. Dust tubers with sulfur. Store in dry sand, perlite, or vermiculite at about 50 degrees.

CANNAS

With bold foliage and colorful flower spikes that grow up to 7 feet tall, cannas have long been a favorite in large gardens. With newer dwarf varieties as short as 18 inches, cannas are equally at home in small spaces and containers.

Cannas bloom best in full sun and thrive in moist soil. After the last spring frost, plant dwarf cannas a foot apart and taller varieties about 2 feet apart. Mix a shovelful of compost into each planting hole, then plant each rhizome 2 to 3 inches deep.

Saving canna rhizomes after frost blackens the plants' leaves is an autumn ritual for many Midwest gardeners. Southern gardeners get to skip this chore, but I don't envy them. Canna rhizomes multiply so rapidly that Southerners have to dig and divide them in spring, anyway.

When I grow cannas in a container, I simply move the pot into the basement and ignore it all winter. The soil in the pot keeps the rhizomes from drying out.

In early spring, I cut the foliage back to near the soil level, slip the rhizomes out of the pot, and cut them into sections, each with two or three plump buds. I then replant three healthy-looking rhizomes in the pot.

To store canna rhizomes that were growing in the garden, I dig up the rhizomes and leave them outside to dry for a day or two. If the weather is below freezing, I set the clumps in the garage or throw a blanket over them.

My favorite storage containers for canna rhizomes are empty dog food sacks. I postpone dividing the clumps until spring, when it's easy to distinguish between sections with plump buds and those that are shriveled.

CALADIUMS

When you start with a shriveled tuber that fits easily in the palm of your hand and a few months later have a handsome shade plant in a coat of many colors, it's almost like turning a frog into a prince.

Caladium tubers planted indoors in March grow into beautiful plants with bold, heart-shaped leaves marked with red, pink, green, and white. You aren't likely to see any flowers, which are tiny and hidden beneath the leaves, but who cares? The leaves themselves are as showy as any blossom.

You could wait until May to buy caladiums already growing. But it's a lot of fun to start your own, especially in March when it's still too early to do much planting outdoors.

Fill pots almost full with potting soil, then add the tubers and cover them with an inch of soil. Water generously, let the excess drain, then put the pots in a warm spot, 70 degrees or more if possible. Caladium

BEST BET

A widespread virus disease is now making it difficult to buy healthy cannas. To be sure newly purchased rhizomes don't have the virus, choose plants grown from tissue culture.

tubers are sensitive to chilling. If your house isn't warm enough to suit them, set the pots on a seedling heat mat.

Wait until the plants start growing before you water again. As soon as leaves emerge, set the pots in bright light and water often enough to keep the soil moist.

Try to be patient while you wait to move your plants outdoors. Temperatures just above freezing aren't good enough for caladiums; they are harmed when temperatures dip below 50 degrees.

Once the weather is warm and settled, give your plants a chance to gradually adjust to outdoor conditions. Then plant them in the shade, either in the ground or in a container. A soil that is rich, moist, and well-drained is perfect. If the site is also protected from harsh winds, so much the better.

Our hot and humid summer weather is ideal for these tropical plants. They're thirsty plants, so be sure to water often enough to keep the soil moist. Pests and diseases are rarely a problem.

Rescue caladiums before the first fall frost. They make fine houseplants but, if space is limited, you can store a lot of tubers in a sack.

GLADIOLI

Amidst all the hoopla over new flower varieties, it's easy to forget old-fashioned favorites like gladioli. That's too bad, because glads have a lot to offer.

Long lasting in cut-flower bouquets, they're a handsome addition to flower beds. Hummingbirds are attracted to the funnel-shaped flowers, which are packed together on tall bloom stalks. The sword-shaped foliage is also a garden asset.

There are glads for any color scheme. They come in a wide range of colors, including cream, pink, purple, red, and yellow. Many varieties are bicolored and a few even offer a blend of three colors. The flowers also come in your choice of plain or fancy, with ruffled edges.

Glads are easy to grow from small corms that look like bulbs. The trick to prolonging the flower show is to plant a few more corms every ten to fourteen days. Expect flowers an average of ninety days after planting. If you plant the first corms right after the last spring frost and make successive plantings until mid-July, you could enjoy blooms for two or three months.

Before planting, enrich the soil with compost. Plant the corms, pointed ends up. The North American Gladiolus Council recommends planting the corms 3 to 5 inches deep and 4 to 6 inches apart.

Most varieties grow 18 to 36 inches tall, although there are also a few that stand only a foot tall. Because most glads are tall, they tend to topple in a storm. There are several ways to reduce that problem. You can hill the soil about 6 inches up around each stalk before bloom time, or plant the corms a little deeper in the first place. You can also stake each one, though that detracts from the beauty. A better choice is to plant glads among sturdy perennials or annuals that will help keep them from flopping.

Although glads are generally easy to grow, sometimes tiny insects called thrips cause problems. Suspect thrips if you see distorted blossoms and browning foliage. You don't have to bring out the big guns to control these tiny pests. Just pick off affected flowers and spray the plants with insecticidal soap every three days for about two weeks.

If blossoms fail to open and the leaves and flowers are streaked or mottled, remove and destroy the affected plant. There is no cure for this virus disease, which is spread by aphids.

A frost or two won't hurt gladioli. After the foliage dies, you can dig up the corms to store or just let the glads go and buy new corms every year. The choice is yours.

Acidanthera, a close relative called fragrant gladiolus or peacock orchid, has similar swordlike foliage but smaller flowers and a less formal appearance. Its blossoms tend to hang their heads rather than stand stiffly upright. Most have white or creamy-white, star-shaped flowers with red or purple centers.

Acidanthera flowers are wonderfully fragrant and the flowering time of each bulb lasts about a month, much longer than the week of flowers from a typical gladiolus bulb.

BEST BET

For any easy way to stretch out the gladioli season for many weeks, plant a mixture of early and late varieties all at one time.

Because acidantheras take a long time to bloom and can't be rushed into cold ground in the spring, they usually don't bloom until late summer or early fall.

ELEPHANT'S EAR

The huge, exotic-looking leaves of elephant's ear can add spice to an otherwise ordinary-looking garden. Non-gardeners would never guess that a plant so dramatic is also very easy to grow.

Actually, there are two different types of plants that share the common name elephant's ear. Close relatives in the same family, each grows from a bulb-like tuber. Both sulk if planted out too soon, but when the weather turns hot, they make up for lost time. Often, by the time I get around to planting the tubers, they are already sprouting in their indoor storage sack.

The cultural needs of the various kinds of elephant's ears differ, making it easy to find the perfect plant for your pot or plot.

If you have a constantly wet spot, the type known also as taro (*Colocasia esculenta*) will prove easy to grow. Its gigantic, heart-shaped leaves measure as much as 3 feet long and almost as wide. You can choose varieties with green or velvety black leaves, some with exotic markings. Others boast attractive red, violet, or blue-green stems.

Elephant's ears in the Colocasia group grow well in full sun or partial shade. The sunnier the spot, the more water they need. You can plant them in the ground, in a pot, or even in a bog or water garden where the water is 1 or 2 inches over the top of the soil.

Plant the tubers in rich soil with lots of compost or other organic matter mixed in the soil. It takes a lot of nutrients to grow such big leaves, so add a liquid fertilizer on a frequent basis when you water.

Elephant's ears in the other group (*Alocasia*) need more shade to keep from burning. While they, too, require moist soil, this type needs good drainage and won't like growing in a bog. Many have exotic silver or white markings on huge, glossy leaves shaped like hearts or shields.

Although elephant's ears are tropical or sub-tropical plants that could never survive a Midwest winter, they're easy to keep from year to year by two different methods. You can grow them in pots as winter houseplants, or store the tubers indoors.

Tuberous begonias bloom in shade, with large, showy flowers that often resemble camellias or carnations. They come in bright colors, including orange, red, and yellow. Some are upright plants while others have a trailing habit, ideal for a hanging basket.

Plant the tubers indoors in March, pressing them hollow side up firmly in the soil but not covered. You can also buy started plants to set in the garden after the weather is dependably warm. To protect the tubers from rotting, take care not to overwater. Also pinch off rotting stems or infected leaves.

Tuberose *(Polianthes)* is an old-fashioned summer bulb with fragrant, white, waxy, tubular flowers that light up the garden. After the last spring frost, plant the bulbs about 3 inches deep in a sunny spot with well-drained soil.

Tuberose bulbs multiply by dividing, with mature bulbs dividing into smaller bulbs that may not bloom for a year or two. So when frost blackens the foliage in fall, dig and store whole clumps in a sack. In spring, break the large clumps into smaller sections containing both large and small bulbs. That way, you're assured of blooms from every group.

Pineapple lily *(Eucomis)* produces spikes of curious and long-lasting flowers arising from a rosette of shiny, strap-like leaves. The flowers resemble pineapples, with an unusual tuft of green foliage atop a dense cluster of tiny greenish-white, starry flowers.

Plant three of the large bulbs in a 12-inch container filled with a mix of potting soil and compost. Set the bulbs so they are just beneath the surface of the soil. A spot that gets morning sun and afternoon shade is ideal.

Tiger flower *(Tigridia)* has brightly colored, triangular flowers with a center cup and tiger-like blotches, surrounded by three outer petals in orange, pink, red, white, or yellow. Blossoms last only a day, but each bulb typically sends up five additional 18-inch-tall bloom stalks over a span of six to eight weeks.

To grow tiger flower, also called Mexican shell flower, plant the bulbs 4 inches deep and 4 inches apart, and place the container in full sun. Store dried bulbs in winter at a cool room temperature.

Peruvian daffodil *(Hymenocallis)* has fragrant flowers that look something like a cross between a daffodil and an amaryllis, only with narrow, feathery petals that produce a spidery appearance. Sometimes called spider flower, this bulb blooms in white or pale yellow, with flowers clustered atop a single 18-inch-tall stalk.

Plant three bulbs about an inch deep in an 8-inch pot. Set the pot in a spot that gets morning sun and afternoon shade. They bloom best when left undisturbed in the pot. Store the pot indoors in winter at a cool room temperature.

Rain lily *(Zephyranthes)* is named for its habit of blooming after each rain in its native Central and South America. Plants grow best in damp soil. Only 6 to 10 inches tall, they have narrow leaves and crocus-like flowers of white, yellow, or pink. Plant a handful of the tiny bulbs in full sun, 1 inch deep and 3 inches apart.

Calla lily *(Zantedeschia)* has exotic trumpet-like flowers that stand upright among arrow-shaped leaves. The blossoms, most often in white or yellow, also come in lavender, orange, pink, rose, or red and are treasured by florists as long-lasting cut flowers.

After danger of frost, plant the rhizomes 3 inches deep in soil enriched with compost. The plants are good candidates for either containers or garden beds, so long as the soil stays moist. Choose a spot shaded from afternoon sun.

CHAPTER 5

SHRUBS

ALLURING ANCHORS

Small shrubs are big. Every year I see more of them in Midwest gardens, where they add year-round structure and contrasting textures.

These pint-size shrubs are easy to love. They fit nicely into today's shrinking yards, partner beautifully with perennials, and produce a lot of flower power with very little maintenance. They enjoy long lives, and you can count on them to fill a void in your winter garden, too.

Best of all, plant breeders are offering an ever-increasing selection of exciting small shrubs.

Take Little Lime hydrangea, for example. If you love the chartreuse blossoms of Limelight hydrangea but can't figure out how to squeeze an 8-foot shrub into your yard, this dwarf form offers the same look in a smaller package. At 3 to 5 feet tall and wide, Little Lime grows only about half as big as Limelight.

Little Lime blooms from midsummer to frost in full sun or partial shade. Like its big sister, Little Lime's flowers change gradually from lime green to pink and make wonderful bouquets, fresh or dried.

A cute little ninebark called Little Devil has the same great reddish-purple foliage that made Diabolo ninebark such a hit, but Little Devil grows only 3 or 4 feet tall and wide. Blooming in June, the pinkish-white, button-like blossoms contrast beautifully with the dark foliage.

Most of the forsythias on our acreage are space hogs, requiring annual pruning to keep them from outgrowing their space. Not so with Gold Tide, a delightful dwarf that grows little more than 2 feet tall. Like other forsythias, it spreads gradually wider, but just a few snips keep it in its place.

Buds of sun-loving forsythias are subject to damage from late-winter cold snaps, but Gold Tide is so short that its blossoms are often protected by snow.

Little Henry Virginia sweetspire is practically perfect. I love its spires of white flowers that attract butterflies in early summer and its outstanding reddish-purple foliage in autumn. And I especially love the way deer tend to avoid browsing on it.

Slightly more than half the size of Henry's Garnet sweetspire, Little Henry grows only 2 or 3 feet tall and wide. It can take full sun but also puts on a surprisingly good display of summer flowers and autumn color in the shade.

Weigelas such as Red Prince and White Knight are fine plants for a shrub border, but too big to partner with perennials in the garden. Not so with Tango and Rumba, Dance series weigelas that grow no more than 3 feet tall.

Midnight Wine is smaller yet. Its mound of dark burgundy-purple foliage stands only a foot tall.

Hummingbirds are attracted to the trumpet-shaped blossoms of weigelas in late spring. Some varieties continue to bloom intermittently throughout the summer.

Some shrubs didn't require the breeders' touch — they're naturally small. Some of my favorites:

New Jersey tea blooms in July, with showy clusters of bright-white flowers that attract both hummingbirds and butterflies.

This small, adaptable shrub grows only 2 to 4 feet tall and thrives in full sun or partial shade, in any well-drained soil. Despite its common name, the shrub is a native not only of the East Coast but of the Midwest, too, appearing in the wild from Canada to Texas, New Jersey to Nebraska.

Potentilla, one of the Midwest's most popular shrubs, has a lot going for it. Drought-tolerant and small enough to tuck into a perennial border, it is also one of the longest blooming of all shrubs, with flowers of yellow, pink, or white often lasting from early summer until frost.

After a few years of neglect, though, this shrub can accumulate a lot of dense, twiggy growth. The number of blooms declines, and the shrub flops open in the center. The cure is simple: cut the shrub back by about half, every year in late winter.

Dyer's greenwood grows about 3 feet high and wide and lights up the garden in June with its bright yellow flowers. Sporadic blooms continue throughout the summer. Green stems add an unusual touch. It tolerates drought and loves full sun, but watch out for rabbits.

Shrubby St. Johnswort blooms most of the summer with exotic-looking flowers at times completely covering the willowy, blue-green foliage. The seed capsules that follow are attractive, and so is the peeling, light brown bark.

Growing only 3 or 4 feet tall and wide, this species of St. Johnswort is a great shrub for a small, sunny space. Tolerant of drought, it easily survives dry years without supplemental watering. In all the years it's grown in my garden, this shrub has never required any maintenance except a couple of times when I had to remove a stem that rotted and died during a wet season.

SHRUBS FOR MIDWEST GARDENS

ALPINE CURRANT *(Ribes alpinum)*
Hardy to USDA zone 4
Exposure: Part shade, shade

ARALIA, VARIEGATED *(Eleutherococcus sieboldianum*
'Variegatus', syn. Acanthopanax sieboldianus 'Variegatus')
Hardy to USDA zone 4
Exposure: Part-shade, shade

AZALEA, NORTHERN LIGHT SERIES *(Rhododendron* hybrids)
Hardy to USDA zone 4
Exposure: Sun, part shade

BLUEBEARD *(Caryopteris* hybrids)
Hardy to USDA zone 5
Exposure: Sun

BOXWOOD (*Buxus* hybrids)

Hardy to USDA zone 4 or 5, depending on cultivar
Exposure: Sun, part shade, shade

BUSHCLOVER (*Lespedeza thunbergii*)

Hardy to USDA zone 4
Exposure: Sun

BUSH HONEYSUCKLE (*Diervilla sessilifolia* and *D. lonicera*)

Hardy to USDA zone 4
Exposure: Sun, part shade, shade

BUTTERFLY BUSH (*Buddleia davidii*)

Hardy to USDA zone 3 to 5, depending on cultivar
Exposure: Sun

CORALBERRY (*Symphoricarpos* hybrids)

Hardy to USDA zone 3
Exposure: Sun, part shade

COTONEASTER (*C. adpressus* and *C. horizontalis*)

Hardy to USDA zone 4
Exposure: Sun

DAPHNE (*D. × burkwoodii*)

Hardy to USDA zone 4
Exposure: Part shade

DOGWOOD, RED-TWIG (*Cornus* species and hybrids)

Hardy to USDA zone 3
Exposure: Sun, part shade

DYER'S GREENWOOD (*Genista tinctoria* and *G. lydia*)

Hardy to USDA zone 4
Exposure: Sun

FORSYTHIA (*F. × intermedia*)

Hardy to USDA zone 3, depending on cultivar
Exposure: Sun

HOLLY, MESERVE HYBRIDS (*Ilex × meserveae*)

Hardy to USDA zone 5
Exposure: Part shade

HYDRANGEA, BIG-LEAF (*H. macrophylla*)

Hardy to USDA zone 4, depending on cultivar
Exposure: Part shade

HYDRANGEA, PANICLE (*H. paniculata*)

Hardy to USDA zone 3
Exposure: Sun, part shade

HYDRANGEA, SMOOTH (*H. arborescens*)

Hardy to USDA zone 3
Exposure: Part shade

JAPANESE KERRIA (*K. japonica*)

Hardy to USDA zone 5
Exposure: Shade, part shade

LILAC, KOREAN (*Syringa meyeri*)

Hardy to USDA zone 3
Exposure: Sun

LILAC, MANCHURIAN (*Syringa pubescens* subsp. *patula*)

Hardy to USDA zone 3
Exposure: Sun

MOCKORANGE (*Philadelphus* hybrids)

Hardy to USDA zone 4
Exposure: Sun

NEW JERSEY TEA (*Ceanothus americanus*)

Hardy to USDA zone 4
Exposure: Sun, part shade

NINEBARK (*Physocarpus opulifolius*)

Hardy to USDA zone 3
Exposure: Sun

POTENTILLA (*P. fruticosa*)

Hardy to USDA zone 2
Exposure: Sun

ST. JOHNSWORT, SHRUBBY (*Hypericum prolificum*)

Hardy to USDA zone 4
Exposure: Sun

SUMAC, DWARF FRAGRANT (*Rhus aromatica* 'Gro-Low')

Hardy to USDA zone 4
Exposure: Sun, part shade

SUMAC, TIGER EYES (*Rhus typhina* 'Bailtiger')

Hardy to USDA zone 4
Exposure: Sun

SUMMERSWEET (*Clethra alnifolia*)

Hardy to USDA zone 4
Exposure: Sun, part shade

VIBURNUM, ARROWWOOD (*V. dentatum*)

Hardy to USDA zone 3
Exposure: Sun, part shade

VIBURNUM, KOREANSPICE (*V. carlesii*)

Hardy to USDA zone 4
Exposure: Sun, part shade

VIRGINIA SWEETSPIRE *(Itea virginica)*

Hardy to USDA zone 5
Exposure: Sun, part shade, shade

WEIGELA *(W. florida)*

Hardy to USDA zone 4
Exposure: Sun

WINTERBERRY *(Ilex verticillata)*

Hardy to USDA zone 3
Exposure: Sun, part shade

....

SHADE-LOVING SHRUBS

After you've chosen trees for the crown of your landscape and grass
and flowers for the carpet, it's time to think about the rest of the story
... the understory.

Many different kinds of shade-loving shrubs can enrich the landscape
with extras such as attractive flowers, fruits, autumn color, varied leaf
shapes, or colored bark. When planted randomly under trees, these
shrubs look right at home, just like nature's own woodlands:

Variegated five-leaf aralia has no spectacular flowers but it shows
off throughout the growing season with beautiful green-and-white
foliage. A slow grower, it reaches about 6 feet tall and wide at maturity.

It's adaptable and easy to grow, thriving in any kind of soil and seldom
bothered by pests or diseases.

Each attractive leaflet is green in the middle with a broad, creamy-
white margin, perfect for brightening a shady border.

Japanese kerria covers itself with bright yellow flowers in spring and
then continues with a reduced but welcome flower show throughout
the season. It's a small and graceful shrub with arching branches of
green stems.

I love both the species and a variegated cultivar, for different reasons. The species blooms heavily in spring but continues to sporadi-
cally light up the shade with yellow flowers throughout the summer.

The white-edged leaves of the variegated variety, known as Picta or Variegata, show off throughout the growing season, although there are fewer flowers.

Japanese kerria tends to sucker, so don't plant it too close to prized perennials.

Bush honeysuckle *(Diervilla)* is an adaptable native shrub that deserves more attention. Not to be confused with the Asian honeysuckle shrubs (*Lonicera*) that are crowding out native plants in some parts of the Midwest, bush honeysuckle is a low shrub that produces pale yellow flowers in midsummer. The small, funnel-shaped flowers attract hummingbirds.

Because this shrub grows only a few feet tall and adapts well to dry, shady sites, I think it's particularly well suited for planting under trees. Its resistance to deer browsing is also a big plus.

Azaleas dress up the shade in spring with their colorful clusters of funnel-shaped flowers. The Northern Lights series, developed at the University of Minnesota, includes some of the hardiest varieties. Some, such as Orchid Lights, grow only 2 or 3 feet tall, perfect for small spaces.

Azaleas require acid soil. Get your soil tested before you plant and amend it if necessary.

Blue Muffin arrowwood viburnum, like many viburnums, will thrive in the partial shade provided by a nearby tree. A compact variety that grows only about 5 feet tall and wide, it offers flat-topped clusters of white flowers in spring and striking blue berries loved by birds in autumn.

SHRUBS FOR WET SOIL

After our daughter and her family moved into a new home, they discovered their yard was the low spot in the neighborhood. Even a moderate rain leaves the lawn squishy, and it isn't unusual to see standing water.

Across the back of the yard, a row of sad-looking arborvitae struggled to survive. They were planted on a soil mound, or berm. This raised area, no doubt, offered some relief from soggy soil when the evergreens were young. As the roots spread, though, they encountered the wet soil where the berm acts like a dam. Water held back from the surrounding hills creates a wet zone that seldom dries out.

Installing drainage tiles is an option. The simplest remedy, though,

1. Love-in-a-mist (*Nigella damascena*)

2. Stocks (*Matthiola incana*)

3. Melampodium (*M. divaricatum*)

4. Scarlet sage (*Salvia coccinea*)

5. Love-lies-bleeding (*Amaranthus caudatus*)

6. Cape daisy (*Osteospermum* hybrid)

7. Dahlberg daisy (*Thymophylla tenuiloba*)

8. Persian shield (*Strobilanthes dyerianus*)

9. Globe amaranth (*Gomphrena globosa*)

10. Cup flower (*Nierembergia* hippomanica)

11. Azure monkshood (*Aconitum carmichaelii* 'Arendsii')

12. Astilbe (*A. x arendsii*)

13. Lenten rose (*Helleborus x hybridus*)

14. October daphne (*Sedum sieboldii*)

15. Spotted dead nettle (*Lamium maculatum*)

16. Angelina sedum (*S. rupestre* 'Angelina')

17. Red barrenwort (*Epimedium* x *rubrum*)

18. Willow bluestar (*Amsonia tabernaemontana*) 19. Yellow meadow rue (*Thalictrum flavum*)

20. Full Moon tickseed (*Coreopsis* 'Full Moon')

21. Maidenhair fern (*Adiantum pedatum*)   22. Goatsbeard (*Aruncus dioicus*)

23. Grape-leaf windflower (*Anemone* x *tomentosa* 'Robustissima')

24. Helen's flower (*Helenium autumnale*)

25. Blanket flower (*Gaillardia aristata*)

26. Blue false indigo (*Baptisia australis*)

27. Snakeroot (*Actaea racemosa*)

28. Bloodroot (*Sanguinaria canadensis*)

29. Cup plant (*Silphium perfoliatum*)

30. Rue anemone (*Anemonella thalictroides*)

31. Rattlesnake master (*Eryngium yuccifolium*)

32. Queen-of-the-prairie (*Filipendula rubra*)

33. Cardinal flower (*Lobelia cardinalis*)

34. Prairie blazing star (*Liatris pycnostachya*)

35. Culver's root (*Veronicastrum virginicum*)

36. Bottle gentian (*Gentiana andrewsii*)

37. Tiger flower (*Tigridia pavonia*)

38. Purple Sensation ornamental onion (*Allium aflatunense*)

39. Striped squill (*Puschkinia scilloides*)

40. Autumn crocus (*Colchicum autumnale*)

41. Magic lily (*Lycoris squamigera*)

42. Calla lily (*Zantedeschia* hybrid)

43. Harry Lauder's walking stick (*Corylus avellana* 'Contorta')

44. Black chokeberry (*Aronia melanocarpa*)   45. Tiger Eyes sumac (*Rhus typhina* 'Bailtiger')

46. Virginia sweetspire (*Itea virginica*)

47. Hummingbird summersweet (*Clethra alnifolia*)

48. Variegated five-leaf aralia (*Eleutherococcus sieboldianus* 'Variegatus')

49. Forever & Ever Together hydrangea (*H. macrophylla*)

50. Winterberry (*Ilex verticillata*)

51. Cypress vine (*Ipomoea quamoclit*)

52. Climbing hydrangea (*H. anomala* subsp. *petiolaris*)

53. Perennial pea (*Lathyrus latifolius*)

54. Passionflower (*Passiflora incarnata*)

55. Moonflower (*Ipomoea alba*)

56. Sunny Lemon Star black-eyed Susan vine (*Thunbergia alata*)

57. Kohlrabi

58. Corn salad

59. Tomatillo

60. Leeks

61. Borage

62. Anise hyssop (*Agastache*)

63. Lemon balm

64. Stevia

is to replace the arborvitae with shrubs such as summersweet and winterberry that thrive in wet soil.

This easy solution is also a good option for people who keep killing their woody plants with an automatic sprinkler system that keeps the root zone constantly wet.

Summer Bloomers

Spring-blooming shrubs are a dime a dozen. But shrubs that light up the landscape in August? Now that's something special!

SUMMERSWEET

Summersweet waits until the dog days of summer to bloom, with spikes of pink or white flowers filling the air with spicy-sweet fragrance and attracting butterflies and bees. In fall, the glossy, deep-green leaves turn a pretty yellow orange.

This adaptable shrub puts on a grand performance in either sun or part shade. It thrives not only in normal garden soil but also in soggy soil with poor drainage, conditions that are fatal to most other plants.

Diseases and pests are seldom a problem. Occasionally, spider mites may attack in hot, dry weather, sucking the deep green from the leaves and covering the foliage with tiny webs. Fortunately, it's easy to stop damage from mites by washing the foliage with water from the garden hose.

You don't need a big yard in order to make room for summersweet. White-flowering Hummingbird and Sixteen Candles grow only about 30 inches tall. Ruby Spice, a pink-flowering cultivar, grows about twice as big. Unlike Rosea, an older pink variety, Ruby Spice flowers hold their color without fading.

If your soil is alkaline, you may need to amend the soil before planting. Scatter about 6 ounces of sulfur evenly on the ground in a 4-foot circle around summersweet every two years in winter to maintain acidity. Watch for yellowing leaves, the plant's clue that it craves a soil that is more acid.

Summersweet gradually increases in width as suckers sprout, but you can keep it in bounds by pulling out any extra shoots. Pruning is seldom needed. Flowers form on new wood, so if you want to trim your plant you can do it in early spring without sacrificing any blossoms.

NINEBARK

Although a North American native, ninebark didn't find its way into many Midwest landscapes until recently. Its growing popularity is due in large part to new varieties that offer exciting choices of foliage color.

White or whitish-pink, button-like flowers bloom in early summer, contrasting beautifully with the dark foliage. In time, older stems develop a handsome peeling bark.

Diabolo was one of the first ninebarks to attract major attention, thanks to its dark mahogany-purple foliage and pinkish-white flowers. But Diabolo is huge, growing 8 to 10 feet tall and wide.

If you like Diabolo's foliage color but don't have room for such a large shrub, you have two choices. You can cut its branches back to the ground every winter. Or you can plant a smaller cultivar such as Summer Wine or Little Devil.

Ninebarks are easy to grow and adaptable to almost any soil. They also offer good drought tolerance. Tough as nails, ninebarks are winter hardy throughout the Midwest. They grow in full sun or partial shade, although those with red or purple foliage need full sun to develop the best leaf color.

Insect pests are seldom a problem, but ninebarks sometimes suffer from powdery mildew if grown in too much shade or without good air circulation.

SHRUB ROSES

If you think roses are a lot of work, think again. These days, hard-to-grow hybrid teas with perfect flower form are pushed to the back burner as rose breeders around the world race to bring gardeners more disease-resistant, easy-care shrub roses that will bloom all summer.

When tough and hardy shrub roses like Bonica and Carefree Wonder kept climbing in popularity while wimpy and disease-prone varieties slipped into oblivion, breeders took note. These days, any disease-prone seedlings end up in the trash.

What do rose breeders wish you knew? That there's nothing

mysterious about growing great shrub roses. That instead of buying special rose food, you can just use the same fertilizer you use for your other flowering plants. That you can forget about routine spraying, since most new varieties offer excellent disease resistance. And that many shrub roses are hardy enough to make it through the winter on their own, even in the country's coldest zones, without elaborate protection.

What can you expect from your new shrub rose? More flower power than any herbaceous perennial in your garden, with wave after wave of blooms lasting until fall frost.

And there's still more good news for those of us who garden in the north: Many rose bushes are now produced not by budding but grow on their own roots. That means that if a rose comes back from the roots after a cold winter kills the top stems, the flowers will still be the same color as the rose you selected. There's no more worrying that any new shoots emerging from the ground might be coming from the plant's unruly rootstock and could overtake the less vigorous rose variety budded on top.

The root structure is stronger and, with no graft union to worry about, planting is easier, too. You won't have to dig as big a hole to place the bud union deep enough to protect it from winter's cold.

Rose experts say that these "own-root" plants also tend to be fuller and have more blooms.

How do you know whether the new rose you're considering buying is budded or grown on its own roots? Many rose producers have their own name for a series of roses grown on their own roots. All Easy Elegance roses produced at Bailey Nurseries, for example, are own-root roses. If roses in garden centers aren't marked, staff should be able to tell you.

You might also be able to tell just by looking at the rose yourself (provided the graft union isn't buried in soil). If you see a swollen knob on the stem, you can be pretty sure you're looking at an unwanted graft union.

HYDRANGEAS

By planting several different kinds of hydrangeas, you can enjoy huge, showy flowers all summer long.

The introduction of bigleaf hydrangeas that bloom on new wood makes it possible for Midwestern gardens to have a long season of pink or blue flowers. While older bigleaf varieties like Nikko Blue often fail to bloom here because their flower buds are killed by cold, the Endless Summer and Forever & Ever series changed the rules.

Even if your bigleaf hydrangea dies back to the ground in a severe winter, this new type of hydrangea will still bloom the following summer. Remove spent flowers to encourage the blossoms to keep coming.

If you plant smooth and panicle hydrangeas, you can also count on a parade of showy white flower clusters from June through September.

The billowing white flowers of a smooth hydrangea such as Annabelle bloom in midsummer. Panicle hydrangeas such as PeeGee bloom several weeks later. To stretch the bloom season into September, plant Tardiva, sometimes called the late-blooming panicle hydrangea.

A spot with morning sun and afternoon shade and moist but well-drained soil keeps bigleaf and smooth hydrangeas thriving and blooming. The more sun they get, the more moisture they need. Panicle hydrangeas bloom best in full sun.

What color are the flowers of bigleaf hydrangea? It depends. If your soil is alkaline, the flowers will be pink. If your soil is acid, you can expect the flowers to be blue.

If you covet blue hydrangea flowers and have alkaline soil, it's difficult but not impossible to change your soil. Start by digging several gallons of pre-moistened sphagnum peat moss into the soil before you plant. Every two years in winter, spread about 6 ounces of powdered sulfur in a wide ring around each plant. Mulch with small pine bark chips, which help keep the soil acid as they decompose.

To encourage good flower production, apply a slow-release fertilizer around all hydrangeas in early spring.

If you mulch the crown of a young hydrangea for winter protection, leave the mulch in place until the weather is warm and settled in late spring. Don't prune the first two or three years, except to remove dead flower heads in spring. Aim to keep the soil consistently moist, not soggy. Use a low-nitrogen, high-phosphorus fertilizer.

The best time to transplant a hydrangea that is failing to thrive, such as one that constantly wilts in the hot afternoon sun, is as soon as new growth begins in spring.

Some of the best summer-blooming woody plants belong to a group called die-back shrubs. Many are not hardy enough for their tops to survive winter in our region and, even if they do survive, look best when cut back to the ground when new growth emerges every spring.

Butterfly bush is one of the most familiar and loved. Bluebeard is another.

Bushclover is a die-back shrub that is too often overlooked for Midwest gardens. It shoots up from the ground to a height of 4 to 6 feet before its long-lasting flower show begins in midsummer. The clusters of pea-shaped flowers are most often rosy-purple, sometimes white.

Fragrant Shrubs

If you long for more of nature's perfume in your yard or garden, fragrant shrubs are perfect. They put the fragrance nearer your nose, so you don't have to stoop to smell the flowers.

When a shrub is called Koreanspice viburnum, you might guess that its flowers are fragrant. And you'd be right. The dense clusters of pinkish buds open to white flowers in spring, releasing a clove-like fragrance into the air.

Koreanspice viburnum and its hybrids, Judd and Burkwood viburnums, are some of the most fragrant shrubs for our region. They're also easy to grow. Although most are medium to large shrubs, there are also dwarf forms like Compactum Koreanspice viburnum that grows only 3 or 4 feet tall and wide.

BUTTERFLY BUSH

Butterfly bush is sometimes called summer lilac and — just like lilac — the fragrant blooms of butterfly bush are ideal for cut-flower bouquets.

If gardeners thought of butterfly bush as a perennial rather than a shrub, perhaps they wouldn't be so quick to worry when the woody branches fail to sprout new leaves in spring. Too many times I've heard of a gardener declaring his or her butterfly bush dead and ripping it out before new shoots had a chance to sprout from the ground.

And when do those shoots sprout? It all depends on weather. The first sign of growth of my butterfly bushes sometimes shows up in early April, sometimes not until late May. I've learned to be patient and to refrain from cutting off the dead top growth until I see new growth — the best practice to help your plant survive.

If you love butterflies but don't have room to fit a big butterfly bush into your landscape, you'll love a miniature version that grows only 2 or 3 feet tall.

My Lo & Behold Blue Chip, the first of the new dwarfs, is covered with fragrant, lavender-blue blossoms all summer long. Cutting off spent blooms makes the plant look prettier but isn't necessary to keep the plant blooming.

This little 2-foot dandy is perfect for growing in a container. You can plant it right outside a window on your deck or patio to get a close-up view of the butterflies and hummingbirds that visit the blossoms.

If you decide to try one of the dwarfs such as Lo & Behold or Flutterby Petite in a container, plan to move it into a garage or other protected spot in late fall to help it survive the winter. Or you might decide to grow it as an annual and just figure you got your money's worth with a summer-long show.

No matter what kind of butterfly bush you grow, you can expect best performance if you plant it in full sun. Well-drained soil is a must and is extremely important for the plant's winter survival.

Deer don't normally browse on butterfly bush and insects are seldom a problem. A few folks have reported spider mites on a butterfly bush in hot, dry weather. If you see the telltale signs of pale, stippled leaves, you can usually control mites with just a forceful spray of water from the garden hose.

LILACS

Of all the fragrant shrubs, lilacs are undoubtedly the best known and most loved. The so-called common lilac is wonderful indeed, provided you have enough space for a large, suckering shrub.

If not, smaller lilacs such as Palibin dwarf Korean lilac and Miss Kim Manchurian lilac offer fragrant flowers on shorter plants that don't produce any suckers.

Good air circulation and plenty of sunshine help prevent powdery mildew, a common disease of lilacs that is caused by a fungus. Palibin, however, is resistant to this disease.

Borers and scale insects sometimes attack lilacs. I've found that annual renewal pruning — fully removing one-third of the oldest branches — helps control both.

If the trunk and branches of your lilacs are regularly covered with clusters of flat scales, you might want to try an early spring dormant oil spray, before leaves emerge, to help get the scale problem under control.

Why does a lilac sometimes fail to bloom? Even if a lilac is blooming in its pot when you buy it, it isn't unusual for the shrub to take a couple of years to get used to its new home before it blooms again. Lilacs also need a spot with plenty of sunlight to bloom well.

Some years, lilac buds may be injured by a late freeze and fail to open.

DAPHNE

If you're up to a challenge, consider planting a daphne. Small shrubs with highly fragrant blossoms, daphnes have a reputation for being finicky.

I'd been enjoying the fragrant, light-pink flowers and variegated foliage of a Carol Mackie daphne for several years when my shrub suddenly died. It eases my feeling of failure a little to know that woody-plant guru Michael Dirr recognizes daphnes' habit of dying for no explicable reason.

BEST BET

If new lilac shoots turn black, blame bacterial blight. When this happens, the best thing to do is prune out any of the affected parts. Be sure to sterilize your pruners between cuts by dipping the blades in a 10 percent chlorine bleach solution or in rubbing alcohol.

Wounds provide easy access for disease, so take care not to bump into your lilac with the mower or otherwise injure lilac stems.

Well-drained soil is a must. A spot in part shade helps provide the cooler temperature daphnes like.

MOCKORANGE

An old-fashioned shrub with fragrant white flowers in June, mockorange is typically a very large plant. Nevertheless, there are some small, compact varieties such as Snow Dwarf, Snowbelle, and Miniature Snowflake that grow only 2 to 4 feet tall.

Fragrance is variable. I think it's best to shop for a mockorange in early summer, when the shrubs are blooming. Then you can find out for yourself if the fragrance of a particular shrub suits you.

Color for Fall and Winter

Shrubs can easily turn a slope or other difficult spot into a blaze of autumn color.

Take Gro-Low fragrant sumac, for example. Years ago, I planted a row of six in a spot where nothing else would grow. Since then, these adaptable shrubs have been thriving there without supplemental watering or any other coddling.

I barely notice the small yellow sumac flowers in spring. The leaves are fragrant, but you have to crush them to enjoy the smell. The fall show, though, is hard to miss. When dressed for autumn, the leaves of fragrant sumac are brilliant shades of gold, orange, or scarlet.

Fragrant sumac is normally a big shrub, but the Gro-Low sumac I planted grows only about 30 inches tall. It will grow in either full sun or partial shade, but you'll get the most spectacular autumn color if you plant it in full sun.

Spreading cotoneaster is another easy-to-grow shrub you can count on for an autumn show. Whether you plant one spreading cotoneaster as an accent shrub or multiple plants to make a hedge, you'll enjoy the showy fall combination of red berry-like fruit and reddish-purple leaves. Sometimes I enjoy a second fall show when a flock of migrating cedar waxwings arrives to feast on the fruits.

Spreading cotoneaster grows 5 to 6 feet tall and 6 to 8 feet wide. If you have only a tiny place to plant a shrub, try Tom Thumb creeping cotoneaster. This dwarf, which turns brilliant red in fall, grows only 8 to 12 inches tall. My Tom Thumb is thriving in the well-drained soil of my sunny rock garden.

Tiger Eyes sumac is gorgeous from spring to autumn. The deeply cut leaflets emerge chartreuse, then change to yellow, creating a beautiful contrast with the fuzzy, rosy-pink leaf stems. In autumn, the leaves put on an even more dramatic show, combining the yellow with scarlet and orange.

Tiger Eyes' form is elegant, too, with branches angling upward, and the lacy leaflets draping downward.

Much smaller than the species (*Rhus typina*), Tiger Eyes grows only about 6 feet tall and wide.

Living on an acreage where staghorn sumac is a common native plant, I never thought I'd get excited about adding a sumac to my garden . . . until I saw Tiger Eyes. It's now earned a place on my list of favorite plants in my garden.

This tough, drought-tolerant native has grown slowly, with no sign of the suckering that creates thick stands of staghorn sumac in the wild and would be impossible to deal with in a garden. However, I've heard from a few gardeners who have seen some minor suckering from Tiger Eyes in clay soils.

Blueberry and black chokeberry shrubs, described in the fruit chapter, also dress for fall with colorful foliage.

If you'd like to stage your own late fall and winter show but have no room for more trees or large shrubs, winterberries are the answer. One called Red Sprite grows only 2 or 3 feet tall and boasts loads of bright red fruits if there is a male variety such as Jim Dandy growing nearby. Against an evergreen backdrop or, better yet, a fresh blanket of snow, the berries are truly spectacular.

A native of lowlands, winterberry thrives in wet soil where many other shrubs fail. I planted mine where they get extra moisture from driveway runoff. Another good spot would be at the base of a downspout.

Although the shrubs grow just fine in partial shade, they produce the best display of fruit when they're planted in full sun.

To provide the acid soil winterberries love, I dug sphagnum peat moss and shredded leaves into the soil before planting. If I notice any yellowing of the leaves during the summer, I make myself a note to add about 6 ounces of powdered sulfur in a wide ring around each plant the following winter. Pretty simple.

Winterberry is a holly, but, unlike the holiday favorite, it's a deciduous holly that drops all its leaves in winter. I've come to think of that as a plus, not a minus. Our region's cold winds often batter the leaves of any broadleaf evergreens. Besides, who would want to hide any of the gorgeous red berries behind leaves?

If you can bear to sacrifice a few branches from the outdoor show, winterberry makes a fine indoor holiday decoration.

We enjoy the coralberry shrubs that color the edge of our woods with their purplish-red fruit from fall through winter. These native suckering shrubs are so numerous my husband, Don, thinks the trickling stream through our acreage ought to be named "Coralberry Creek."

The berries are very tiny, usually less than one-fourth inch diameter. Nevertheless, when seen in mass they can be quite colorful. I like to cut armloads of the arching branches to add to outdoor planters for winter color.

Whether in the wild or in my planters, the berries remain all winter.

Plant breeders have been at work, crossing coralberry with its other close relatives, including snowberry. The result: small, easy-to-grow hybrids that have bigger, showier berries than the native species.

One exceptionally lovely variety is Amethyst coralberry, which shows off in the autumn and winter garden with large purplish-pink fruits. Another variety, called Magic Berry, produces lilac-pink berries.

Coralberry shrubs are exceptionally cold hardy and aren't at all picky about soil as long as it is well drained.

A suckering habit makes these shrubs ideal candidates for planting as a ground cover or on a slope to help control erosion.

Garden color isn't doomed after the birds polish off all the fruit from berried shrubs. Many shrubs boast bright, colorful bark.

Against the subdued backdrop of the winter landscape, red-stem dogwoods add a welcome splash of bright color. Against a backdrop of snow, their red is nothing short of spectacular.

Exceptionally cold hardy, these native shrubs are adaptable and easy to grow in sun or partial shade. Compact varieties allow you to accent your winter landscape with red even if you don't have a lot of room. A red-stem dogwood named Arctic Fire, for example, grows only 3 or 4 feet tall and is not likely to produce suckers.

Kelsey dwarf dogwood is even smaller, growing only 2 or 3 feet tall.

I'm always impressed with a dogwood named Isanti. Slow-growing and dense, this University of Minnesota selection grows 5 or 6 feet tall and has not only red stems and twigs but also abundant white fruit and pretty reddish-purple fall leaves. Firedance is similar, but more compact.

Ivory Halo has a compact, rounded shape that grows at most to about 5 feet tall and wide. It owes its popularity to its beautiful green-and-white variegated leaves in summer as well as its attractive red stems that show off in winter.

If you really want to heat things up in your winter landscape, add some yellow, too. Arctic Sun has both colors on one compact shrub, with rich yellow stems tipped with blood red. Like the red-stemmed Arctic Fire, Arctic Sun grows only 3 or 4 feet tall.

Winter Flame is just a bit bigger, with a rounded shape 3 to 5 feet tall and wide. Its stems are yellow at the base but deepen to fiery orange and red at the tips.

No matter which of the dogwood shrubs you grow, regular pruning is the key to keeping the stems colorful. Because the youngest stems always have the brightest color, prune out about a third of the thickest, oldest stems every year in late winter or early spring.

Stem cankers, which dogwoods often develop if stressed by environmental conditions such as drought, are also best controlled by pruning. Make cuts well below any stem wounds. Dip the blades of your pruners in a bleach solution (1 part chlorine bleach to 9 parts water) between cuts to avoid spreading disease.

In the flamboyant summer garden, it's easy to think of green as a background color rather than the main show. But in the mostly brown winter garden, I treasure the green stems of Dyer's greenwood and Japanese kerria.

Harry Lauder's walking stick, a classic shrub for winter interest, is at its best when the leafless stems show off their bizarre curled and twisted shapes.

Easy to grow in sun or partial shade, the shrub does have one flaw. Most specimens are produced by grafting, and the straight-stemmed European filbert used for the roots has a tendency to send up straight stems from the base. To preserve the shrub's curly appearance, you must diligently cut out any of these straight stems.

If you can find a Harry Lauder's walking stick on its own roots rather than a grafted plant, that's the best bet.

BROADLEAF EVERGREENS

Any shrub that has evergreen foliage is a winter garden treasure. Unfortunately, most needled and broadleaf evergreens require cages or sprays to protect them from deer and rabbits. Boxwoods, however, are a happy exception.

Some hardy boxwoods for this region include Green Mountain, Green Velvet, Chicagoland Green, and North Star. All are small, compact shrubs that never need pruning.

Plastic holly often serves as an indoor decoration, but you seldom see real evergreen holly growing in a Midwest garden.

Why? For one thing, many kinds aren't hardy enough to survive our winters. For another, when the ground is frozen, even the hardiest evergreen hollies have trouble. If the roots can't take up water from the soil to replace water lost through the evergreen leaves, holly foliage dries up.

Despite the problems, some Midwest gardeners do succeed in growing evergreen hollies. The key is to start with one of the hardy Meserve hybrids, such as Blue Girl, Blue Maid, Blue Princess, or China Girl.

These female varieties are capable of producing bright red berries, but only if there is also a male plant nearby to pollinate them. You can easily tell the girls from the boys by their names. Some of the hardy male hollies include Blue Boy, Blue Stallion, Blue Prince, and China Boy.

The ideal place to plant holly is in a spot protected from the wind and afternoon sun. The soil should be rich, moist, acid, and well-drained. Mulch the soil to help preserve moisture and water in winter anytime the ground isn't frozen.

To give your hollies extra winter protection, spray the leaves with an anti-transpirant such as Wilt-Pruf. Made from pine resin, this non-toxic product creates a clear, protective covering that preserves moisture. Be sure the temperature is above freezing when you apply the anti-transpirant, so the liquid won't freeze on the leaves. One spraying is usually effective about four months.

Pruning

Unlike people, shrubs can be made young again. Annual renewal pruning does the trick.

It's a relatively simple process. Just take out at ground level about one-third of the largest, oldest stems.

If you repeat the process of renewal pruning every winter, you'll end up with forever-young shrubs that maintain their natural shape and never get too big for their space.

With renewal pruning, no single stem is ever more than three years old. Diseases and other problems of old age never have a chance. Increased air circulation around foliage also helps keep the plants healthy.

And what about "the rule" for pruning spring-blooming shrubs such as forsythia and lilac? The time-honored rule says you must not prune in winter but instead wait until after the blooms fade, lest you cut off all the flower buds. That rule does indeed apply if you were to trim back individual branches, a process known as heading back.

But who says you have to do any heading back? With annual renewal pruning, there are often no wayward branches left in spring to head back because the oldest stems removed each winter also tend to be the longest.

Renewal pruning allows you to turn an ungainly shrub such as forsythia, for example, into a shorter, narrower shrub with a delightfully graceful shape. This shrub will still produce an abundance of spring flowers on the remaining stems, all the more delightful because there won't be so many stems packed together.

Winter is my favorite time for renewal pruning because there are few other outdoor chores and no nesting birds to worry about disturbing. If there is deep snow piled around the crown of the shrub, though, I may not get the job done until spring or even summer. Fortunately, timing is not critical.

A small, handheld pruning saw is ideal for renewal pruning, particularly for those shrubs that grow so densely that it's difficult to get to the base of interior stems with any other kind of tool. I'm not much good with a saw, though, and depend on ratchet loppers whenever possible.

Although renewal pruning is fairly easy when done every year, it can be overwhelming when a common lilac or other large shrub has been long neglected. In that case, it's acceptable to cut all the branches back to about a foot from the ground.

This butchering will speed up the pruning, but be prepared for the shrubs to take time to regain their good looks. In the meantime, you'll lose a season of flowers as well as the privacy that large shrubs normally provide.

Although initially stressed, barberry, cotoneaster, honeysuckle, lilac, and privet will regain their good looks within a year or two after such drastic pruning. Small shrubs like Japanese spirea and potentilla will recover even quicker.

While winter renewal pruning works for most shrubs, there are exceptions. To control the size or shape of evergreen shrubs such as yews, arborvitaes, and junipers, wait until spring so that new growth will quickly cover any cuts. Prune as much as you like, but avoid cutting any branch beyond green growth, into the brown interior. Such a branch will not recover.

I also postpone pruning cut-back shrubs such as butterfly bush and bluebeard until spring. Sometimes called sub-shrubs, they're best cut back to a live bud just above the ground after the first signs of new growth appear.

Yet another group of shrubs grown for their colorful foliage thrives with this kind of maintenance: Cut them off near the ground every year in early spring. Then revel in their bright new growth every summer and fall.

This "forcing" of new shoots from a purple-leaf smokebush, for example, encourages more purple. Such drastic pruning sacrifices the "smoke" — pink, hairy plumes that normally would grow on flower stalks. But it produces brighter, prettier leaves.

And there's another plus. When you're planning to cut the shrub to the ground every year anyway, it doesn't matter if the stems die back in freezing weather. This means gardeners in the upper Midwest, above the normal range for smokebush, can enjoy growing these purple-leaf varieties.

The same technique works on colorful willows. Only the young, new stems of Britzensis coral bark willow, for example, are a bright and beautiful orange red.

The beautiful Hakuro-nishiki dapple willow, usually considered hardy only to USDA zone 5 or 6, does fine in my zone 4 garden. If the above-ground growth doesn't survive winter, no matter. The brightest pink and white leaves grow in sun or partial shade on the vigorous new shoots, anyway.

European elderberries grown for their colorful foliage also respond well to pruning back almost to the ground in early spring.

Both Black Beauty and Black Lace elderberries sprout leaves so dark purple they look almost black. And, unlike many other dark-leaf plants, the color doesn't fade in hot weather in full sun. Hard pruning keeps these ornamental elderberry bushes small enough to fit in even a small garden.

During winter pruning, I bypass roses. They're best shaped up in early spring by removing weak, damaged, and crisscrossed canes when the leaf buds begin to swell. Also make a pruning cut several inches below any abnormal swelling near the base of a cane, which could be caused

BEST BET

Wait until a smokebush, willow, or elderberry is well established and growing vigorously before you start an annual regimen of removing all its branches. With such major surgery, a young seedling might never show its face again.

either by borers or by a bacterial disease called crown gall. Sterilize pruners between cuts by dipping the blades in a 10 percent chlorine bleach solution.

PRUNING HYDRANGEAS

Hydrangeas are easy to prune, but knowing when and how to do it sometimes gets confusing. That's because it all depends on what kind of hydrangeas you have.

Do you have a smooth hydrangea like Annabelle? Its large, showy, rounded clusters of white flowers start blooming in June. Or maybe you have a later-blooming panicle hydrangea like Tardiva, with white, cone-shaped flower clusters that gradually change to pinkish bronze as they age?

Late winter to early spring is the right time to prune both of these types of hydrangeas. They bloom on new wood, so you don't have to worry that you'll be cutting off any flower buds. Cut each stem back to about 2 feet to produce a sturdy plant that blooms well.

If, on the other hand, your hydrangea has big pink or blue globe-shaped or lace-cap flower clusters, it's probably one of the bigleaf hydrangeas. If you prune Nikko Blue or most other varieties of this type of hydrangea in spring, you have no chance of seeing any blooms. After the last spring frost, just remove faded blossoms from the preceding autumn.

Some newer bigleaf hydrangeas like the Endless Summer and the Forever and Ever series bloom on both old and new wood. But that doesn't really change the pruning rules for this species. If you cut these rebloomers back in late winter, you'd not only lose all the flower buds formed on the old wood, you'd also set your plant back so it would be later to bloom on new wood, too. Instead, just cut off spent flowers and prune out any dead wood.

Like most other northern gardeners, I rarely see blooms on my oak-leaf hydrangea. But, although the tender flower buds are easily killed by winter's cold, the handsome oak-like leaves and fall color are reasons enough to plant this shrub.

In the parts of the Midwest where oakleaf hydrangeas do bloom, prune them after the blossoms fade.

CHAPTER 6

VINES

THE RIBBONS ON THE PACKAGE

Vines fit almost anywhere: on a trellis or post, covering a fence, tumbling over a tree stump, even scrambling up a shrub or tree.

The perfect finishing touch, vines "knit" together all of the other elements of a garden.

Vines are also great for concealing eyesores, covering structures, and connecting other elements of the landscape.

To conceal the electric meter on a post in front of our house, for example, my husband, Don, boxed in the post with several sheets of lattice. He then cut a hole for reading the meter. A perfect support for vines, the lattice now supports an American wisteria.

Hardscape features such as chain-link fences, garden arches, trellises, and retaining walls always look best when covered with vines. The John Clayton honeysuckle vine that twines its way over the arch at the entrance to my main garden is a real joy. I love its yellow blossoms, produced faithfully from June through frost, and also the steady parade of hummingbirds the flowers attract.

Although most of us think of vines as climbing plants, they also make great ground covers. You could use a few clematis vines scampering across the ground, for example, to visually connect the garden to the surrounding landscape.

While you wait for an old stump to decay, vines scrambling over it can turn the eyesore into a garden asset.

Practice patience when you plant perennial vines. Most need at least three years to get established. There is truth in the old adage: "First they sleep, then they creep, then they leap."

If you're in a hurry for vines to provide privacy, to shade the patio, or to screen out an ugly scene, plant seeds of annual vines in spring. Morning glory, purple hyacinth bean, and other fast-growing annuals do the job beautifully while giving perennial vines time to grow.

Twiners, Claspers, Clingers

If your Boston ivy won't climb your chain-link fence, don't blame the ivy. Blame the chain link.

All vines can climb, but not all the same way.

A twining vine, such as honeysuckle or Dutchman's pipe, easily wraps itself around chain-link fabric. Clasping vines, such as clematis and perennial pea, can also climb a chain link fence, holding on with small, specialized stems called tendrils.

Boston ivy, on the other hand, is a clinging vine. While it can't hold onto a wire fence, it can scramble up a wall or wooden fence post, adhering to the flat surface with its aerial roots, called "holdfasts."

If your house is made of brick or stone, you can grow clinging vines such as ivy, trumpet vine, or Virginia creeper right on the walls. As long as the mortar is sound, the vines won't damage the wall. If the mortar is already crumbing, the vine's aerial roots may worsen the situation. Keep the vine pruned below the roofline, so the aerial roots can't dislodge shingles.

Wood siding, on the other hand, is apt to rot if covered with vines. You can give the wood some breathing space by providing trellises for your vines. If a trellis is attached to the overhang with hooks, at painting time you can easily unhook the trellis and lay it on the ground, vines and all.

What about climbing roses? Roses are a good candidate for growing on a fence or trellis although they aren't really climbers at all. They're simply roses with extra-long canes you can tie to a vertical support.

TWINING VINES (CLIMB NETTING, LATTICE,
STRING, WIRE, OR A SLENDER POLE)

Perennial: Akebia, bittersweet, cinnamon vine, Dutchman's
pipe, honeysuckle, silver lace vine, wisteria

Annual: Cardinal climber, climbing snapdragon, cypress
vine, firecracker vine, mandevilla, moonflower,
morning glory, purple hyacinth bean

CLASPING VINES (TENDRILS WRAP TIGHTLY
AROUND WIRE, STRING, OR NETTING)

Perennial: Clematis, perennial pea

Annual: Passionflower, sweet pea

CLINGING VINES ("HOLDFASTS" ADHERE TO
TREES AND OTHER FLAT SURFACES)

Perennial: Boston ivy, climbing hydrangea, English ivy, trumpet
vine, Virginia creeper, wintercreeper euonymus

Annual: None

Clematis, Queen of Flowering Vines

One of the most popular of all vines, clematis comes in sizes and colors
to fit any sunny garden. You can choose from varieties that have giant
flowers up to 10 inches or great masses of tiny blossoms. The flowers
of some resemble clusters of dangling bells while others are shaped
more like flat disks.

Some grow so tall they can scale a tree, while others are a perfect fit
for a small obelisk. Most are somewhere in between.

Clematis flowers come in your choice of many colors, including blue,
lavender, pink, purple, red, violet, white, yellow, and bicolor. After the
blooms fade, the wispy seedpods are also beautiful.

This vine prefers cool "feet," easily provided by a layer of mulch covering the soil or with low-growing plants at the vine's base. Well-drained soil is a must.

You'll see more flowers if your clematis gets five or six hours of sunlight each day. Nevertheless, it's okay to plant clematis in the shade, so long as the vine can climb into bright sunshine.

When planting clematis, protect its crown by setting the plant 1 or 2 inches deeper than it was growing in its pot.

If you want to grow this clasping vine on a post or split-rail fence, first fasten a piece of fence fabric to the wood so the tendrils will have something to grab as they climb.

Wet soil encourages clematis wilt and may also cause clematis leaves to yellow. Yellowing leaves may also be caused by a magnesium deficiency. If you suspect magnesium deficiency, sprinkle one-fourth cup of Epsom salts on the soil around the plant.

Why Doesn't My Wisteria Bloom?

Wisteria is pretty picky and, worse yet, there's some conflicting advice from experts on the secret to getting a wisteria vine to flower.

But wisteria is worth the effort, because it is one of the most beautiful of all flowering vines, with pendulous flower clusters, often blue-violet or lilac-purple. Growing to heights of 20 or 30 feet, the vine is dramatic on a (sturdy!) fence, trellis, or arbor.

If you have a wisteria you haven't been able to coax into bloom, here are a few clues to help:

Blame cold temperatures for killing the flower buds. Although some kinds of wisteria are root-hardy to minus 30 degrees, their flower buds

> **BEST BET**
>
> If a clematis vine suddenly wilts and dies, a fungus disease called clematis wilt is the likely culprit. Large-flowered varieties are most susceptible. Don't be too quick to give up on your plant. New shoots often appear, if not right away at least by the following spring. Cut and remove the dead stems, then wait.

aren't. American wisteria (*W. frutescens*) is a much more dependable bloomer in the Midwest than the more common Japanese wisteria (*W. floribunda*) because the American species blooms on new wood later in the season. Kentucky wisteria (*W. macrostachya*) is another species with increased cold hardiness. Both North American species also have more restrained growth, which means they're less likely to topple your arbor.

Start with a grafted plant. Seedlings sometimes take ten years or more to bloom.

Restrict feeding and watering. Add no nitrogen, which may make the vine grow more vigorously but will discourage flowering. Spread a layer of compost as mulch around the vine. Water a mature plant only if there's a drought.

Prune off any suckers at the base of a grafted plant. The suckers can crowd out the more desirable part of the plant.

If your plant still won't bloom, consider root pruning. Slice down through the soil with a sharp spade, as if you were starting to dig up the plant.

Bittersweet

Growing American bittersweet (*Celastrus scandens*) is easy. The native vines with their glowing-orange berries grow like weeds, scrambling up fences along rural Midwest roadsides. Planted by birds, the plants need no help from a gardener.

Trouble is, until recently you had to live on an acreage to have enough room to grow your own bittersweet. Here's why: Only female plants produce berries and in theory you had to have room for both a female plant and a male plant to pollinate it. In practice, it's hard to identify young male and female plants when you buy them, so gardeners have often been disappointed with a lack of berries unless they had room to plant a half dozen bittersweet vines.

Now from Bailey Nurseries (www.baileynurseries.com) comes a bittersweet revolution. Appropriately named First Editions Autumn Revolution, this bittersweet has mostly "perfect" flowers. A perfect flower has both male and female parts, so you can be sure that even if you plant only a single vine you will still get loads of berries.

If you provide a sturdy trellis for this twining vine to climb, you can grow your own berries even in a small yard. The berries produced by Autumn Revolution are not only prolific but also bigger than those of wild bittersweet, making quite an impression.

Bittersweet grows in sun or light shade and is not at all picky about soil. The vines are hardy throughout the Midwest.

Supported by a trellis, bittersweet can grow 15 feet tall or more. You can also grow bittersweet on a fence or, if you have lots of space, let it scramble on the ground over rock piles or tree stumps.

Leafspot and powdery mildew are occasional problems.

Don't be disappointed if at first your berries are not brightly colored. When they first appear, they are encased in pale-orange capsules. As soon as the covering on the capsules splits in autumn, brilliant red-orange fruits are exposed.

If you want to gather clusters of bittersweet for autumn arrangements, do it before a hard frost. Any berries you leave on the vines will provide a feast for birds.

When buying bittersweet vines, avoid Chinese bittersweet (*Celastrus orbiculatus*). Also known as Oriental bittersweet, it is invasive, threatening nearby trees and shrubs.

Vines for Shade

Nature designed most shade-loving vines, such as climbing hydrangea and English ivy, to cling to tree trunks. Their aerial roots, or holdfasts, can stick to any large, flat surface, including not only tree trunks but brick and stone walls, too.

But what if you want to grow vines on a trellis in the shade? That was the dilemma I faced when I needed a vine that could climb a trellis on the north side of a shed. Here are a few possibilities, all hardy to USDA zone 4:

Woodbine honeysuckle *(Lonicera periclymenum).* Honeysuckle vines grow and flower best in full sun, but some species will tolerate light shade. With less sun, you can expect a honeysuckle to flower less. That's why I chose one called Harlequin, which has variegated foliage. With green leaves edged with white, plus pink highlights, it provides some color even though its yellow and pink blossoms are sparse in the shade.

Dutchman's pipe *(Aristolochia macrophylla).* The small brown flowers are so insignificant they are seldom seen, but this old-fashioned twining vine boasts beautiful large, dark-green, heart-shaped leaves. Undemanding, it will thrive in any light, from full shade to full sun. A fast grower, it can cover a trellis in a single season and prefers moist, well-drained soil.

Silver lace vine *(Fallopia baldschuanica, syn. F. aubertii).* This vine doesn't seem to care whether it's growing in sun or shade and thrives even in dry soil. In late summer and early fall, it covers itself with showy sprays of small white flowers, flowering more in a sunny site but usually putting on a respectable show in the shade, too.

....

WHEN TO PRUNE YOUR VINES

....

Bittersweet: Late winter or early spring
Clematis, spring bloomer: After flowers fade,
   just enough to keep plant in bounds
Clematis, summer bloomer: Cut back by half in early spring
Clematis, autumn bloomer: Cut back hard,
   to 3 feet or less, in early spring.
Honeysuckle: Early spring
Ivy, Boston and English: Whenever necessary
   to keep plants within bounds
Trumpet vine: Early spring
Virginia creeper: As necessary to keep plants within bounds
Wisteria, Japanese: Pinch back side shoots after flowers fade
Wisteria, American or Kentucky: Early spring

....

Tender Flowering Vines

If you've ever battled bindweed in the garden, you'll understand why early gardeners were reluctant to plant morning glories that look a lot like that aggressive weed.

But then in the 1930s, along came Heavenly Blue, with huge sky-blue blossoms. Gardeners were hooked.

Heavenly Blue is still one of the most popular morning glories, and gardeners still count on its quick-growing vines filled with large, heart-shaped leaves to provide welcome shade and camouflage.

Scarlet O'Hara, another early favorite still popular today, won an All-America Selections award in 1939 for its 4-inch, wine-red flowers.

Once morning glories caught on, offerings expanded to include varieties with trumpet-shaped blossoms of crimson, lavender, pink, violet, and white, as well as bicolors.

Moonflower, a close relative of morning glories, was quicker to catch the fancy of gardeners. Victorian ladies, who preferred to stroll in their gardens after the sun went down, cherished the 6-inch, white, trumpet-shaped blossoms that open at nightfall, emitting a pleasant clove-like fragrance.

Cardinal climber, another Victorian favorite, is once again popular in gardens. This morning glory relative is prized for its small red trumpet-shaped blossoms and dainty leaves. Cypress vine has similar flowers and ferny foliage. Both attract hummingbirds and, after decades of obscurity, both are readily available in catalogs and on seed racks.

There's no need to fertilize morning glories and their relatives. These vines bloom best when none is added. Planting in full sun also helps encourage blossoms.

Morning glory, moonflower, cardinal climber, and cypress vine are all twining vines that spiral around supports as they grow. They can easily wrap around netting, lattice, string, wire, or a slender pole. Once you help the vines get started at the bottom of the support, stand back and watch them grow.

BEST BET

As long as you soak the seed overnight before planting, morning glories and their relatives are easy to grow. Not all are quick to bloom, though. If you want to hurry yours along, give the seeds an early start in individual pots indoors about four weeks before the last spring frost.

Sweet peas, with their sweet scent and multi-flowered stems of delicate, sunbonnet-shaped blossoms, are always a delight. Unfortunately, they'd rather grow in the cool, moist weather of England than put up with the Midwest's hot and sometimes dry summers.

Still, they're worth a try if you plant the seeds early, as soon as the frost is out of the ground. You can speed up sprouting by soaking seeds overnight in warm water before you plant, then plant the seeds 2 inches deep.

Choose a place with morning sun and afternoon shade to shield the plants from midday heat. Spread compost 2 or 3 inches thick on the ground, then spade deeply before you plant.

To keep flowers coming, remove faded blossoms before they start to set seed.

By the time annual sweet peas fail in summer's heat, the hardy perennial version (*Lathyrus latifolius*) is in full bloom, providing similar blossoms in shades of pink or white. Although the flowers lack the sweet scent of sweet peas, they are great for bouquets and the plants are exceptionally easy to grow.

OTHER ANNUAL VINES

Black-eyed Susan vine *(Thunbergia)* is a twining vine that quickly scales a 5-foot trellis or cascades from a window box. Dark-eyed flowers of gold, orange, cream, white, rose, or yellow bloom nonstop in sun or partial shade. Buy plants or give seeds an early start indoors.

Firecracker vine is an unusual but elegant vine with long tubular flowers that are red at the base and yellow at the tip. Easy from seed, plants do best if shaded from the hot afternoon sun.

Passionflower vine produces large, exquisite flowers of purple or blue that attract butterflies. Although there are never a lot of flowers at one time, one or two are pretty enough to grab attention. Passionflower thrives in hot, sunny weather. Because starting plants from seed is difficult and time-consuming, most gardeners prefer to purchase plants.

Mandevilla boasts 4-inch, trumpet-shaped blossoms that look like giant morning glory flowers. Glossy foliage is another plus for this sun-loving vine. Purchase a container-grown plant. If you grow it in a pot, you can cut the vine back in autumn and move the pot indoors for the winter.

Purple hyacinth bean is an ornamental bean that's as easy to grow from seed as pole beans in the vegetable garden. It boasts striking lilac blossoms, shiny purple pods, purple-veined leaves, and purple stems. It needs full sun and may require protection from rabbits when young.

Climbing snapdragon *(Maurandella,* formerly *Asarina)* covers itself with small bell-shaped purple flowers. Despite a delicate appearance, the vines are actually strong and both quick and easy to grow from seeds. They look as good cascading from a hanging basket or window box as they do climbing up a trellis or fence.

Vines You Can Eat

Some vegetables grow on vines so pretty you wouldn't hesitate to grow them on a fence or trellis in front of the house. Malabar spinach, for one. Although seldom seen in the Midwest, it thrives in our region's hot summer weather.

Even if you never ate a single leaf, you'd enjoy the 6- or 8-foot tall vines with their red stems and thick, dark green leaves. But you can also pick your fill of tender greens to cook or use raw in salads all summer.

Malabar spinach is easy to grow but requires a long growing season, so it's best to start the seeds early indoors and transplant them outside after the last spring frost. The first leaves will be ready to pick in early summer soon after regular spinach gives out.

Scarlet runner bean, an old-fashioned favorite, is another dual-purpose vine that is back in style. As easy to grow as any other pole bean, scarlet runners produce pretty flowers from July to frost. Hummingbirds find the trumpet-shaped, scarlet flowers irresistible.

The young pods, which have few strings, are great for eating fresh. Or you can harvest mature pods for pretty purple-and-black shell beans.

CHAPTER 7
VEGETABLES

THE GARDEN OF EATIN'

With soaring food prices and concerns about food safety fueling renewed interest in growing vegetables, I predict that many who take up the challenge will be permanently hooked by something else: the superior taste and freshness of homegrown produce. It happened to me.

I'm also hooked on harvesting at just the right stage to suit my own preferences, such as sweet corn picked slightly immature or tender asparagus tips snapped off soon after they push up from the ground.

If this kind of eating sounds good to you, winter is the ideal time to start planning your own gourmet vegetable garden. You'll have time to dream over catalog descriptions and find varieties that tempt you. For me and countless other gardeners, this winter gardening done from an armchair is not only valuable planning time but also a pleasure not to be missed.

If you're just getting started, here are a few tips:

- If you don't have a garden spot that gets at least six hours of sunlight, make the most of any sunny spot by growing vegetables in containers placed at the edge of the driveway or on the deck. You might even put your containers on wheels and roll them around to follow the sun.
- Work miracles by adding compost to the soil before you plant. Compost nourishes plants, improves the soil, and sponges up excess moisture, holding it until needed by the plants. If you're growing your veggies in containers, add about one-third compost to two-thirds potting soil: it will reduce the need for frequent watering.

- Choose disease-resistant varieties whenever possible.
- Blanket the ground between plants with a 1-inch layer of grass clippings, shredded leaves, or ground corn cobs. This mulch holds in soil moisture, prevents weed seeds from sprouting, provides slow-release nutrients, improves garden soil, stops the spread of soil-borne diseases, and allows walking in the garden when soil is wet.

A slow-to-decompose mulch such as bark chips works great around berry bushes and a perennial crop like asparagus. Chips aren't ideal, though, in parts of the vegetable garden where you plan to till the soil annually. Instead, you need some material that will decompose by the end of the season, when you till it into the soil.

Grass clippings are my favorite. They look nice and do a wonderful job of keeping down weeds. As the season wears on and the mulch starts to break down, I add additional clippings as I have them.

But don't pile fresh clippings directly against plant stems, and refrain from using clippings if the grass has been treated with an herbicide.

Some gardeners claim you have to dry the clippings before you use them because, they say, fresh clippings could "burn" the plants. Maybe that would happen if you piled on a deep layer right up against plants, but in decades of mulching with a 1-inch layer, I've never seen anything but good come from mulching with fresh clippings. Besides, dry clippings don't work nearly as well to stop weeds.

Getting enough grass clippings to cover my whole vegetable garden is often a problem, especially now that we often use a mulching mower to help our grass grow stronger. When I'm short on clippings, I spread a layer of newspaper, a page or two thick, and top it off with a thin layer of whatever clippings or shredded leaves I have. I avoid a thicker newspaper layer, which could keep light rain from reaching the soil. Dipping the papers in water before spreading makes them easier to handle.

Soil, Compost, and Garden Cleanup

The success of a garden lies beneath the surface, in the decomposed organic matter known as humus. Not nearly as exciting as the latest plant discovery, humus is nevertheless more crucial.

Is your soil too clayish? Too sandy? Too soggy? Too dry? Too compacted? Humus can help. Even if your soil is nearly perfect, humus can help keep it that way.

So . . . where do you get humus? From just about any plant or animal wastes, such as leaves, sawdust, manure, small prunings, or fruit and vegetable peelings. Dig the organic materials into your soil. As they decay, they turn into humus.

Better yet, layer a mixture of organic materials into a compost pile so they can partially decompose first.

When the last of the paste tomatoes and bush beans have been picked, the plants are ready to pull. In the flower garden, tubs quickly fill with yellowing leaves, faded flowers, and declining annuals. What's a gardener to do with it all?

The quickest, easiest (and best) answer is a compost pile.

It's too bad that so many myths abound about composting, keeping some gardeners from trying this simple way to turn garden wastes into a valuable source of humus to enrich soil.

Contrary to some of the myths, a proper compost pile is not a trash pile. It doesn't smell. It doesn't attract varmints. And you don't have to be a soil scientist to make good compost.

Finished compost looks just like crumbly, rich soil, and it smells sweet and earthy. Research proves what gardeners have known for decades: Plants grown in soil enriched with compost are healthier. A 1- or 2-inch layer of compost not only adds valuable minerals but also increases soil aeration, helps prevent soil crusting, and decreases the need for watering.

Don't let fancy compost recipes keep you from starting a compost pile. While it's true that some methods make compost faster than others, there's nothing mysterious about composting. It's simply a way to hurry along nature's own decaying process.

You won't go wrong if you simply alternate 6- to 8-inch layers of plant material (a mixture of both green and dry) with 1-inch layers of garden soil.

If the weather is extremely dry, you can add a little water to help get the pile "cooking."

Some gardeners like to turn their compost piles every few days with a pitchfork. The turning adds air that hurries along the cooking process. But if the work of turning a compost pile doesn't appeal to you, don't worry. Started in autumn, your compost's contents should be completely broken down and ready to use by spring, anyway.

You can buy a compost bin or make your own enclosure with wire, wood slats, or concrete blocks. If you don't have room for a traditional compost pile, just put your compost ingredients in a trash bag, sprinkle them with little water, and hide the bag under an evergreen or shrub while the contents decompose.

What can you put in a compost pile? Spent plants, grass clippings (if lawn was not treated with an herbicide), autumn leaves, weeds (minus any mature seed heads), fruit and vegetable peelings, egg shells, coffee grounds. In short, just about anything that was once living is a go, except for meat scraps or oils.

Cover each fresh addition of kitchen garbage with a little garden soil.

Cleaning up the garden at the end of the growing season makes gardening a lot easier in the long run by reducing potential disease and pest problems. Here's a sampling: Septoria leaf spot and early and late blights of tomato; Colorado potato beetles; corn borers; corn smut; squash bugs; grasshoppers; and bean, cucumber, flea, and asparagus beetles.

Visitors sometimes tell me I have an exceptionally pretty vegetable garden. I wonder if they realize that it's the volunteer flowers like cosmos and cleome that are responsible. The flowers earn their keep by attracting beneficial insects to the garden.

BEST BET

After you finish garden cleanup in autumn, spread a 2-inch layer of compost over the bare soil. The compost doesn't have to be completely "cooked" and you don't even have to dig the compost into the soil. Earthworms will easily accomplish that job by spring.

Itching to get started planting? No need to wait until after the last spring frost. While some vegetables are easily damaged by cold temperatures, others aren't fazed by frosty leaves.

COOL-SEASON CROPS

VEGETABLES TO PLANT ABOUT A MONTH BEFORE THE FROST-SAFE DATE

Beet

Broccoli

Cabbage

Carrot

Cauliflower

Kohlrabi

Lettuce

Onion

Pea

Potato

Radish

Swiss chard

WARM-SEASON CROPS

VEGETABLES TO PLANT AFTER THE FROST-SAFE DATE

Bean

Cucumber

Eggplant

Melon

Pepper

Squash

Sweet potato

Tomato

Second-Chance Garden

An especially fun aspect of vegetable gardening is the repeated chance for a new beginning. When one crop comes out, there's room for another crop to go in.

While summer is too late to plant more tomatoes or peppers, it's perfect for sowing seeds of many other crops.

SUMMER PLANTINGS FOR A SECOND-CHANCE GARDEN

Bush bean: June, July

Cabbage: June, July

Carrot: June, July

Cauliflower: July

Corn salad: August

Cucumber: June, July

Endive: July

Florence fennel: July

Kale: July, August, September

Kohlrabi: June, July, August

Lettuce: August, September

Pea, snow: July

Pea, sugar snap: June, July

Radish: August, September

Spinach: August, September

Sweet corn, early variety: June, July

Swiss Chard: June, July

Turnips: August

Zucchini and other summer squash: June, July

Solanaceae: Tomatoes and Their Relatives

TOMATOES

What kinds of tomatoes do you want to grow? Most gardeners are pretty opinionated. Some opt only for colorful heirlooms like Cherokee Purple or Big Rainbow. Others prefer hybrids bred to stand up to diseases that can infect tomato plants.

Those who plant a pot rather than a plot like to plant a determinate variety such as Celebrity. This type won't produce a runaway vine that could swamp the container.

I always plant at least one Early Girl because it's quick to produce, disease resistant, and dependable no matter what the weather. I also like its taste. And taste is, after all, the most important of all criteria in choosing favorites.

Every year I also plant a half dozen different kinds of cherry and grape tomatoes. They're great for snacking right in the garden and fun for informal tomato tastings when visitors tour.

No matter what varieties you choose, follow these tips to keep your tomato plants healthy:

- Rotate tomatoes and their relatives (potatoes, peppers, and eggplants) to a different part of the garden every year or grow your tomatoes in fresh soil in pots.
- If there's a walnut tree growing near your garden, plant tomatoes in pots to escape the toxic effect of juglone produced by walnuts. (A standard-size tomato requires an 18-inch-deep container, while a small patio-type variety will grow in an 8-inch-deep pot.)
- Allow enough space for good air circulation between plants.
- Use sturdy cages to support plants.
- Immediately after planting, cover the ground surrounding each plant with mulch.
- Avoid overhead watering.

GROWING TOMATOES THAT TASTE GREAT

The best-tasting tomatoes come from plants grown in soil enriched with compost or other organic matter. Tomatoes grown in lean soil and fed with chemicals just don't measure up.

You'll also notice better flavor if you delay picking until tomatoes are fully colored. If you pick them sooner, store them at room temperature out of direct sunlight, not in the refrigerator.

The denser the foliage of a tomato plant, the better its tomatoes taste. And that makes sense: plants manufacture sugars in their leaves.

It seems strange that for years the going wisdom recommended pinching off all the side shoots so plants could easily be tied to a stake. Thankfully, most tomato plants now are grown in cages and are allowed to keep all their leaves.

Still, disease often takes a toll on the foliage, particularly in rainy seasons or if the garden is routinely watered with an overhead sprinkler. With great-tasting tomatoes in mind, it pays to do what you can to keep the foliage healthy.

Start by planning for good air circulation. Spacing most varieties 4 or 5 feet apart should leave enough room to easily walk between the tomato cages, with plenty of space for air to circulate.

As soon as you get your tomato plants in the ground, cover the bare ground around them with mulch. It will keep splashing rain from spreading fungus diseases from soil to tomato foliage. The mulch also retains soil moisture, thereby reducing cracking, splitting, and blossom-end rot of the fruits.

There's no question that some tomatoes have more built-in resistance to disease than others. To make sure I'm never without tomatoes during the growing season, I always include a few tried-and-true varieties such as Early Girl and Celebrity. I know I can count on these two even if it turns out to be a bad year for tomatoes.

Some gardeners tell me their tomato plants look fine but just aren't setting on any fruits. Large beefsteak type tomatoes and some kinds of

BEST BET

If the bottoms of the first tomatoes to ripen are rotten, don't panic. This condition, called blossom-end rot, results from uneven water absorption. Weather, such as heavy rains followed by a dry spell, is often the culprit. Keep plants mulched, and water in dry weather. While there is nothing a gardener can do about heavy rains, blossom-end rot rarely persists throughout the season. Later ripening tomatoes aren't usually affected.

heirlooms, which demand perfect conditions for fruit set, are the most likely to suffer. Another possible cause of no fruit is too much nitrogen, which can happen when a high-nitrogen fertilizer such as one intended for use on the lawn is used in the vegetable garden.

When you haven't yet had your fill of ripe tomatoes, you'll want to prolong the harvest as long as possible. That means covering the plants if frost threatens. Floating row covers such as Reemay, sold by many garden centers and mail-order garden supply catalogs, are my favorites. Made of polyester or polypropylene fabric, they're light enough to rest directly on the plants without breaking them. Better yet, they allow air and light to pass through the fabric, so there's no rush to uncover the plants the next day before they "cook."

When heavy frost threatens, I pick any remaining firm green tomatoes and pack them in a single layer in shallow boxes. Stored in the cool garage, they continue to slowly ripen over a number of weeks.

PEPPERS

Today's peppers come in a mind-boggling assortment of bright colors and interesting shapes, in flavors to suit every palate.

If you're ready to break from the traditional green and red, you can substitute peppers in chocolate brown, lavender, orange, purple, or yellow. Even more interesting is Blushing Beauty, the All-America Selections winner that starts out ivory, then blushes to pink, then rosy red as it matures.

At our house, where enchiladas are a long-time family favorite, jalapeno and cayenne chili peppers are also a must.

Peppers tend to be even easier to grow than tomatoes, because peppers aren't nearly as prone to diseases.

Think you don't have room to grow your own peppers? Not to worry. Pepper plants are pretty enough to grow in the flower garden. With most varieties growing only 18 to 24 inches tall, they're also a good size for growing in containers where you can enjoy the beauty of the fruits at close range.

Pepper plants need full sun and a spot sheltered from harsh winds. I postpone setting out pepper plants until a week or two after I plant tomatoes because pepper plants resent chilling.

In the garden, space plants 12 to 18 inches apart. Dig a shovelful of compost into each planting hole, along with a light sprinkling of organic vegetable fertilizer.

If you want to grow a pepper in a pot, a 2-gallon container is ideal. Peppers growing in pots require additional feeding, such as liquid fish fertilizer, during the growing season.

Some kinds of peppers grow large enough to require a small cage or other support when they're bearing a heavy load of fruit. The flimsy cages often sold as tomato cages aren't big enough to contain most tomato plants but they're perfect for peppers.

Hot peppers develop their full spiciness in hot, dry weather. If it's spicy you want, go easy on watering.

As hot peppers mature from green to red, I string up a dozen or so by their stems with needle and thread and hang them to dry. Later, I'll run some of the dried peppers through the blender to add to a shaker jar.

Besides adding flavor to foods, hot peppers also work wonders at repelling both animal and insect pests. When squirrels made a mess by digging in my containers, I grabbed my shaker jar and sprinkled the soil with ground hot pepper. It worked!

The effect lasted about a month. When the squirrels started in again, a repeat application shooed them away.

EGGPLANT

The dog days of summer are just what eggplant craves. The hotter the weather, the more an eggplant produces.

The purple flowers and velvety leaves are so pretty, I think eggplant would be worth growing even if we didn't want to eat any.

BEST BET

Pepper varieties that produce big, blocky fruits are sometimes finicky, failing to produce if the weather is too hot or too cold. For a dependable harvest even in bad pepper years, also plant a small-fruited variety such as Gypsy or an Italian roasting pepper like Carmen.

You don't have to settle for traditional white, egg-shaped fruits. Some eggplants are pink, green, lavender, purple, or almost black, sometimes with stripes. Shapes vary, too. I especially love long, skinny varieties for slicing on pizza.

The size of the plants ranges from foot-tall dwarfs, perfect for growing in pots, to 4 feet tall.

Eggplants are subject to some of the same diseases as tomatoes, peppers, and potatoes. Rotating the whole family to different parts of the garden helps keep plants healthy.

If the weather is dry, water the soil to keep eggplants producing. You might also need to stake eggplants for support when they're loaded with fruits. Use shears to harvest fruits that are glossy and fully colored, when pressing with a finger leaves only a slight depression. Discard over-mature fruits that are soft and have dark seeds. Regular picking helps keep the plants producing.

Eggplants would be as easy to grow as they are pretty if it weren't for one bugaboo: flea beetles. Tiny insects that jump like fleas when disturbed, they weaken the plants by riddling the leaves with small holes.

Flea beetles feed on a wide variety of vegetables and flowers, but eggplants are their favorites. Their larvae do their dirty work out of sight, feeding on the roots.

Hosing off the eggplant foliage with a strong jet of water from the hose in midday is sometimes enough. If that doesn't do the trick, consider spraying the plants with a product containing pyrethrin, such as Safer Yard and Garden Insect Killer or Pyola.

Another option is dusting the leaves with wood ashes or lime early in the morning while the leaves are still wet with dew. Also clean up plant debris after harvest to eliminate places where flea beetles could hibernate in the garden.

POTATOES

If you've never tasted a fresh-dug, home-grown potato, you can't imagine how moist and flavorful a potato can be.

With the dozens of different varieties of seed potatoes available today, growing your own spuds can be a real adventure. Besides the old standbys like white Kennebec and red Pontiac, you can also grow a yellow-fleshed potato like Yukon Gold that looks buttery without adding a teaspoon of fat. Long, slender tubers called fingerling potatoes offer excellent flavor and texture, ideal for potato salad.

A week or two before planting, I spread my seed potatoes in a single layer indoors to sprout at room temperature. The day before planting, I cut them into egg-size pieces, each with several "eyes."

To keep disease problems to a minimum, plant potatoes in a part of the garden where neither potatoes nor tomatoes have grown for a couple of years. Space the cut pieces 12 to 15 inches apart and cover with 6 inches of soil.

I often plant some early potatoes a month or more before the last spring frost but wait until about the time dandelions bloom to plant the main crop. That's because potatoes are more apt to be attacked by fungi and bacteria if the soil is below 50 degrees.

But potatoes don't grow well in hot soil, either. Here's how to keep it cool: When the plants are 6 to 10 inches tall, hill the soil up around them. Then apply a thick layer of straw or other mulch to shade the soil. The extra soil and mulch also prevent another problem: sunburned tubers.

For a dependable harvest, it's hard to beat Kennebec. This variety tolerates drought and resists late blight.

Red Norland resists scab, a fungus disease that makes brown, corky patches on a potato's skin.

Yukon Gold, my favorite for taste, is also the best I've ever grown for long-term storage.

Midwesterners don't often have to deal with a widespread outbreak of late blight, the fungus disease that caused the great Irish potato famine in the 1840s. That's thanks to our normally hot, dry summers. Late blight does its dirty work when the weather is rainy and the temperatures are mild. An infection can't get started unless the leaves are wet.

Still, the problem with late blight seems to be getting worse, with so-called exotic new strains of the fungus spreading more aggressively to both potatoes and tomatoes. Just in case the growing season turns out to be wet and mild, follow these simple precautions:

- Plant only certified seed potatoes. Reject any tomato plants that have brown lesions on the stems or white fuzzy growth on the underside of leaves.
- Hedge your bets by planting some potatoes that have shown resistance to late blight. Although as of now there is no immune variety, both Kennebec and Rosa potatoes offer some resistance.
- Rotate both potatoes and tomatoes to new ground every year.
- Because late blight survives only on living plant tissue, pull up and destroy any volunteer potato or tomato plants as well as nightshade weeds, which are close relatives.
- Allow room for good air circulation between plants.
- Never use overhead watering for potatoes or tomatoes.
- Pull any potato or tomato plant that shows symptoms of late blight: Purple-brown lesions on leaves and stems; greasy, dark lesions on fruits. Destroy the diseased plant with a propane flamer, put it in a trash bag, or bury deep in soil.
- At the end of the season, clean up all spent potato and tomato plants.

TOMATILLOS

Tomatillos, just as easy to grow as tomatoes, are a must for salsa. Like tomatoes, they need a five- or six-week head start indoors. You can choose varieties with either green or purple fruits. Harvest when the papery husks split, revealing the plump fruits inside.

The Cabbage Family

BROCCOLI

Broccoli, a strong, easy-to-grow plant, thrives when the weather is cool and the soil is fertile. You can usually avoid disease problems simply by rotating broccoli and other members of the cabbage family to a different garden spot every year.

Depending on variety, broccoli takes fifty-five to eighty days from setting out plants until harvest. Seeds sown directly in the garden take about twenty days longer. For the quickest harvest, I like to include a few plants of an early variety like Packman.

When you see yellow or white cabbage butterflies flitting around your plants, it's a sure bet that your broccoli will soon be wormy unless you take action. You can either exclude the butterflies with a fabric row cover or spray plants every ten days with *Bacillus thuringiensis* (*Bt*), an organic control.

Although broccoli grows best in cool weather, the plants will produce side shoots all summer long. Planting more broccoli plants for a fall crop isn't usually necessary if you keep the side shoots harvested throughout the summer. Once the weather cools, the new shoots grow bigger and tastier. The only reason for planting a new crop is if you're hung up on harvesting a large central head. But I figure I'd be cutting a big head apart anyway to cook the broccoli, so why care?

Some varieties, including Packman, are particularly good at sprouting side shoots. If you planted a variety that isn't producing any, you may still be in luck. Take a look where the plants come out of the ground, and you may discover that your tired old spring plants have already sprouted a new plant at the base of each trunk-like stalk. All you have to do is remove what remains of the original plants to make room for the new.

CABBAGE

After my first taste of an amazingly sweet and tender savoy-type cabbage, I abandoned growing all other cabbages. Savoy cabbage is perfect for salads and slaws. When cooked, it doesn't stink up the kitchen like other cabbages.

Savoy cabbage is also extra beautiful in the garden, with its crinkly, blue-green leaves.

Most savoy cabbages take about 11 weeks after transplanting to mature, a little longer than early varieties of regular cabbages. I'm willing to wait.

BEST BET

Dipel and other *Bt* products are poisonous only to caterpillars and won't harm birds, people, or beneficial insects. But this bacterium kills the larvae of all butterflies, so use it only to spray broccoli and other members of the cabbage family where the larvae of desirable butterflies don't dine.

For the earliest harvest, set out cabbage transplants in mid-spring. For a later crop, you can grow cabbage from seeds planted directly in the garden in mid-spring.

Plant cabbage again in June or July for a fall harvest. Cabbage is at its best after touched by a light fall frost.

CAULIFLOWER

In the Midwest, growing white cauliflower is a challenge. Growing purple cauliflower is easy.

White cauliflower is so finicky that many commercial growers make small plantings every week rather than risk losing a large crop to adverse weather.

Choosing a weather-tolerant variety such as Snow Crown, I set out just a few young transplants every spring. If we have perfect weather, I'm delighted with a harvest of beautiful heads in June. But I don't count on it.

If the cauliflower suffers any stress, such as temperature too high or too low, or rain too much or too little, I'll get button-sized heads, or no heads at all.

When weather is perfect and my white cauliflower plants begin developing heads in June, I use a clothespin to fasten the surrounding leaves over each head. (Unless growing a self-blanching variety, excluding sunlight is necessary to preserve the pure white color.)

I peek under the leaves every day, hoping to harvest each head at its peak of perfection. When the weather is hot, though, I know the texture of the cauliflower will change overnight from crisp to "ricey."

Meanwhile, the whims of the weather have little effect on my Violet Queen cauliflower. These plants tolerate hot temperatures and don't require blanching. The pretty purple florets, although they turn green when cooked, are fun to serve raw with dips or in salads.

Actually part cauliflower and part broccoli, purple cauliflower apparently gets its undemanding nature from its broccoli heritage.

More challenging is lime-green Italian Romanesco cauliflower, known for its unique spiraled heads and nutty flavor. I admit to more failures than successes with this finicky variety, though I'm still trying.

Success with Romanesco is most likely when the seeds are planted in June so that the plants mature in cool fall weather. The plants must be babied with fertile soil and plenty of water, though, to have a chance at success.

If you want to take a stab at growing a white cauliflower for fall harvest, plant seeds of Snow Crown in July.

Cabbage butterflies seem to find cauliflower's thick leaves less attractive than broccoli plants for laying their eggs.

KALE

Although ornamental varieties of kale are edible, they don't taste as good as they look. The leaves are not nearly as sweet and tender as kale varieties that are bred for eating.

Of the vegetable kales, Winterbor is the classic. Growing 2 feet tall or more, this vigorous variety is blessed with outstanding cold hardiness. It's pretty, too, with ruffled dark-green leaves. Another variety that stands up exceptionally well to cold is Dwarf Blue Curled Scotch, a low-growing kale with curly blue-green leaves.

Red Russian, an heirloom variety that's regaining its popularity, offers flat, toothed-edged, gray-green leaves with purple veins. Purple stems add to this variety's good looks in the garden.

Kale connoisseurs wait until cold weather to harvest the leaves because low temperatures convert starches to sugars for a sweeter taste. Most varieties bred for eating are even hardier than ornamental varieties. Grown in a cold frame or under a row cover, kales can be harvested for much of the winter.

Kale is best eaten soon after you pick the leaves. The young, tender, outer leaves are ready to harvest just twenty-five days after sowing the seeds. Large leaves, best for steaming, casseroles, or stir-fries, require twice as long.

KOHLRABI

The sight of kohlrabi growing in the garden makes me smile. Leafy stems sprout from odd-looking, above-ground balls, like little alien spaceships. I usually plant both purple and white varieties because they look pretty growing together, but once they're peeled they all look alike.

Once the plants are up and growing, thin kohlrabi to 4 inches apart. Most types of kohlrabi are ready to harvest in about six weeks, as soon as the swollen stems swell to about 2 inches in diameter. The white flesh is sweet and crisp, like an apple. Some people eat kohlrabi lightly cooked, but I think it's at its best served raw with dip.

Although kohlrabi can be grown throughout the growing season in the Midwest, plants maturing in the fall hold best in the garden without getting woody.

TURNIPS

August is the time-honored month for planting turnips. Tender, sweet roots about 2 inches in diameter are ready to harvest in forty to fifty days. Young turnips the size of radishes, a delicacy served at some of the finest restaurants, are ready for eating just thirty days after you plant turnip seeds.

Legumes

BEANS

Fresh-picked green beans are a superb taste treat I look forward to every summer. Luckily, beans are easy to grow and produce a bumper crop in little space.

The first picking of most kinds of bush beans begins in about fifty-five days. If you make your first planting in May, do a second planting in June to ensure a continuous supply.

If space permits, it's fun to grow some purple and yellow beans, too. I also like to plant some Italian flat-pod beans, which hold up best in stir-fries. For a gourmet treat, plant one of the French filet types, called *haricots verts*. These are the very slender beans served in upscale restaurants.

If you find it difficult to bend over to pick bush beans, plant pole beans instead. Pole beans produce over a much longer period and many gardeners find the taste superior. Kentucky Blue is an award-winning variety that produces sweet and tender beans. Support pole beans on a fence, trellis, or pole teepee. You'll not only get a huge harvest in a small space, you'll also be able to pick the harvest from a standing position.

Beans require a sunny spot with well-drained soil. Soak seeds in a jar of water for an hour or more before planting, particularly if the weather is dry. If you have a new garden or haven't planted beans in recent years, pick up a package of legume inoculant at the garden center. Before planting, drain off the water used to soak the seeds, sprinkle a little inoculant over the wet seeds, and shake the jar. The good bacteria in the inoculant will help your beans grow better and produce more.

Go easy on fertilizer. Too much nitrogen invites problems.

Thin bean plants to stand about 6 inches apart.

To control diseases, choose disease-resistant varieties, stay out of the garden when the plants are wet, rotate beans to a different spot in the garden each year, and clean up dead plants in the fall.

Bean beetles, which eat the foliage and damage the beans, may require control in Midwest gardens. If necessary to save my beans, I use a pyrethrin product such as Pyola or Safer Yard and Garden Insect Killer. Although these products are approved for organic gardens, I use them only as a last resort because pyrethrin is a broad-spectrum product that is also toxic to beneficial insects.

Once the beans start to produce, regular picking every few days is a must. Frequent picking ensures the best quality harvest while also encouraging the plants to keep producing. Strive to pick the pods before the seeds inside them start to swell. If you're growing one of the French filet varieties, forty-eight hours is the absolute maximum between pickings.

Green-seeded soybeans, called edamame, make a delicious high-protein snack. With the rising popularity of edamame growing, there are now soybean varieties developed especially for eating at the fresh-shell stage. A short-season variety called Envy is ready to eat just seventy-five to eighty days after you plant the seeds in the garden.

To prepare edamame, just boil fresh soybeans five or ten minutes, then pop them out of their shells like peanuts.

Rabbits adore soybeans, so be prepared to protect your plants with an enclosure or repellent spray.

PEAS

What do you need to successfully grow peas in the garden?

For most kinds, an extra-early start. As soon as the snow melts and the ground thaws, it's time to plant garden peas. Early planting helps them get established before hot weather arrives.

Sugar snaps are a different story. High sugar content makes these seeds more apt to rot in cold ground. I usually postpone planting sugar snaps until mid-April, but then I keep planting more sugar snaps on and off all summer because they are more heat resistant than garden peas. Since the debut of this vegetable several decades ago, sugar snaps have been a favorite in our household and in countless others. Everyone, it seems, loves the sweet, crunchy, pea-filled pods, whether they're served raw or lightly steamed.

Sugar Snap, the original All-America Selections award-winning variety, grows on vigorous 6-foot vines that require a fence or other support. I still grow this variety, but I also enjoy the benefits of some of the newer varieties of sugar snaps. Super Sugar Snap, which is a little shorter, offers more disease resistance. Sugar Sprint grows only 30 inches tall and is earlier, virtually stringless, and disease resistant.

New varieties of garden (English) peas make that vegetable easier to grow, too. Mr. Big, another All-America Selections award-winner, is at the top of my list of favorites. As you might guess from the name, the pods are big, filled with eight to ten peas.

What impresses me most about Mr. Big, though, is its tolerance of heat and disease. While most varieties shrivel and die by the Fourth of July, my plantings of Mr. Big often keep on producing several weeks longer.

Snow peas, wonderful in stir-fries, are my choice for a fall crop. I always plant a mildew-resistant variety like Oregon Giant because mildew is rampant in cool autumn weather. The flat pods are ready for harvest about sixty days after planting.

To make sure the 30-inch-tall vines stay upright, I poke some short, twiggy branches into the soil when I plant.

Cucurbits: Vine Crops

SQUASH

"What's the big deal about zucchini?" a non-gardening friend asked me. "If gardeners are so overwhelmed with the harvest that they have to sneak zucchinis off on unsuspecting friends or strangers, why don't they just plant less?"

Since he's never grown zucchini, he had no idea that the harvest from just a plant or two could overwhelm a small family.

Worse yet, more often than not that prolific supply shuts off suddenly. Vine borers kill squash plants seemingly overnight. Squash bugs take more time to do their dirty work but can be just as deadly. Sometimes a virus disease is the culprit. Then that same gardener who couldn't give away enough zucchinis is left wishing for more.

While it's nearly impossible to produce exactly the amount you need at any given moment, you don't have to choose between feast and famine. The trick is to plant seeds with restraint, then a few weeks later plant again.

In early May, I prepare a single circle of ground about 18 inches in diameter, spading a sprinkling of organic fertilizer and a bucketful of compost into the soil.

Into the prepared ground, I push five or six seeds, spaced about 2 inches apart. Later, after the plants are up and growing, I pull out the weakest plants, leaving only two or three to mature.

About four weeks later, I repeat the process in another part of my garden. By the time this second planting is producing, the first plants are often faltering. I love being able to rip out the old, tired-looking plants and enjoy the harvest from these vigorous new plants.

When a squash plant suddenly wilts and dies, blame squash vine borers. If you slit the stem, you'll likely find a fat white worm inside.

If a squash plant dies a slower death, squash bugs are the likely culprit. Both pests are common in Midwest gardens and require diligence to control.

Of all the controls I've tried for vine borers, I've had the best luck wrapping the main stems for several inches near the base with strips of old pantyhose as soon as the stems are sturdy enough to wrap. As the stems continue to grow, the fabric expands, keeping the stem covered.

If my wrapping efforts fail and I find a wilting vine, I look for a hole on the stem surrounded by stuff that looks like sawdust. When I find one, I use a syringe to shoot a solution of Dipel or other *Bt* product into the hole to kill the borer, then mound soil over the injured stem. This method often yields good results but, believe me, it's easier said than done.

Control of squash bugs requires a multistep approach. Diligence pays, because insecticides don't have much effect once squash bugs mature.

Here's what works for me: Lay a small board at the base of each plant. Every morning, lift the board and destroy any of the large, dark-colored adult squash bugs you find hiding there. If you start early in the season, you can make a noticeable difference.

Throughout the summer, check squash leaves for copper-colored egg masses, usually on the underside of leaves. Scrape off all you find. Spray insecticidal soap on any groups of newly hatched babies you see. To deprive squash bugs of a place to hibernate, practice autumn garden cleanup.

Butternut squash is a gardener's dream. Why? Because the vine borers that devastate other kinds of squash and pumpkins in Midwest gardens virtually ignore butternut vines.

Another reason I love butternut squash is that it's an exceptionally good keeper. We store ours on a shelf in the basement, where they stay in good condition until spring.

Compared to many colorful kinds of squash, butternuts don't look like much. Cylindrical but with a bulb-shaped end, they're a nondescript tan. Inside, though, the flesh is bright orange, like a pumpkin. In fact, cooked and mashed, it makes a flavorful substitute in any recipe that calls for pumpkin. Truth be told, my "pumpkin" pies are actually butternut.

To grow butternut squash, start with a packet of seeds. If your garden is small, choose a space-saving variety such as Burpee's Butterbush or Early Butternut Hybrid. If you have more room for vines to ramble, you can count on an old favorite named Waltham to produce lots of 4- to 5-pound butternuts with rather small seed cavities.

CUCUMBERS

Good fences make good neighbors, they say. Good fences also make good cucumbers.

A chain-link fence is perfect. So is any other fence or trellis that cucumber vines can clasp.

The fence's value is clear: the fruit from vines allowed to sprawl on the ground is often curled, while fruit from vines with vertical support grows long and straight.

Growing cucumbers on a fence also saves a lot of space.

Cucumber vines love hot weather, but if they don't get enough water they'll produce bitter-tasting fruit. Fortunately, most of the bitterness is concentrated in the stem end. If you slice off and discard the stem end, the remaining part of the fruit usually tastes fine.

There's another good reason to keep cucumber vines watered in dry weather. Stressed plants attract cucumber beetles, the biggest threat to a good cucumber crop in Midwest gardens.

Cucumber beetles are about the size of ladybugs, only yellow. As they feed, they spread a disease called bacterial wilt, which will wipe out cucumber and melon vines in a jiffy. Once a vine is infected, there is no way you can save the plant. If a vine suddenly wilts even though the soil is moist, pull and dispose of that plant before the disease spreads.

The easiest way to thwart cucumber beetles is to grow a cucumber variety they don't like, such as County Fair, a pickling variety, or a non-bitter slicer such as Diva.

When the number of cucumber beetles is high, you may need to resort to an organic pesticide that contains pyrethrin for control. It will knock down pests fast but not linger long to create a problem for the environment or for those who eat the produce. Always spray in the evening, when bees aren't active.

Even if you can't use one more cucumber at the moment, it's important to keep on picking. The more cucumbers you pick, the more the vines produce. Any unpicked fruits left to yellow on the vine will signal the plant it's time to quit producing.

MELONS

Homegrown melons can be a challenge in the Midwest, but one taste of success is all it takes to keep most gardeners trying.

For an extra-early melon harvest, I start seeds indoors in mid-April in individual pots. In three or four weeks, when the weather is warm and settled, the little plants are just the right size to plant in the garden.

The most serious insect pest of Midwest melons: cucumber beetles, both spotted and striped varieties. They do a double whammy on the plants, with the adults chewing on the leaves and blossoms, and their larvae feeding underground on the roots.

Worse yet, cucumber beetles spread bacterial wilt, a disease that sooner or later proves fatal to the plant.

To get my young melon plants off to a strong, pest-free start, I cover them with a lightweight fabric row cover such as Reemay. Soon after they start to bloom, I have to remove the cover so the bees can pollinate the blossoms.

Many years, no other control is needed. But if, after the cover comes off, I see a lot of quarter-inch yellow beetles with black stripes or spots, pyrethrin may be warranted. Spray only in the evening, when bees aren't active.

Because stressed plants are more likely to attract cucumber beetles, I try to water often enough to keep the soil moist. But wet foliage encourages disease, so overhead sprinkling is out. A soaker hose is better.

Harvesting juicy melons is a gardener's delight. Knowing when to harvest is sometimes a gardener's dilemma.

I know all the signs of a ripe watermelon: a dull look with a yellowish underside, the tendrils closest to the melon dark and shriveled, the stem dark and crisp, and the small leaf where the melon's stem is attached to the vine pale. Still, I tend to wait too long.

I prefer picking cantaloupes, which signal approaching ripeness by changing to yellowish-tan, then fall off with a very gentle tug. Before I slice it, though, I press a fingernail into one of the "seams." If I hear a crunch, I give the melon another day or two on the kitchen counter.

Honeydew melons are trickier. I look for a creamy white or yellow color, with no greenish tint and a slight "give" when I press the melon with my finger.

Once in a while, even a ripe melon is a disappointment. Blame poor flavor on cloudy or rainy weather when the melon was ripening, a diseased plant, or poor soil.

Root Crops

CARROTS

The taste of carrots depends a lot on variety. Nantes types are known to be some of the sweetest. Chantenay-type carrots tend to be less sweet but better keepers.

Don't rush to harvest: carrots generally reach full sweetness several weeks after they develop full color.

The roots grow best in cool weather and are undeterred by a late spring frost. Early to mid-April is a good time to make a first planting. Planting more carrot seed in July works well, too. Maturing in autumn when nights are cool, carrots develop more natural sugars and better flavor.

It's fun to grow not only orange carrots, but red, purple, white, and yellow varieties, too. The bright colors are a hit on relish trays and offer additional nutrients, too.

Because carrot seeds are so tiny, I often have a hard time getting an even stand. It helps to mix the seeds with sand before sowing, but it's still hard to avoid a few patches where the carrots are growing too close together. To give carrots a chance to develop, thin crowded plants to 2 inches between plants.

If you prefer, you can buy easier-to-handle pelleted seed for better spacing and less time spent thinning.

BEETS

Canned beets never ranked high on my list of childhood favorites, but fresh beets from the garden are something special.

I'm particularly fond of the colorful and nutritious beet tops, ready to start picking just three to four weeks after planting. They're beautiful and tasty in salads and also good lightly steamed, like spinach.

Baby beets, ready in five or six weeks, are sweet and tender. Full-size beets harvested at seven or eight weeks maintain their sweet flavor, provided the plants are kept watered whenever the weather turns dry.

The many different varieties available to home gardeners make growing beets extra fun. Some are round while others are long and skinny, like a carrot. I love to grow Bull's Blood for its deep red tops that are gorgeous mixed with salad greens, and Chioggia, an Italian variety with roots that have alternating interior rings of pink and white.

April is an excellent time to plant beets because the seeds sprout quickest when the soil temperature is still cool but not cold. The colors of beets are also brightest when the weather is cool.

Beets need a sunny spot with well-drained soil and respond well to a 2-inch layer of compost dug into the soil before planting. Avoid excessive fertilizer, which increases the chance of misshapen beets.

For a constant supply of top-quality beets, plan to sow small amounts of seed every two weeks. Because beets can be slow to sprout, I hurry them along by soaking the seeds overnight before planting.

A beet seed is actually a dried-up fruit containing multiple seeds, so thinning beets has always been a necessity. Plant breeders have been working on that problem, though, and now there are a few varieties that contain only a single seed. After your beets are up and growing, thin as necessary so the seedlings stand at least 2 inches apart.

Problems with growing beets are few. Don't let them dry out in dry weather, which can make the roots bitter, hard, and woody. Good cultural practices such as fall clean-up, crop rotation, and mulching will protect beets from most other problems.

If leaf miners regularly ruin beet leaves in your garden, spread a floating row cover over your plants to prevent the flies from laying their eggs. Control leaf spot infections by picking off any damaged leaves.

ONIONS

The secret to growing good onions is early planting and plenty of nitrogen. Plant seeds, sets, or plants in spring as soon as the snow melts and the soil is dry enough to work. Don't worry about the cold. Onions are hardy to 15 degrees and won't be hurt even if their tops turn yellow from cold.

BEST BET

Plant some radish seed in the same row as beets. The quick-to-sprout radishes will break up the soil, making it easier for the beets to emerge. Radishes mature so fast that they'll be long gone by the time beets need more space.

A steady supply of nitrogen fertilizer helps onion tops grow big before the bulbs start to form, resulting in bigger bulbs to harvest.

A raised bed is perfect for onions. The soil dries out fast for early planting, and good drainage prevents rotting.

If you start with seeds, thin seedlings to allow 4 inches between plants.

Water onions in dry weather and mulch to conserve soil moisture. If stressed by lack of water, onions may send up seed stalks and won't be good keepers, even if you remove the stalks.

If the onion leaves show signs of streaking or browning, suspect thrips. Control them with a spray of insecticidal soap.

Plan to harvest your onions soon after the tops of the plants fall over. Cure the bulbs for a week or two to toughen the skins. To cure, just lay the plants in a dry, shady place or hang small bunches in a shed or garage.

After the bulbs are cured, clip off the tops to within an inch of the bulbs. Sort out any split or damaged bulbs to use right away and store the remaining bulbs in mesh bags hung in a dry, cool, frost-free place.

For flavor, onions earn their keep. *If* they keep.

If you find your onions sprouting and rotting in storage, salvage as much of the onion crop as possible by chopping and freezing them. No pre-treatment is necessary.

Another option: dry chopped onions in a food dehydrator.

Next spring, take steps to insure better luck with your onion crop. First, choose a variety such as Copra, widely recognized as an excellent keeper. A storage variety like Copra should keep all winter without sprouting or rotting.

While the varieties that store well start out pungent, they become milder when stored or cooked. After their pungency is lost in cooking,

BEST BET

For long-term storage onions, always start with onion seeds or plants rather than the tiny onion bulbs called sets. Onions grown from sets are often the first to produce seed stalks, which ruin storage potential.

many cooks think that storage varieties actually have flavor that is superior to sweet onion varieties.

The onion varieties that hold up well in storage, though, won't provide the sweet raw slices you want on your hamburger. For that, you'll have to also grow a sweet onion such as Candy and eat the bulbs soon after harvest.

GARLIC

Growing good garlic is a lot like growing daffodils. Nothing could be easier, but you need to plant the bulbs in the fall. Spring planting — too late for daffodils — is also too late for garlic.

With fall planting, garlic bulbs will have time to put their roots down deep so they can produce big, plump cloves by the time the tops of the plants die down next summer.

You don't need much space to grow a lot of garlic, but you do need a spot with full sun and good drainage. I always plant garlic in a raised bed for the good drainage that it provides. Before planting, I spread compost 1 or 2 inches deep over the bed, then dig it into the soil.

When choosing garlic bulbs, you'll find three different kinds. The soft-necked type has braidable foliage. Elephant garlic, which is closely related to leeks, produces huge cloves that are sweet and mild. Hardneck garlic, also known as rocambole or stiffneck garlic, produces not only a bulb but also a flower stalk topped with small bulblets.

I've enjoyed growing all three kinds but it is hardneck garlic that I've found most likely to survive Midwest winters.

To plant, separate each garlic bulb into individual cloves. Plant them pointed-end up, 4 inches apart, covered with 1 or 2 inches of soil.

After the soil surface freezes, spread a 1-inch layer of shredded leaves or other mulch on the ground over the bulbs for winter protection.

Don't think you've failed when the foliage starts to dry up by midsummer. Like onions and tulips, the dying foliage just announces that these bulbs have reached the end of their growing season. It's your signal to harvest the bulbs, keeping back the biggest and best to replant in the fall.

I learned the hard way not to delay digging garlic bulbs once the plant tops are mostly dead. Too much rain at this stage can easily cause the bulbs to rot. Instead, dig up the bulbs and spread them out for a few days to dry in a dark, airy place protected from rain.

Garlic bulbs keep best when stored at cool temperatures just above freezing.

LEEKS

After the last of the tomatoes and peppers are long gone, the harvest of fresh leeks is still going strong.

Leek plants look like onions, only they never form a bulb. The thick, white stems taste like mild, sweet onions and are especially good in soups and stews.

More cold hardy than most vegetables, leeks can be dug all winter if protected with mulch and row covers so the ground doesn't freeze. Even without protection, the leeks won't be ruined. You can eat them in early spring, as soon as the ground thaws enough for digging. Soon after, over-wintered leeks begin to develop bloom stalks. While leek flowers are beautiful (I often leave a few leeks to bloom just for fun), blooming leeks develop a woody core that makes them unfit for consumption.

Leeks take a long time to mature, but they are easy to grow and seldom troubled by pests or diseases.

You can give leek seeds a start indoors in January or February, then transplant seedlings to the garden after the last frost. I usually take the easy way out and sow my seeds outdoors in a raised bed in early spring. You can also buy leek seedlings in spring by the bunch, ready to transplant to the garden.

The best leeks have long, white stems, produced by excluding light when the plants are growing. The process is called blanching and there are two ways to do it. You can hill up the soil around the stems several times during the growing season. Or, if you're setting out transplants, you can start by digging a trench 6 to 8 inches deep. Then plant the seedlings in the bottom of the trench and let the rains gradually fill in the soil around the plants as they grow.

With plants spaced 5 inches apart, you can grow a lot of leeks in a small area. Harvest leeks as needed any time after they're at least a half-inch in diameter.

SWEET POTATOES

The first time I grew sweet potatoes, an old gardener advised me to handle the tuberous roots as if they were eggs. Decades later, I still heed his advice when I harvest my sweet potatoes and carefully tuck them away for long keeping.

And what long keepers they are! Even as I'm squirreling away the autumn's harvest, a few year-old sweet potatoes remain in prime condition, tucked away in a cardboard box. That makes the sweet potato unique: it's the only home-grown vegetable we can eat fresh year-round.

Unlike Irish potatoes, which store best at temperatures just above freezing, sweet potatoes do best with a storage temperature of 50 to 60 degrees. That's easily doable for just about anyone. At our house, a closet under the basement stairs works perfectly.

Just before — or immediately after — the first fall frost, I clip off the vines near the ground and dig up the sweet potatoes. I sort out those with cracks or soft spots, as well as any that I accidentally injure with my spade. I put these roots in a sack to use within the next couple of weeks, although they taste better if we wait at least a week to consume them. The roots need a little time to convert their starch to sugar.

I also set aside one perfect sweet potato, just the right size to suspend in a quart jar. This potato will serve as the "mother" for next year's plants, which I'll start rooting in March. After wrapping it in newspaper, I put it in a separate sack.

The remaining sweet potatoes are wrapped individually in newspapers and tucked into a cardboard box. When I get the box back to the house, I set it in a warm room for about a week so the roots can "cure" before I move the box to the cooler basement closet for long keeping.

Sweet potatoes are normally one of the easiest vegetables to grow, needing little care throughout the growing season except, perhaps, a fence to exclude rabbits or deer.

One year, the vines looked unusually spindly. As I dug them up in the fall, most of the roots had been hollowed out. There was no question what had happened when my spade brought up a surprised vole along with the root he was eating.

Now I protect my crop from voles by setting mouse traps baited with peanut butter around the vines. To keep pets and wild birds safe, I invert a clay pot over each trap.

To grow your own sweet potato plants, start in March. Put one sweet potato, stem end up, in a jar of water. As shoots grow, take 3- or 4-inch cuttings and root them in water.

After roots form, pot each cutting individually and continue to grow the plants indoors until the weather is warm and settled in mid- to late May.

The Salad Garden

Renee Sheppard compares spring greens to fine wines. Owner of Renee's Garden, a specialty seed company, she points out that salad crops come in many colors with subtle or complex flavors that are sometimes earthy, sometimes sweet.

While you can occasionally buy lettuce transplants, you'll never harvest a full range of flavors without starting your salads from seeds.

If you're eager to fill your salad bowl with sweet and crunchy greens, plant seeds as soon as the soil dries out enough to be crumbly, not soggy. You could be picking your first leaves in just three or four weeks.

Salad mixtures, called mesclun, come in blends to suit any taste, from mild to tangy. Some include a mix of different lettuce varieties. More adventurous mixes also include a variety of greens such as arugula, beet, peppergrass, and mustard.

The advantage of buying mesclun: you get to harvest an interesting assortment of salad greens from a single seed packet.

Nitrogen is important for all leafy crops. To make sure my salad greens get the nutrients they need, I spread a 1- to 2-inch layer of compost on the ground before planting, and then dig it into the soil. A light sprinkle of a slow-release, organic vegetable fertilizer provides extra nitrogen.

The more greens you pick, the more leaves the plants produce. That's why they're sometimes referred to as cut-and-come-again crops. You can either pick individual leaves or, if you have a lot of plants, simply shear off one part of the planting at a time. Cut down to about an inch from the ground.

Expect the harvest of quality crops to continue three or more weeks. Make small, successive sowings every two or three weeks to insure a continuous supply of fresh young leaves.

To keep garden-fresh salads on our table in hot weather, I suspend a piece of shade cloth over plants to help them keep their cool. And I grow heat-tolerant summer-crisp varieties of lettuce, also called Batavian lettuce. They're as easy to grow as leaf lettuce, almost as crisp as head lettuce, and have flavor that's in a class of their own.

Endive's curly-leaved heads can spark up your salads with the tangy flavor of their leaves. Bitter if harvested in hot weather, endive is at its best when harvested in fall.

For the most delightful flavor, blanch by excluding light for two weeks before harvest. One easy way to do it is to hold the older leaves together with a rubber band to shade the younger inner leaves beneath. You can also encourage self-blanching by thinning just enough to leave only about 8 inches between plants, so the older leaves have little space to spread.

SPINACH

Sow the season's first spinach seeds as soon as the snow melts. This allows plenty of time to produce a fine crop of leaves before lengthening days encourage flower stalks. Spinach leaves produced during cool weather also taste best.

The first picking of baby spinach leaves begins only three weeks after seeds are sown and will normally continue for three or four more weeks. By picking off only the largest leaves the plants produce, you can

BEST BET

For the earliest spring salads, sow seeds of hardy crops like spinach, miner's lettuce, and corn salad in the fall. Often these plants will survive a Midwest winter and start growing again as soon as the snow melts. A continuous blanket of snow or a winter-weight floating row cover increases their odds of survival. It's never guaranteed, but it succeeds often enough to be worth the gamble.

encourage spinach to keep producing new leaves for a while, until long days and hot temperatures take their toll.

To prevent leaf miners from ruining spinach leaves with light-colored patches, cover plants with cheesecloth or other lightweight cover. For a fall crop, sow spinach seeds again in August and September.

Malabar spinach isn't really spinach, although the young leaves taste like spinach. Instead, it's a gorgeous twining vine. Unlike true spinach, it keeps right on producing through summer's heat.

RADISHES

Growing good radishes is child's play. It must be, because radishes rank high on the list of easy, quick, dependable crops recommended for children's gardens.

But when radishes aren't easy, they're impossible. A lot depends on the weather.

What do radishes want? Cool weather and moist soil. That means radishes grow best when planted in early spring or in late summer, for a fall crop. If the weather is too hot or dry, the radishes grow pithy and taste too hot.

Radishes don't want a lot of nitrogen. Planted in rich soil, they make beautiful tops with puny roots. Too little sunlight may also result in underdeveloped roots.

When you grow your own radishes, you can choose from many different varieties — in your choice of colors. Small round types mature in just twenty to thirty days.

Winter radishes, traditionally sown for a fall crop, grow bigger and take about sixty days to mature. They make excellent storage radishes, keeping for several months in a plastic bag in the refrigerator. Some old standbys include Chinese Rose and Chinese White, which grow long like a carrot, and Round Black Spanish.

Thinning is a must if you want to grow good radishes. When the seedlings are an inch or two tall, thin small, globe-shaped varieties to about an inch apart. Thin winter radishes to 4 to 6 inches apart.

SWISS CHARD

Easy to grow from seed, Swiss chard stands up to spring and fall frosts and thrives in summer's heat, too. Soak seeds overnight to speed their sprouting.

Bright Lights Swiss chard looks especially pretty in a container. With its crinkled, dark-green leaves and stems in a rainbow of colors, it's as colorful as any flower.

Where rabbits are a problem, growing chard in a big pot out of reach is practical as well as pretty.

Young chard leaves taste great in salads, while larger chard leaves lightly steamed make a good substitute for spinach, particularly after the spinach crop succumbs to summer's heat. Lightly steamed, the stalks have a mellow flavor, like a mild asparagus.

CORN SALAD

For a cold-weather treat, plant corn salad seeds in August. Also known as mache or lamb's lettuce, corn salad's fist-sized rosettes are ready to harvest in about fifty days. I love its nutty flavor.

Corn salad is exceptionally easy to grow and thrives in cool weather. Sometimes I even dig under the snow to harvest its perfect leaves for gourmet salads in winter.

CHINESE ARTICHOKES

Chinese artichokes are tiny, knobby, white tubers. Known in France as *crosnes* (pronounced "krones"), they're mild and sweet, with the crispness of water chestnuts.

The tubers are great sliced raw into salads or added to stir-fries with other vegetables.

Chinese artichokes belong to the mint family and are pretty plants with mint-like leaves and pale purple or pink flowers. Like mint, they can spread rapidly into a dense mat. They won't get away from you, though, as long as you dig the plants up at the end of the growing season and pluck off the tubers. The roots are shallow and easy to dig, and the white tubers are hard to miss against the dark soil.

After tucking away most of the harvest in plastic bags in the refrigerator for winter eating, I replant a small bed with tubers placed about 3 inches deep and a foot apart.

I always miss a few tubers and need to thin out extra plants in the spring. Well-spaced plants produce bigger tubers, a decided plus when you're scrubbing dirt off. Shear off the tops when the plants are about a foot tall to avoid energy wasted on flowering.

For best results, Chinese artichokes need moist soil. Dig compost into the soil before planting, mulch, and water in dry weather. Plant tubers in fall or early spring.

CELERIAC

Also known as celery root, celeriac is ugly. But once you peel it, the knobby, round, 3-inch root reveals white flesh that is crisp and packed with pure celery flavor. You can shred celeriac to eat raw in salads or use it as a replacement for celery in soups and stews. It's also great roasted with other root vegetables or added to stir-fries.

In the Midwest celeriac is easier to grow than celery; although, like celery, it grows best in rich, moist soil.

It's rare to find celeriac plants for sale, so starting from seed is often the only choice. Give the seeds a twelve-week head start indoors because celeriac needs a long time to mature.

Waiting until after light fall frost to harvest both enhances the flavor and gives the roots more time to grow. Stored in the refrigerator, celeriac stays in good shape for many weeks, providing a fresh taste from the garden even in winter.

FLORENCE FENNEL

Bulbing fennel, also called Florence fennel, is at its best when seeds are sown in midsummer for fall harvest. The bulbs form at the soil line, developing readily in the cool weather.

A pretty plant with feathery tops and a long taproot like a carrot, fennel is ready to harvest when the flattened bulbs measure 2 to 4 inches across. Use a knife to cut just under the bulb.

To serve, cut the leaf stalks from the top. Each bulb consists of layers of increasingly larger curved sections that wrap partly around each other. When separated, they look something like short stalks of celery.

Crunchy with a sweet flavor that's something like a combination of licorice and anise, fennel is ideal to serve raw with dip. It also adds zip to a salad or makes a tasty addition to stir-fry recipes. Cooking mellows the flavor.

Count on harvesting mature bulbs about eighty days after planting Florence fennel seed. (If you've grown fennel before but have never seen any bulbs, chances are you planted common fennel. An herb that looks like dill, this type is grown for its flavorful leaves and seeds.)

Sweet Corn

Whether you pluck your sweet corn from a backyard plot or pick out ears at the farmers' market, you can thank plant breeders that you don't have to hurry.

Old-timers advised putting water on to boil before going out to harvest corn, and they weren't kidding. The reason: The minute the ears were picked, the sugars started turning to starch. If you wanted your corn sweet, you had to eat it quick.

Then came the first super-sweet hybrids. These new varieties held onto their sweetness much longer. Not everyone was happy, though. While some of us loved the taste, others bemoaned the lack of "real corn" flavor. Less vigorous, the seedlings also proved harder to grow. If planted near other types of corn, the taste was easily ruined by cross-pollination.

So plant breeders kept working. Now, a new generation of hybrids offers everything you could want: Extra-sweet, long-lasting flavor, tender kernels, and old-fashioned taste. In the garden, these vigorous new varieties are easy to grow and can be harvested over a longer period without loss of eating quality.

Think you don't have room to grow your own? These days, gardeners are growing corn in raised beds or even in large tubs.

The secret to success with a small patch of sweet corn? Group plants close together, so the wind can easily blow the pollen from the male tassels to the female silks, filling out the ears with plump kernels. To aid pollination, I avoid planting in single rows and instead plant in a block of "hills" spaced 30 inches apart in each direction, three plants per hill.

Sweet corn is a thirsty crop, particularly when the silks first appear, so keep it watered. Expect to start harvesting two to three weeks after you see silks, with ears maturing fastest when the weather is hot. When the ears are firm and the silks are brown and dry, harvest by pulling the ear down with a little twist.

When husking an ear, you might find an unpleasant surprise, a corn earworm. Damage is often limited to the tip of the ear, though, so just break off and discard it, earworm and all.

Better yet, stop earworms while they're still feeding on the silks, before they invade the ear to feed on kernels. I've had good luck controlling the pests by spraying the silks once or twice with Bt (*Bacillus thuringiensis*). Another time-honored control for earworms: Put five or six drops of mineral oil on the silks just as they begin to brown.

If raccoons are beating you to the harvest, the National Garden Bureau suggests sprinkling baby powder on the stalks and leaves. I've had good luck surrounding the corn patch with a tangle of squash and melon vines.

Asparagus

You can count on one planting of asparagus to provide an annual harvest of succulent spears for twenty years or more.

One bundle of twenty-five crowns, enough to plant a 40-foot row, will satisfy an average family. Early spring is the best time to plant bare-root asparagus.

For the most productive plants, select an all-male variety such as Jersey Giant. With a male variety, there will also be no volunteer plants to weed out.

Dig a trench 6 inches deep and wide enough to easily accommodate the roots. Shovel a small mound of compost along the middle of the trench, then spread the roots evenly over the compost mound.

For weed control, spread a layer of mulch over the ground. Select a mulch such as shredded leaves or ground corn cobs that is free of weed seeds.

One year after planting, begin harvesting a few spears. Take only those that are at least as big around as a pencil and limit your first year's harvest to a three-week period. In subsequent years, harvest all spears for six weeks, then allow the ferny tops to grow to strengthen the roots for the next year's crop.

Don't bother with a knife for harvest. Just snap spears off by hand where they easily break, leaving the tough part behind in the garden.

In late fall, clean up dead asparagus ferns. This thwarts asparagus beetles by eliminating their favorite hiding places and also helps control fungus diseases. Then boost available nutrients and replenish soil humus by spreading a 2- or 3-inch layer of compost on the ground around the plants.

CHAPTER 8

FRUITS

FLAVOR TO SAVOR

There are many good reasons to grow your own fruit, but the best reason is taste. Fruit picked at the peak of ripeness and popped into your mouth simply tastes better.

Growing fruit doesn't necessarily require a lot of space, particularly if you choose berry bushes and dwarf fruit trees. You can save even more space by training fruit trees to grow flat against a wall or trellis, called espalier.

If your yard has some space that gets six hours of sunlight per day, you can grow almost any fruit. (If you have only shade, you'll have to settle for shade-tolerant bushes such as gooseberries and currants.)

I prefer to buy bare-root fruit trees and shrubs, which come in the largest choice of varieties, usually at a substantial savings. Early spring is the best time for planting bare-root nursery stock.

Some fruit trees require two different varieties for pollination. These include apples, sweet cherries, pears, and American plums. A single variety is all you'll need for others, including apricots, peaches, pie cherries, and European plums. Most berry bushes are also self-fruitful, although blueberries will often produce a bigger, better crop if you plant two different varieties.

You can make growing fruit a lot easier simply by choosing the right varieties. Eliminate most of the need to spray by selecting disease-resistant varieties such as Liberty apples and North Star pie cherries.

If you plant dwarf fruit trees, you won't have to drag a ladder around when you prune or harvest. A bonus: dwarf trees start producing fruit years before a standard variety would.

Selecting a Dwarf

Success with dwarf fruit trees lies in the roots. Sure, the top part of the tree above the graft is important, too. That's what determines the looks and the taste of the fruits the tree produces. But it's the roots that determine how tall the tree will grow and how hardy it will be.

Depending on which rootstock is used, a dwarf apple tree might grow only 4 feet tall or as much as 14 feet tall, with a corresponding increase in width. With two different varieties required for cross-pollination, the size difference could be critical where space is limited.

Although dwarf trees are easier to spray, prune, and harvest, some dwarfing rootstocks have such a small root system that the tree has to be staked to keep from blowing over in the wind. Some rootstocks also make the tree more prone to disease or less apt to survive the winter. This is a complex subject, but here are the basics:

An apple tree grafted on an M26 rootstock, for example, will be cold hardy but apt to suffer from fire blight. It is usually self-supporting, but if your site is windy the tree might require staking. You can expect the top of the tree grafted on an M26 rootstock to grow 8 to 14 feet tall.

An apple tree grafted on an M27 rootstock, on the other hand, will grow only 4 to 6 feet tall. Perfect for growing in a container or tiny yard, the tree will not be as cold hardy as an M26 tree and it will definitely require staking.

Confusing? Wait, there's more! Some trees are twice grafted, with an additional "interstem" between the top part of the tree and the rootstock. These trees are practically perfect in many ways, tending to be both strong survivors like standard-sized trees and dwarf sized to fit small spaces. Twice grafted trees are also more drought-tolerant and less prone to blowing over in a strong wind.

But twice-grafted trees are also more expensive and have a tendency to produce lots of extra shoots, called suckers. To limit the sucker problem, plant the tree so that the lower end of the interstem graft is covered with 2 or 3 inches of soil. The upper graft, on the other hand, should be 2 or

3 inches above the ground. Otherwise, the top part of the tree might grow roots of its own and thus lose the dwarfing effect of the rootstock.

So how do you know what you're getting? Plant tags often note the rootstock used. Some mail-order catalogs and online sources also offer detailed information to help you choose the rootstock that is right for you. Before you select your fruit trees, it pays to take a little time to study and ask questions. Midwest Fruit Explorers offer additional information at www.midfex.org.

Apples

Whoever said "easy as pie" probably didn't own an apple tree. But by the time we're eating the apple pie, my husband, Don, and I agree it's worth the effort.

Autumn is one of those times when extra effort is required. When harvesting the apples, we sort them into perfect fruits to refrigerate for later use and flawed fruits to process immediately.

Thank goodness for the food mill that can separate steamed apple quarters from their skins and seeds. Even the grandchildren love to make applesauce using this hand-cranked, low-tech machine. Combining the flavors and textures of all of our apple varieties makes the best sauce.

As we deal with the apple harvest, we also take the time to pick and dispose of any dried-up "mummies" still on the trees and to rake up leaves and pick up fallen fruit. This autumn cleanup is one of the easiest and most important ways to control disease and pest problems, particularly apple scab, which is the Midwest's most serious apple disease. It results in spotted leaves falling early and malformed fruits developing cracks and corky patches.

Choosing disease-resistant varieties also reduces potential problems. Our Liberty apple has shown no signs of scab, cedar/apple rust, or fire blight even though we haven't sprayed it with any fungicides. Liberty apples taste good, too. The maroon-red fruits are firm and juicy, ideal both for eating fresh and for cooking.

As perfect as Liberty is, it needs at least one other companion unless there are other apples for cross-pollination in your neighborhood. I chose Pristine, Redfree, and Enterprise, all disease-resistant varieties.

They ripen at different times and keep fresh apples coming from late July to mid-October.

You can't tell just by color when apples are ready to harvest. Instead, give each one a gentle tug. They'll release easily when ripe. For long keeping, we sort out the perfect apples, wrap each one in white tissue paper, and store them in perforated plastic bags in an extra refrigerator, or in a barrel buried in the ground.

Apples that fall from the tree are a bit overripe and apt to be bruised. Although they won't make good keepers, they're great to gather up to cook or process within a few days.

Pears

A home-grown pear is a taste treat, and the tree itself is a handsome addition to the landscape.

You can't tell when to pick pears just by looking. Unlike most fruits, pears are best picked before they're ripe. (Seckel and Asian pears are an exception to this rule.)

You can't go by the calendar, either. Depending on variety, pears can ripen any time from August through October in the Midwest.

BEST BET

It's easier to control apple maggots and worms with traps than sprays. Red balls covered with sticky Tangle-Trap Insect Trap Coating catch the larvae of apple maggots. Use six traps per dwarf tree, starting by June 1. Hang them 5 to 6 feet off the ground, about 18 inches into the tree canopy.

To catch coddling moths before they lay their eggs, use a recycled gallon-size milk jug with a banana peel, 1 cup sugar, and 1 cup vinegar, then add water to near the top. Hang one trap per tree by petal fall.

Clean and renew sticky traps and replace the solution in the milk jugs as needed.

The best way to judge is to give full-sized, yellow-green pears a squeeze. If the flesh gives slightly to the touch and the pears release easily from the tree, they're ready. Stored at room temperature, the pears will soften and develop full flavor in a week to ten days.

To keep pears longer, store them in the refrigerator when first picked. Remove a few at a time to finish ripening as needed.

Pears are generally easy to grow and have few problems except fire blight, a serious disease in the Midwest. Caused by bacteria, it's easily recognized: infected branches look like they've been burned by fire.

The first line of defense against fire blight is planting varieties that come with built-in resistance, such as Moonglow and Starking Delicious.

If your pear tree gets fire blight, tackle the problem with a pruning saw and pruning shears.

In winter, routinely inspect not only pears for blackened areas but also other plants that are sometimes infected: apple, crabapple, cotoneaster, flowering quince, hawthorn, mountain ash, and serviceberry. Remove any blackened branches you see, cutting at least 10 inches below the visible damage. Sterilize your tools after each cut by dipping the cutting blades in a 10 percent solution of chlorine bleach.

Also pick up and dispose of fallen twigs and dried fruit mummies.

Stone Fruits

PIE CHERRIES

Fresh cherries for pies and preserves are a summer treat not readily available at any price. Fortunately, sour cherries are one of the easiest tree fruits to grow.

You don't need much space to produce a bounty of pie cherries, either. Unlike apples, pears, and sweet cherries, all of which require two different varieties for cross-pollination, sour cherries are self-fruiting; a single tree will suffice.

North Star, a natural dwarf that's exceptionally cold hardy, produces loads of red cherries on a tree only 8 feet tall. Meteor, a slightly bigger dwarf, produces a big crop on a 10-foot-tall tree.

If bucketsful of homegrown cherries sound good to you, spring is the perfect time to plant a cherry tree. Look for a site that offers full sun, well-drained soil, and good air circulation.

What problems can you expect with cherries? Birds are the biggest complaint. Some gardeners hang aluminum pie pans, flashing tape, or unwanted CDs in the cherry tree. Others resort to covering the tree with netting, a job made much easier if the tree is a dwarf.

Two fungus diseases, leaf spot and brown rot, sometimes attack cherries grown in the Midwest, although North Star offers some natural resistance to both. Raking up leaves in fall, removing dried mummies, and pruning out dead twigs and sunken lesions help control both diseases. If necessary to get a severe disease problem under control, spray the cherry tree with wettable sulfur, starting when the petals fall.

What about gum oozing from the bark? The two most likely culprits are borers, which you can dig out with a knife, or southwest injury, which you can prevent with a coat of interior white latex paint on the trunk every fall.

If the gum oozing from a sunken area smells sour, bacterial canker is the probable cause. If it's on a limb, not the main trunk, prune the branch 10 inches below the canker, then sterilize the pruners with a 10 percent chlorine bleach solution.

Cherry fruit flies, which look like small houseflies, lay their eggs under the skin of immature cherries. The eggs soon hatch into cherry "worms," or maggots. As a first line of defense for my cherries, I use the same red sticky traps that I use for trapping maggots in my apple trees.

BLACK KNOT AND BROWN ROT

The color you want to see on your plum trees is purple, not black.

Dark, corky swellings on the twigs and branches are sure signs of black knot, a fungus disease. If allowed to persist, the infection will

BEST BET

To keep birds from eating your cherries, grow some wild fruits for the birds. Serviceberries and mulberries often prove so popular that the birds seem not to notice that the pie cherries are ripe.

stunt branches then gradually kill them. Black knot sometimes infects cherry trees as well as plums.

In late winter before new leaves emerge, inspect trees for these black swellings, which are sometimes small, sometimes more than a foot long.

If you find any, the solution is simple. While the tree is still dormant, prune any affected twigs or branches, making the cut 2 or 3 inches below the swellings. If the infection occurs on a large limb you don't want to sacrifice, remove the affected portion by cutting down to the wood. The cut should be at least an inch deeper and wider than the visible infection.

Another common problem that affects plums, cherries, peaches, and apricots is a fungus disease called brown rot. Fuzzy gray patches appear on the ripening fruit, spreading rapidly when the fruit matures in mild, moist weather.

A little cleanup in winter will help control this fungus disease, too. Prune out any dead twigs or branches with sunken lesions where the fungus might be lurking. Remove any dried fruits that are still on the tree. If black rot is still a problem, spray wettable sulfur.

ORGANIC DISEASE CONTROL

APPLES

Spray: Wettable sulfur plus spreader-sticker
Controls: Scab, cedar/apple rust
Timing: When buds show green, again when blossoms first
   show pink, again after petal fall, and again ten days later

CHERRIES

Spray: Wettable sulfur plus spreader-sticker
Controls: Cherry leaf spot, brown rot
Timing: Every two weeks through harvest,
   starting when flower petals fall

PEACHES, PLUMS

Spray: Wettable sulfur plus spreader-sticker
Controls: Brown rot
Timing: At first sign of symptoms

Grapes

If experience has lowered your grape expectations, maybe it's time for another look. With disease-resistant, winter-hardy varieties and a better understanding of how they grow, producing grapes in the Midwest is easier than ever.

Some of the best grapes for this region come from the work of the late Elmer Swenson who bred hardy, disease-resistant grapes in northern Wisconsin for decades.

Swenson Red, a disease-resistant red grape known for its unique, fruity flavor, is ideal for eating fresh or making wine. Edelweiss, a superhardy white table grape, is also blessed with exceptional resistance to disease. Esprit bears large clusters of white wine grapes.

Most hardy grapes have seeds, no problem if you're making jelly or wine. If you want seedless grapes for eating fresh, the list of winter-hardy varieties is short. Mars, a blue, and Reliance, a red, are two of the most reliable for the upper Midwest.

Grapes ripen from mid-August through September but they look ripe before they are. Wait for the stem of each cluster to turn brown, with darkened seeds. Then taste a few to be sure.

The ideal location to plant grapes is in full sun with good air circulation to thwart fungus diseases. Avoid gusty winds, which break tender shoots and tatter leaves.

February is the traditional month in the Midwest for annual grape pruning — a necessary step to keep grapes healthy and productive.

Vigorous grapevines can become a real tangle of canes in a single year. I find it easy to see what I'm doing if I start my pruning by removing all the old canes that have already produced fruit. They're easy to recognize; they're the ones that have shaggy bark.

Directions for training grapes can be confusing, but this simple method works for me: Maintain a central trunk with four vigorous canes, or "arms," shortened to about a dozen buds each. Also leave four short renewal spurs, each with a bud or two, to become next year's arms.

After I finish pruning, I spread a 1-inch layer of compost and 3-inch layer of mulch around grapevines. By covering any diseased grapes on the ground with mulch, they're prevented from releasing spores to infect the new crop with black rot, one of the most serious of grape diseases.

Grapevines grow well on any support, such as a trellis or arbor. Growers who want a lot of grapes often install a simple system with two parallel wires connected to heavy posts.

Berries

STRAWBERRIES

For strawberry lovers like me, growing two different types of strawberries is a must.

A June-bearing variety such as Sparkle or Surecrop allows for gorging on fresh berries, with plenty of extras to make jam and stash in the freezer during the intense two- to three-week harvest in early summer.

A day-neutral variety such as Tristar or Tribute, on the other hand, provides the season's first taste of ripe berries and then a small but steady harvest of fresh strawberries that continues until frost. Ideal for busy people, day-neutrals produce just enough berries for eating fresh over the entire growing season.

Managing these two different kinds of strawberries requires different techniques.

As soon as the June bearers' harvest ends, we get out the mower. With the blade set as high as possible, we mow off the entire patch.

The mowed strawberry patch looks dreadful for a couple of weeks, but this mowing of the June-bearers serves a purpose. It rejuvenates the patch by removing the oldest plants, which have the highest crowns. Only the young daughter plants, sprung up from runners, are left to carry on.

After mowing, we replenish the soil by spreading a 2-inch layer of compost around the plants. Next, we spread fresh mulch around the plants plus a heavy layer of mulch between rows to maintain walking paths. Because strawberries have shallow roots, we make sure to water the young plants in dry weather.

That's it. Treated to this annual renewal, a patch of June-bearing strawberries stays vigorous and productive for up to ten years.

To maintain day-neutral varieties, on the other hand, mowing is out. Since we're counting on them for a continuous harvest, we wouldn't want to mow off their tops.

Fortunately, day-neutral varieties don't produce as many runners as June-bearers and thus aren't nearly as quick to grow too crowded. You can always just pull out a plant here and there, if necessary.

To replenish the soil for day-neutrals, I wait until fall to spread a 2-inch layer of compost around the plants, then top it with fresh mulch.

All strawberries require sun, but I've found that a little afternoon shade seems to help day-neutral varieties keep producing during the hot weather in mid- to late summer.

There are a host of things that can go wrong in the strawberry patch, but — on the home garden scale — most of them never happen. You can prevent most troubles by protecting blossoms from late-spring frosts, mulching to keep berries from contact with the soil, and picking often to keep berries from rotting in the patch.

Strawberries are usually sold bare-root in bundles of twenty or twenty-five plants. Soak the roots in water about an hour before you plant. Potted plants are sometimes offered for sale, but they cost a lot more and offer no particular benefit unless you want to buy just a few day-neutral strawberry plants to grow in a container.

For maximum production, plant your strawberries where they'll get sun at least six hours a day. Avoid low-lying frost pockets, where early blossoms are likely to suffer damage. Don't choose a spot that has been part of the lawn because grubs, which are more numerous in sod, can injure strawberry roots.

Strawberries require well-drained soil. If you have soggy soil, plant your strawberries in a raised bed or container.

Before planting, spread a 2-inch layer of compost over the soil and dig it in. Set each plant in the ground so that the soil comes to the base of the crown; then fan out the roots. Firm the soil around each plant, water thoroughly, and immediately mulch with straw or shredded leaves. The mulch not only helps keep the soil from drying out but also helps protect the new plants from wind.

To help the plants get a good start, pinch off any blossoms on day-neutral strawberries for the first six weeks. Once you stop removing blossoms, expect to be picking your first ripe berries in about four weeks. For June-bearers, pick off all the blossoms the first growing season and look forward to a huge harvest of fruit the following summer.

For June-bearers and day-neutral strawberries alike, wait until after the ground freezes before adding a blanket of straw over the top of the plants for winter protection.

In late winter, check the mulch in the strawberry patch and add more if necessary. If alternating cycles of freezing and thawing have pushed the plants up to expose roots, use your foot to push the plants back where they belong.

In spring, cautiously remove the mulch a little at a time, but leave it nearby in case you need to throw it back over blooming plants to protect the blossoms from a late frost.

After about ten years, strawberry harvest declines as virus diseases take their toll. That's your signal that it's time to begin again with new virus-free plants planted in a new garden spot.

RASPBERRIES

Fall-bearing raspberries are late summer's refreshing reward. Plump, ripe berries fall easily into your hand with the slightest pressure. When you grow your own, you can pop some of the sun-warmed berries into your mouth as you pick.

As easy to grow as they are delicious, fall-bearing raspberries ripen over a period of many weeks, often continuing right up to the first fall frost. Year after year, my patch of Heritage raspberries produces a near-perfect, problem-free crop.

When it comes to pruning the plants and fending off diseases,

BEST BET

Fertilizing strawberries is tricky because too much nitrogen makes mushy berries. Use only slow-release fertilizer or compost to keep an established patch well fed.

fall-bearing varieties such as Heritage have several advantages over summer-bearing raspberries like Latham. With the fall-bearers, you can just mow off all the canes at ground level anytime in winter or early spring and remove them from the patch. Not only is this much less tedious than the pruning required for summer-bearing varieties, it also insures that no canes infected with disease remain to infect new shoots.

There's no worry about damage from cold temperatures or winter-browsing rabbits and deer, either, since you aren't aiming to save anything above ground anyway.

After removing the canes, I spread a 1-inch layer of compost over the soil and pile on fresh mulch to control weeds in the raspberry patch.

Because fall-bearing raspberries are so easy to grow and maintain, I stopped growing summer-bearing raspberries, which require more difficult selective pruning to remove only the old canes after harvest. It's a prickly, difficult job that must be performed in the heat of summer just as soon as the harvest is over.

It doesn't take a lot of raspberry bushes to produce your fill of raspberries. Ten plants spaced 3 feet apart will quickly fill in to make a dense hedge that will supply bucketsful of fruit.

Choose a sunny spot with well-drained soil for raspberries. You can plant container-grown raspberries anytime, but if you're willing to wait until spring to plant bare-root plants, it will cost less.

BLACKBERRIES

Growing blackberries recently got a lot easier, thanks to varieties that produce fruit on new canes.

BEST BET

Ready to plant your own raspberries? Resist the temptation to take free plants offered by friends. Instead, buy virus-free plants from a reputable nursery. Also remove any wild brambles growing on your property. There's no cure for virus diseases, so it's better to be safe than sorry.

Prime-Jim, Prime-Jan, and Prime-Ark 45 are primocane-fruiting blackberries that grow a cane and produce fruit in the same season, just like fall-bearing raspberries.

That means there are no more lost crops when winter's cold kills the canes and no more tedious summer pruning to remove old canes while keeping the new. With the new varieties, you can simply mow off all the canes anytime during the winter.

I experimented with two plants each of Prime-Jim and Prime-Jan. As soon as I tasted the big and delicious berries, I couldn't wait to dig out my conventional blackberries.

Many gardeners are disappointed to learn that the new primocane-fruiting blackberries have wicked thorns. I've found that thornless blackberries do not produce a reliable crop in most of the upper Midwest. I'm willing to undergo a little pain for the pleasure of popping ripe blackberries in my mouth in summer.

To make summer picking as painless as possible, I narrow my blackberry hedge by pruning out at ground level any cane that sprouts outside a 4-foot-wide row. I also remove any weak, damaged, or dead canes and thin out crowded canes, leaving at least 6 inches between those that remain.

BLUEBERRIES

Since Mother Nature didn't provide my garden with the acid soil that blueberries require, I almost missed the pleasure of homegrown blueberries. I don't usually fight Mother Nature, but my love of blueberries and the encouragement of blueberry expert Dan Hartmann finally convinced me to give blueberries a try.

Here's the method, suggested by Dan, which has made my blueberries a success:

- For each blueberry plant, stuff a five-gallon bucket of water with sphagnum peat moss. After the moss soaks up all the water, dump the bucket's contents into the planting hole and mix it into the soil.

  (A note about using sphagnum peat moss: Although reputable companies are now using sustainable practices in the harvest of sphagnum peat moss from bogs, I recommend its use only when necessary to lower the soil's pH. For other plantings, compost works great as a soil-builder.)

- Mulch each blueberry bush with pine bark chips, pine needles, or shredded oak leaves. As the mulch decomposes, it helps keep the soil acid and also provides organic matter that blueberries need. Add fresh mulch as the old breaks down.
- Every two years in winter, spread 6 ounces of powdered sulfur in a wide ring around each plant.

You don't ever have to wonder whether your acid-loving plants need another winter sulfur treatment: pale, anemic leaves during the growing season and sparse flowers and fruits are sure signs that they do.

Half-high blueberries such as Northland and North Blue grow 2 to 4 feet tall and are hardy throughout the Midwest. Highbush blueberries like Blue Jay and Blue Crop, hardy through USDA zone 4, grow 5 to 7 feet tall.

Planting at least two different varieties provides the best fruit set. You can harvest blueberries from July to September if you have room to plant early-, middle-, and late-season varieties.

Blueberries prefer to grow in full sun and well-drained soil. Plant in spring, allowing 3 feet between half-high varieties, 5 feet for highbush blueberries.

Diseases and insects have not been a problem for my blueberries, but protecting ripening blueberries from birds is a must. My husband, Don, solved that problem for me with a framework over the shrubs

BEST BET

If you want to give blueberries a try but don't know whether your soil is acid or alkaline, start with a soil test. You can find a simple, inexpensive kit to measure your soil's acidity or alkalinity — called pH — at any garden center.

Soil pH is measured on a 14-point scale, with pH 7 being neutral, and higher numbers increasingly alkaline. Healthy blueberries require pH 5.5 or lower. If you need to lower the pH, follow the steps described above.

that supports half-inch green poultry netting and allows room for me to stand up to harvest.

I soon learned that blueberries are thirsty plants, requiring supplemental water whenever the weather is dry. I keep my blueberry shrubs forever young by removing any stems more than five years old.

I planted blueberries because I adore the fruit. Little did I know that their fall foliage would make the shrubs an autumn favorite, too.

Now, after the summer harvest of delicious berries ends, I look forward to October, when the bright crimson leaves of the blueberries rival the beauty of any other shrub. After the colorful autumn leaves fall, the branches add a subtle beauty to the winter landscape with their handsome red sheen.

ARONIA BERRIES

Black chokeberry (*Aronia melanocarpa*) has long been one of my favorite shrubs. It boasts white flowers in spring and showy, long-lasting, purple-black berries that remain on the plant most of the winter. In autumn, its wine-red foliage makes a fine show.

Adaptable and easy-to-grow, black chokeberry is a Midwest native. It thrives in full sun or partial shade, and in wet or dry soils. I've never seen any kind of pest on the foliage or fruit, and my plants have never suffered from any disease.

Many years ago I planted several black chokeberries partly to provide a late-winter food source for birds, but I never had any intention of eating the berries myself. Visitors who dared to sample a berry usually ended up spitting it out.

When I first heard about the new demand for aronia berries because of their high antioxidant content that exceeds wonder crops like blueberries and elderberries, I was skeptical. I figured the fruit was so sour it would require a huge quantity of sugar to make the berries palatable.

Well, I was wrong. Turns out the berries' dry, puckering taste comes from high tannins. The trick is to freeze the berries before use to break down the tannins.

Now I fill small bags with chokeberries in fall and freeze them.

Throughout the year we enjoy the richly colored, flavorful fruit in smoothies, muffins, and pancakes.

Unlike most fruits, there is nothing critical about harvest time of chokeberries. I usually harvest the berries in small batches as time allows in September and October.

A variety called Viking, which can grow about 6 to 8 feet tall and wide, is recommended for its large, plentiful berries. If your space is limited, try compact Autumn Magic or dwarf Iroquois Beauty. All are self-pollinating, producing berries even if you have room for only a single plant.

Rhubarb

Unlike some perennials in our ornamental gardens, rhubarb is reliably winter hardy and long lived.

As long as it's planted in full sun and well-drained soil, rhubarb pretty much takes care of itself. It doesn't even seem to care whether you harvest any stalks or not. It'll be there, ready to eat, when you get hungry for a rhubarb pie.

To plant, spade in some compost and then set rhubarb with the crown — or growing point — covered with about 2 inches of soil. Space plants about 3 feet apart. Two plants will produce plenty for an average-size family.

Allow the plants a year to get established before harvesting any stalks. After the plants are growing vigorously you can harvest spring through July, but take no more than half the stalks at any one time.

If your plants send up any flower stalks, remove them.

Late November is the easiest time to ensure the continuing health of rhubarb. Simply removing dead foliage at this time goes a long way toward preventing problems. Rhubarb crown rot, a fungus disease known also as stem rot or foot rot, lives on infected plant debris and in the surrounding soil. So do other rhubarb diseases, including leaf spot, anthracnose, and verticillium wilt.

For good measure, also clear the nearby area of grasses and weeds, especially curly dock, which can harbor two rhubarb pests, the stalk borer and the rhubarb curculio.

Right after you clean up the foliage is an excellent time to feed rhubarb plants. Their preferred diet: a 2-inch layer of compost or aged manure spread on the ground around the plants. Top it off with a layer of fresh mulch to control weeds, and you'll have little left to do in the coming year except enjoy the harvest.

After about five years, spindly rhubarb stalks are a sign that it's time to dig and divide rhubarb clumps. That job is best done in early spring, as soon as new leaves emerge. If possible, choose a new garden spot to replant rhubarb divisions.

CHAPTER 9

HERBS

FRAGRANT FINDS

Two paths lead to an herb garden.

On the first path are great cooks who learn to grow herbs to ensure a fresh supply of top-quality seasonings.

The second path is taken by people like me — passionate gardeners who want to experience as many different kinds of plants as possible.

Along the way, I think I've become a better cook. I'd hate to return to the days when I didn't have plenty of summer savory to flavor the beans or enough sweet basil for every tomato dish. But I have to confess: Some of my herbs still serve no useful purpose. I grow herbs such as pineapple sage and anise hyssop just because they look pretty and smell good.

Herbs don't require much coddling. Most are drought tolerant and need little or no fertilizer. Fertile garden soil can actually be too much of a good thing for many herbs, which tend to develop stronger scents on less-rich soil.

Many herbs, including chives, lemon balm, sage, English thyme, and French tarragon, are hardy perennials that come back dependably year after year in my Midwest garden. Others, including cilantro, dill, summer savory, fennel, and borage, are annuals that grow quickly from seed sown directly in the garden. So does parsley, provided you remember to soak the seeds overnight before planting, to speed its germination.

Basils are easy to grow from seed, but I like to give them a six-week head start indoors for earlier harvest. Oregano, mint, rosemary, and pineapple sage are best purchased as plants.

By August, the harvest of favorites such as oregano, thyme, basil, and sage for long-term storage is in full swing. For best flavor, herb leaves should be harvested before the plants bloom. If they get ahead of me, I just pinch off and discard the blooms.

Because the flavor of herbs peaks in the morning, I try to harvest the leaves as soon as the dew dries. Then I wash the dust off the leaves and pat them dry.

I usually dry herbs in my food dryer, but culinary herbs can also be tied together in bunches and hung upside down to dry out of direct sunlight. You can also use a microwave; check your manual for instructions.

Stored in glass jars in a cool spot, properly dried herbs keep indefinitely, although they eventually lose some of their flavor.

BASIL

One of the most popular of the culinary herbs, sweet basil is also one of the easiest to grow — but only if you wait to plant until the weather is warm and settled. It doesn't take a frost to kill basil plants. Anything below 50 degrees can do them in.

While waiting for warm weather, I keep young basil plants in my coldframe. There they have time to adjust to strong sunlight and wind. When the temperature drops too low, the automatic vent closes, protecting the plants from cold.

The traditional Genovese-type Italian basil is my favorite for pesto to serve on pasta, poultry, and fish, and for tomato sauces. Greek or fine-leaf varieties such as Spicy Globe offer great flavor, too, as well as small, compact plants ideal for growing in a pot.

Basil grows best in full sun. When setting out plants in the garden, I pinch the plants back by about half.

I try to squirrel away plenty of basil leaves for winter while the weather is still hot because, once cool temperatures arrive, basil stops growing. I freeze forty-leaf portions in plastic freezer bags for winter pesto and also dry some leaves to crumble into soups and sauces.

Even if basils weren't favorites for flavoring, their heavenly scent would be reason enough to grow them. When I'm working in the garden, I enjoy running my hand over the leaves just to enjoy the fragrance.

Basils are pretty enough for the flower garden, too, with leaves of purple or green, plain or ruffled, big or small. Purple-leafed varieties, although not as flavorful for cooking, look beautiful as a garnish, in salads and in herbed vinegars. It's fun to grow cinnamon and lemon basils for herbal teas, or just to sniff. Siam Queen, a Thai basil, merits space in my garden for its reddish-purple flowers, though I seldom use any of its licorice-flavored leaves in cooking.

The choice of varieties is huge, particularly if you're willing to grow basil from seed.

Although basil is usually free of problems, some gardeners encounter fusarium wilt. A fungus disease carried by infected seed, it causes sudden wilting and death of the plants.

Quality seed is now tested for fusarium, but that doesn't prevent the problem where the soil is already infected. The fungus can live in the soil for years.

If a part of your garden is already infected with fusarium wilt, don't plant basil there again. One good solution: Plant basil in fresh soil in a container. And when you work in the infected area, be sure to clean your trowel or hoe before moving on.

Downy mildew is another fungus disease that can infect sweet basil. If the leaves of one of your plants start to yellow, remove that plant immediately before the disease spreads.

HERBS FOR SHADE

Mostly shade? No problem. Although most culinary herbs are from sun-baked regions and prefer full sun, many also perform surprisingly well in partial shade.

Parsley is not only one of the most shade-tolerant herbs, it's also one of the prettiest. For a garnish, I prefer the dark green, curly kind. For cooked recipes, I want the more flavorful Italian flat-leaf type.

Parsley is easy to grow, but you may want to plant more than you think you'll need for the kitchen. Larvae of the beautiful swallowtail butterflies are particularly fond of parsley and can quickly eat all the leaves. If my parsley crop is at risk of disappearing, I gently move the large caterpillars off the parsley onto an alternative food source, such as volunteer dill or fennel plants.

Peppermint, spearmint, and other mints also do quite well in shade. Often used for teas, their chopped leaves are also delicious in fruit salads.

Because flavor of mint seedlings is quite variable, start with purchased plants. To keep less flavorful volunteer plants from growing, trim off any flowers before plants go to seed.

Not all mints are winter hardy, but those that are can be invasive. To keep perennial mints from spreading, plant them in large pots. Add compost to potting soil for a rich, moisture-holding mix. After planting, sink each pot into the ground. Refresh the pot every spring by dividing the mints and adding fresh soil and compost.

Sweet cicely is a hardy, long-lived perennial with ferny, dark-green foliage and clusters of small white flowers. You can toss in a handful of its finely cut leaves when stewing fruit to add sweetness and an anise-like flavor. This herb is ideal for naturalizing in a woodland garden. The white flowers atop ferny foliage look like a giant Queen Anne's lace.

Chervil is another culinary herb you can grow in the shade. These plants have a fine-textured, delicate appearance and are best grown from seeds sown where you want them to grow. After the initial planting, chervil often self-sows additional crops. Sometimes called gourmet's parsley, chervil is used to season salads, soups, vegetables, and poultry.

BEST BET

While it's fun to experiment with some of the lesser-known herbs like chervil and sweet cicely, if you're a shade gardener who longs to grow basil and other sun-loving herbs, you have several choices. Plant your herbs in pots so you can move them to any spot on the deck or patio that gets some sun. Or limb-up some trees to let more sunlight into the yard.

Angelica is the most dramatic herb for the shade, shooting up 4 feet tall or more in its second year and topped with large clusters of greenish-white flowers. Although sometimes behaving like a perennial, angelica is typically a biennial that dies after the second year. If you allow the seeds to drop on the ground, angelica often self-sows.

Although angelica is so pretty you'd want to grow it even if you had no intention of using it as an herb, its sweet-scented leaves are a good addition to fruit salads. Candying the stems for a sweet treat is another time-honored role for angelica. My favorite use: chop angelica stems to add to rhubarb, reducing the need for sugar.

Both the stems and leaves of angelica are best harvested early in the season, before the herb produces flowers.

CILANTRO

With the zooming popularity of salsas and other Mexican dishes, many gardeners are discovering that it's quick and easy to grow their own cilantro from seed.

It's a waste of money to buy cilantro plants because they don't last long. Once cilantro goes to seed, the plants die.

In the beginning, you'll want to plant a few more seeds every three or four weeks for a continuous supply of the bright green, ferny leaves. Eventually cilantro will keep itself going, provided you allow some of the seeds to fall to the ground to grow a fresh supply of young plants. The seeds germinate best in cool soil.

Growing directions for cilantro always recommend full sun, but I've found that growing it in partial shade may actually help the plants last longer in hot summer weather.

LEMONY HERBS

With a pot of lemon balm by the back door, who needs a lemon from the grocery store? A couple of leaves of lemon balm in a glass of iced tea or a fruit salad pack all the lemony flavor of the fruit.

A hardy perennial, lemon balm is easy to grow in full sun or partial shade. So easy that, if you're hoping for a small patch of lemon balm in the garden, the biggest problem you're apt to encounter is keeping it small. Lemon balm would gladly take over if allowed.

Harvest often to encourage a fresh crop of new leaves, to keep plants looking their best and to prevent flowering.

Besides lemon balm, many other lemon-scented herbs can help satisfy your craving for citrus in food or potpourri. All you need is a sunny spot with room for a few pots.

Lemon verbena, a handsome, shrubby plant with a heavenly lemon scent, is my favorite. The plant performs best when allowed to summer outdoors in the sun and winter indoors in a bright, cool spot. If whiteflies attack, spraying with insecticidal soap usually takes care of the problem without poisoning the leaves.

Lemon grass looks just like grass, but its lemony fragrance is hard to miss. Popular in Asian recipes, lemon grass grows amazingly fast from a tiny plant in spring to a big clump by fall. To save it from frost, I bring a small division indoors for winter. My little plant often languishes under lights in the basement, but then quickly regains its vigor when moved back to a sunny spot outdoors for the summer.

BORAGE

Borage, with its starry blue flowers, is as pretty as it is useful. Easy to grow by planting seed directly in the garden, it grows into a handsome, bushy plant 2 feet tall and wide.

A few young borage leaves chopped and tossed into the salad bowl add a cucumber-like flavor, especially welcome early in the season while you're waiting to harvest your first cukes.

The flowers, besides adding beauty to the herb garden, are also fun to eat. Float a few in cool beverages or candy some blossoms for decorating desserts.

Sounds like the perfect plant, right? Not quite. Borage doesn't hold up very well in our region's summer heat and, soon after flowering, the plants often collapse.

However, once you've grown borage in your garden, there always seem to be a few volunteer seedlings you can use to fill the void. Never self-seeding to the point of becoming a problem, borage has nevertheless kept itself going for many years in my garden. When one plant collapses, I just rip it out and replace it with a fresh volunteer.

FRENCH TARRAGON

Snip some French tarragon in midsummer and you'll be doubly rewarded. Cutting stems back not only stimulates new growth but also provides leaves that can really perk up a salad dressing.

Some say French tarragon tastes like fresh licorice. Others describe it as a mild anise flavor. Just make sure you have the French version. Russian tarragon, sometimes identified only as tarragon, is tasteless.

French tarragon is a perennial herb. Start by buying a small plant. You can't grow it from seed because, unlike Russian tarragon, the few seeds produced by the French type are usually sterile. Growing about 2 feet tall, it's a pretty plant with narrow, fine-textured, dark-green leaves.

You'll find French tarragon easy to grow if you plant it in a sunny spot with well-drained soil, and just as easy to kill if you plant it in a soggy spot. During rainy spells, some stems may rot at the base. If that happens, just clip off the affected stems. To prevent mildew, avoid crowding this herb. With room to breathe, it's usually a trouble-free plant.

You can use fresh French tarragon to flavor soups, salads, sauces, and meats. Jars filled with tarragon herb vinegar are beautiful and make a tasty salad dressing. Herb vinegar is also one of the best ways to preserve tarragon for winter use.

DILL AND FENNEL

Even though dill and fennel are exuberant self-seeders, it's hard to have too many of these sun-loving herbs. They pack extra flavor for soups and salads. The plants also serve as a prime food source for swallowtail butterfly caterpillars. And both sun-loving herbs have fine, feathery foliage that looks gorgeous almost anywhere. I like to use extra plants for contrast with the coarser texture of a wide assortment of ornamental plants, in containers as well as in the garden.

When I find a swallowtail caterpillar devouring the leafy top of a carrot or a parsley plant, I simply move the worm to a dill or fennel plant in the background, where the damage will be hidden from view.

Dill, a must for flavoring pickles and useful in many other dishes, usually grows about 3 to 4 feet tall. Fennel grows about as tall, producing tender, sweet leaves for flavoring salads, dressings, fish, and potatoes.

With a mixture of bronze-red and deep-green varieties planted for contrast, fennel is a pretty addition to the garden.

Both dill and fennel produce flowers arranged in open clusters that resemble umbrellas. This type of flower is extremely attractive to beneficial insects, such as small parasitic wasps and predatory lacewings. With the beneficials well fed, they'll stay to help fight garden pests. What a deal!

COMMON SAGE AND ITS RELATIVES

A perennial herb hardy at least to USDA zone 5, garden sage has fragrant gray-green leaves that are a must for flavoring poultry and stuffing.

My single sage plant is decades old and requires little care. I simply cut it back to near the ground in early spring after the first new leaves appear. Full sunlight and well-drained soil keep this herb thriving. Division of the old woody crowns isn't recommended.

Closely related to garden sage are sages grown primarily for their ornamental foliage. There's purple sage and golden sage. Tricolor sage has purple, green, and white fuzzy leaves. As the weather cools in autumn, its leaves grow ever more handsome, with accents of brighter purple and pink. None of the ornamental sages are as winter hardy as common sage. Although they can be used for seasonings, common sage is still the best for culinary use.

Pineapple sage has two great things going for it. The strong pineapple scent of its leaves is heavenly. And, in late summer when the plant is topped with bright-red flower spikes, I love to watch the hummingbirds enjoy the nectar.

Pineapple sage isn't winter hardy in the Midwest, but I don't mind. The pleasure it gives makes it well worth buying a new plant each spring. A large, bushy plant, it grows 4 feet tall and wide in a single season. Like other sages, it thrives in full sun in well-drained soil and is seldom bothered by diseases or pests.

STEVIA

These days, some gardeners are growing their own healthy sweetener in the garden or even in a pot on the windowsill.

It's stevia, a super-sweet herb that aficionados say has none of the drawbacks of sugar or artificial sweeteners. Almost calorie-free and never responsible for a spike in blood sugar, stevia is a boon for diabetics and dieters alike.

Before frost kills stevia plants, I dry some of the leaves for winter use. You can also bring a potted stevia plant indoors and grow it in bright light all winter.

Stevia is an undemanding plant that is easy to grow as long as you have well-drained soil. If you don't, you can still grow stevia in a container. One stevia plant is a good fit for a 12-inch pot. Outdoors, you can grow stevia in either full sun or light shade. Indoors, put a potted plant in a sunny window or under a grow light.

I've given stevia seeds an early start indoors and had no germination problems, but some other gardeners find the seeds hard to sprout. As the fame of stevia spreads, stevia transplants are becoming widely available in spring wherever herbs are sold. Since most gardeners would need only one or two stevia plants, buying transplants probably makes more sense than buying a packet of seeds.

A variety called Crazy Sweet eliminates the "licorice" or bitter aftertaste sometimes experienced after consuming stevia.

More Tips for Success with Herbs

Thyme. There are many different kinds, some hardy, some not. The key to winter survival of hardy varieties like English thyme is a sunny spot with well-drained soil where water never stands. Use grass clippers to shear plants whenever they start to look ratty.

Chives. Both the round, pink flowers and mild, onion-flavored leaves are edible. Shear after spring flowers fade to promote new growth. Plants thrive in sun or partial shade.

Summer savory. The "bean herb" grows rapidly from seeds sown in a sunny spot, with the first sprigs ready to pick in about six weeks. Plant some seeds every few weeks during the summer to insure a continuous supply.

Winter savory. Although not quite as flavorful as the annual, the perennial version is particularly welcome early in the season before summer savory is ready to harvest. Winter survival isn't guaranteed, but good soil drainage helps.

Greek oregano. There is considerable variation with plants sold as oregano. To be sure you're getting a flavorful plant, crush a small leaf and sniff it before you buy. Grow oregano in full sun and well-drained soil, and refrain from trimming until plants are actively growing in spring.

Herbs on the Winter Windowsill

The harvest of indoor herbs will never rival the quantity of scented leaves I gather from the summer garden. But when the outdoor garden is sleeping, the indoor herbs are indispensable.

My potted herbs come in handy for occasional snippets of fresh leaves, but I treasure them most for something more: a sniff or two of the wonderful and diverse fragrances can transport me back to the summer garden, even when snow covers the ground.

Rosemary is one of my favorites. I love its spicy flavor and dark-green, needlelike leaves. Of all the herbs, though, it's the most temperamental to grow indoors. It needs the bright light of a sunny window but doesn't like dry air or toasty temperatures. It balks if it's over-watered or allowed to dry out.

One mistake I've made with rosemary is crowding it together with too many other plants. The lack of good air circulation resulted in a bad case of powdery mildew.

Rosemary has an easier time making the transition from outside to indoors and back again if grown year-round in a pot.

Thyme and oregano like their soil drier and the temperature hotter. Both do well in a sunny window, provided the soil in their pots dries out between waterings. If they get too much water or not enough light, they'll let you know by developing mildew or rotted roots.

Parsley is one of the easiest herbs to grow as a houseplant. Although it likes bright light, it can get by on less than most of the others. And parsley isn't as sensitive to overwatering; it prefers moist soil. I like the flat Italian type for cooking, but curly-leaf parsley is a prettier houseplant.

Bay makes a fine potted plant. A tender perennial, it can summer outside but must come in for the winter. Like many other herbs, it likes to grow in full sun and dry soil.

Chives grow well indoors. Put a clump in a pot in September but leave it out to chill until a hard freeze threatens before bringing it to a sunny window.

Sweet basil's heavenly fragrance makes it worth the trouble to grow this annual herb indoors. Easy from seed, sweet basil requires bright light. Small-leaf varieties are the best for growing inside.

Some annual herbs aren't good candidates for growing indoors unless you're willing to plant new seeds every few weeks. Dill and cilantro, for example. Both grow tall and lanky, then fall over. If you want fresh leaves to snip for flavoring, you'll need new plants coming along for replacements.

Ornamental Herbs

Some herbs are so pretty, they're just as much at home in a sunny flower border as the herb garden.

Lavender, with its silvery foliage and purple flower spikes, is one of my favorites for planting at the feet of roses to cover their bare ankles.

This pretty herb has a long history of use as an insect repellent. Its sweet smell makes lavender ideal for potpourri and sachets, as well as dried bouquets and crafts. Lavender is even becoming popular as a culinary herb, with fresh flowers tossed in salads and leaves substituted for rosemary.

Because lavender is so much fun to use, it's hard to grow enough. Luckily, the more it's cut, the more it blooms. Best time for harvest is just as the flowers begin to open.

In just a few extra minutes, you can easily start extra lavender plants by "layering." Just bend some of the uncut stems down to bare soil and use a stone or mound of soil to hold the middle of the stem in place. Before long, roots will form where each stem touches the soil. These young plants are more likely than the mother plant to survive the winter.

When you're cleaning up your garden in early spring, just walk on by lavender plants with your pruners in your pocket. No matter how bedraggled the lavender looks at this time of year, the plants are much more likely to survive if you force yourself to wait until new growth emerges in spring before you trim off dead foliage.

The reason: dormant pruning makes lavender plants more susceptible to damage from fluctuating temperatures.

If you have poorly drained soil, lavender is unlikely to survive the winter. Fortunately, we have Lady, an award-winning lavender that produces plentiful flowers even when grown as an annual.

Anise hyssop (*Agastache*), another pretty perennial for the flower garden, produces mauve-purple flower spikes from midsummer until frost. It's also considered an herb, thanks to its licorice-scented, dark-green leaves that are used in tea, potpourri, and salads.

This showy plant grows about 3 feet tall and thrives in sun or partial shade. It's a favorite of hummingbirds and butterflies but ignored by deer and rabbits. Sometimes called licorice mint or anise mint, it shares only the common name, not the aggressive nature, of most mints.

Growing Herbs in Containers

Ideal for growing in pots near the back door, many easy-to-grow herbs are as beautiful as they are useful. By combining different colors and textures — whether planted in one large container or in individual pots grouped together — you can create your own masterpiece of beauty and taste.

With a container of basil close at hand on your deck or patio, the delight of fresh pesto can't be far behind. Besides being tasty, a collection of basils can be beautiful, too, especially when you plant an array of different varieties.

A well-behaved dwarf dill called Fernleaf remains green and attractive all season, adding a fine, feathery texture to a container and providing fresh snippings to perk up soups and salads.

Dark green and curly, parsley's foliage looks every bit as pretty as that of any ornamental plant in a container. With parsley, though, there's also a long-lasting harvest, with plenty of leaves to spice up your meals.

Gold-leaf varieties of lemon balm contrast beautifully with dark-green plants such as parsley. Don't be afraid to pick some leaves to flavor teas and salads; more will grow to replace the ones you pick.

Any container looks best when some plants are allowed to cascade over its edges, and there are plenty of pretty herbs that are up to the task. Semi-trailing varieties of thyme are perfect. Prostrate rosemary is another attractive, low-growing plant ideal for trailing over the edges of a container. Snip its needle-like leaves as needed to flavor your meat and potato dishes.

Ornamental varieties of sage and oregano are new favorites for growing in containers. While the old-fashioned culinary varieties have these newcomers beat for flavor, the ornamental varieties make great additions to an herbal composition.

APPENDIX

January

- Before you order new seeds, try this simple test to see if leftovers are still good: Spread ten large or twenty small seeds from the packet on a damp paper towel. Roll up the towel like a scroll and store it in a closed plastic bag. Check daily for sprouted seeds. If nearly all sprout, your seeds are still fine. If only half sprout, don't buy new seeds but plan to plant twice as many as normal. If few or none sprout within two weeks, it's time to toss the old seeds.

- Give your Christmas tree a second life in the garden. Cut the branches into 8- to 10-inch pieces to use as protective winter mulch for perennials or strawberries. Or tie the tree to a fence post to provide winter shelter for birds.

- Give houseplants periodic showers in the kitchen sink to wash off dust and to prevent an outbreak of red spider mites. Flush excess salts from the soil by allowing the water to run freely through the pots for several minutes. If a pot is too heavy to carry, scrape away the top several inches of potting soil and replace it with fresh.

- Use yellow sticky traps to detect houseplant problems with white flies, aphids, or fungus gnats. (Buy ready-made traps or make your own with yellow plastic lids or plates and a sticky product called Tangle-Trap.) If your houseplants are infested with large numbers of these small pests, spray them with insecticidal soap.

- Minimize midnight raids of bird feeders by opossums and raccoons by using animal-resistant metal feeders or filling feeders with only the amount of seeds that the birds can eat in one day. Check feeders for moldy or rancid seeds; if necessary, empty the feeder and scrub with hot, soapy water. Dry thoroughly before refilling.

- If you're tired of shoveling snow from the driveway, resolve now to plant shrubs this spring to serve as a living snow fence.
- Visit a public garden to glean ideas for plants with colorful fruit or attractive bark that could liven up your own landscape next winter.

VEGETABLES, FRUITS, AND HERBS

- Prevent disappointments in your summer harvest by ordering disease-resistant varieties whenever possible.
- For a tangy addition to sandwiches or tossed salads, sow seeds of curly cress in a pot indoors. Set the pot in bright light and keep the soil moist. Begin harvesting in about ten days, when the plants are about 2 inches tall.

FLOWERING PLANTS

- When paperwhite narcissus bulbs stop blooming, toss them; they aren't winter hardy in the Midwest. Save other forced bulbs such as daffodils, hyacinths, and tulips to plant outdoors in spring, but don't expect blooms for a year or two while they recover from forcing. For now, pinch off faded flowers and continue to treat these bulbs as houseplants until the foliage withers and dies.
- Bring potted bulbs still in cold storage out now to force early blooms indoors.
- Take cuttings from begonia, coleus, impatiens, or other plants you're overwintering indoors. After removing the lower leaves of each cutting, root it in water. Change the water every day or two. Take geranium cuttings, too, but root them in damp sand, not water.

AROUND THE YARD

- To reduce the need for deicing salts, which can harm outdoor plants, remove snow from the sidewalk and driveway before walking or driving on it. Whenever possible, use sand or kitty litter, not salt. If necessary, add a little salt to the sand or kitty litter. Never use sodium chloride, also known as rock salt. Best bet: a product made with calcium magnesium acetate, which is less harmful to plants than rock salt.

- Check evergreens after a heavy snowfall or ice storm. Prune any damaged branches to prevent further tearing. Use a broom to brush snow from the ice on the water garden. Also stomp around trees and shrubs to eliminate hiding places for rodents that might otherwise feast undetected on the plants' tender bark.
- Renew deer and rabbit repellents. Alternate among several different products.
- To avoid wearing a path in the lawn, don't walk on frozen grass blades.
- When the proverbial January thaw arrives, slowly trickle water on the ground around boxwoods, hollies, rhododendrons, and other evergreens.

February

- To prepare for starting seeds indoors, collect containers such as milk cartons, paper cups, or cardboard boxes and punch drainage holes in the bottoms. If you want to recycle pots left over from last year's bedding plants, rinse them out and run them through the dishwasher, or sterilize them in a 10 percent solution of chlorine bleach.
- Use a ready-made, soilless mix formulated for indoor seedlings.
- Get mower blades sharpened now, before the spring rush. Buy an extra blade, too, so you'll always have a sharp blade on hand.
- Build a coldframe to stretch your garden season in both spring and fall.
- Stockpile empty milk jugs. As you have time, cut the bottoms from the jugs to get them ready to provide temporary protection for your new garden transplants this spring.
- To brighten the house with fresh flowers, bring in branches of crabapple, flowering dogwood, flowering quince, forsythia, magnolia, pussy willow, redbud, or serviceberry. Put the branches in a vase of warm water. Every day or two, change the water. Keep the vase out of direct sun. Expect the buds to start opening in several weeks.

- Sketch a plan for your vegetable garden. Remember to rotate each crop (especially tomatoes and all members of the cabbage family) to a new spot to decrease problems with diseases and pests.
- Start broccoli, cabbage, celery, head lettuce, leek, onion, and pepper seeds indoors.
- When you prune grapes, keep in mind that the vines bear fruit only on year-old wood. Leave four branches on the central trunk, plus four short shoots that can grow to produce next year's crop. Remove any mummies, which can spread disease.

FLOWERING PLANTS

- Watch for blooms of the season's first tiny bulbs such as multicolored snow crocuses, white snowdrops, and yellow winter aconites. On warm days watch for the unfurling of the strap-like yellow petals of vernal witch hazel flowers.
- If you didn't get your tulips and other hardy spring-flowering bulbs planted last fall, don't try to save them until this coming autumn. Instead, plant them as soon as a patch of ground thaws enough for digging the planting holes.
- Start seeds of begonia, geranium, lisianthus, pansy, snapdragon, stock, and viola indoors.
- Check stored cannas, dahlias, and other bulbs and tubers in storage. Throw out any that are rotted, shriveled, or riddled by pests.

AROUND THE YARD

- During any prolonged warm spell, check shallow-rooted plants such as chrysanthemums and strawberries. If alternating freezing and thawing have pushed the roots out of the soil, use your foot to gently push the plants back into place. Shovel extra snow over perennials to help protect them from fluctuating temperatures, but avoid using snow from areas where you've applied deicing salts.
- Inspect trees and shrubs for damage from rabbits. If necessary, install a cylinder of wire mesh or other barrier to prevent further damage.

- Use mild days to get an early start on pruning trees and shrubs. Remove any broken, diseased, or rubbing branches. If a young tree has two leaders, remove one. Also remove any thin, upright shoots arising from previous pruning cuts or from the ground. Prune oaks now while they're dormant to avoid attracting insects that can spread oak wilt.
- For pruning jobs too big to tackle with hand tools, call a professional arborist. Don't let anyone talk you into "topping" a mature tree, which not only looks bad but also encourages weak, fast-growing, upright sprouts from every cut.
- Renew shrubs such as forsythia and lilacs by removing at ground level one-third of the thickest branches.

March

- If your soil routinely stays too wet for early spring planting, plan to build a raised bed where the soil can dry out and warm up faster.
- As soon as indoor seedlings sprout, provide plenty of light from a sunny window or, even better, a shop-light fixture with fluorescent tubes. Adjust the fixture so the tubes are only 2 or 3 inches above the tops of the plants, and leave the lights on twelve to fourteen hours a day.
- Keep young indoor seedlings healthy by avoiding the four things that encourage damping off: overwatering, poor air circulation, containers with no drainage, and crowded seedlings.
- If indoor seedlings grow too tall and leggy, decrease heat and increase light. Another possibility: move the seedlings outside to a coldframe.
- Repair damaged trellises or other garden structures. As soon as the frost is out of the ground, reset wobbly bricks or pavers in garden paths.
- Repot houseplants that have outgrown their pots as the plants begin a growth spurt in response to longer days. Also resume fertilizing houseplants now that longer daylight is encouraging new growth.
- Root cuttings of houseplants such as wandering Jew and purple heart to use in outdoor containers this summer.

- If snow still covers the garden, scatter a light sprinkle of wood ashes saved from the fireplace on the snow. Besides hurrying the melting, ashes add nutrients.
- As soon as a squeezed fistful of soil crumbles apart easily without caking, plant lettuce, onion, pea, radish, and spinach seeds. Also set out onion plants and sets. (Wait until April for sugar snap peas; their high sugar content makes them more likely to rot in cold soil.)
- Plant a mix of salad greens in one bed, then cover with a floating row cover such as Reemay to boost the temperature and speed up the first harvest.
- Give seeds of warm-weather crops such as tomato, eggplant, pepper, and basil an early start indoors.
- Suspend a large sweet potato in a jar of water, stem end up, with three toothpicks stuck into its "waist" to keep its "head" above water. As shoots grow, take cuttings to root for the vegetable garden.
- Control black knot in plum and cherry trees by pruning 2 or 3 inches below any black, swollen area.
- Inspect apple and pear trees for the blackened branches typical of fire blight. Prune 10 inches below any visible signs of the disease, sterilizing the pruners between cuts by dipping the blades in a 10 percent solution of chlorine bleach.
- Cut off everbearing raspberries such as Heritage at ground level and remove old canes from the patch. (To avoid sacrificing the whole crop of a summer-bearing variety such as Latham, delay pruning of those raspberries until after the crop is harvested.)
- Save tedious hand weeding later on by hoeing or tilling the soil two times, starting several weeks before you plant, particularly where you'll be planting small or slow-growing seeds such as beets and carrots. Before tilling, spray the tiller blades with vegetable oil to reduce sticking and help prevent rust.
- Plant asparagus and rhubarb. If you have old rhubarb plants that are no longer producing large stalks, dig and divide those plants. If emerging rhubarb is exposed to freezing temperatures, discard any stalks that show signs of damage.

- Cut and remove dead tops of asparagus plants if you didn't already do it in late autumn.

- When the snow melts, sow seeds of cool-season flowers such as bachelor button, calendula, larkspur, and poppy.
- Plant seeds indoors of warm-weather annuals such as impatiens, petunias, and flowering vinca.
- If you have old-fashioned roses that bloom only once a year, postpone pruning until immediately after the flowers fade this summer. If you have roses that bloom all summer, prune them when their leaf buds begin to swell. Remove canes that are weak, crossed, or damaged. Make cuts at a 45-degree angle, one-fourth inch above an outward-facing bud. Seal cuts with white glue to keep out carpenter bees and other boring insects.
- Gradually remove any soil you mounded over tender roses in the fall.
- Give tuberous begonias and caladiums an early start indoors. Cover caladium tubers with an inch of potting soil. Just press begonia tubers into the soil, hollow side up. Water, then set the pots in a warm spot.
- Remove last year's withered foliage of iris, daylily, and other perennials before new growth begins.
- Delay raking mulch off perennials, which might expose the plants to damage in a cold snap.
- Postpone digging and dividing chrysanthemums until nighttime temperatures stay consistently above 25 degrees.
- Delay pruning lavender, butterfly bush, blue-mist shrub, and Russian sage until after new shoots appear.

AROUND THE YARD

- Top off mulches with a fresh layer to stop overwintering fungus diseases such as gray mold and leaf spot from spreading to new growth.
- Flush the soil in areas near the sidewalk, driveway, or street with water to wash away any deicing salts left over from winter's snow and ice storms.
- Rake bare spots in the lawn as well as matted "snow mold" areas. Add topsoil to any low spots, then reseed with a disease-resistant grass-seed blend.

- To keep the lower branches of hedges healthy, prune so the shrubs are broader at the base than at the top.
- Clip ornamental grasses back almost to the ground. If you'd like to skip tedious raking, tie all the top growth of each plant together with twine before you cut. Dig and divide any grasses that have died out in the center of the clump.
- When pruning trees and shrubs, save small limbs to prop up floppy garden plants later in the season.
- Prune established summer-blooming clematis vines back by half. Prune autumn-blooming varieties back hard, to 3 feet or less. (Postpone pruning spring-blooming clematis until after its flowers fade.)
- If trees or shrubs such as euonymus or lilac have been plagued with scales, aphids, or mites in the past, spray plants with dormant oil. Wait for a day when the temperature is over 50 degrees and not expected to drop below freezing for twenty-four hours.
- Don't panic if your evergreens look discolored. Wait until late spring to give new growth a chance to cover any damaged needles.

April

- To clean pots encrusted with mineral deposits, soak them overnight in a solution of 1 tablespoon vinegar in a gallon of water, then use a wire brush to remove deposits from a clay pot. If your pots are plastic, use a knife for scraping the deposits.
- If you buy perennials or cold-hardy annuals that have been growing in a greenhouse, allow them to stay in a somewhat protected spot for several weeks to get used to outdoor conditions before you plant them in the garden.
- If bare-root roses, shrubs, or trees arrive before you can plant, give them a temporary home in the garden. Dig a shallow hole, lay the plants at an angle, and cover the roots with soil.
- If cats or dogs are digging in your garden, lay a piece of welded wire fence fabric on the soil as soon as you plant.

- Put bottomless gallon-size plastic jugs over new transplants to offer temporary protection from wind and cold. Mound soil against the sides of the jugs to keep them from blowing away. If you screw the caps on the jugs on frosty nights, remember to remove the caps in the morning.
- If slugs are damaging your plants, control them with a product such as Sluggo that contains iron phosphate, a substance so safe it's used to fortify bakery foods.
- Destroy any volunteer potato plants, which may harbor disease that could infect this year's tomatoes and potatoes.
- For a quick onion crop, plant dime-sized bulbs (called sets) an inch or two deep if you want green onions, or barely covered for big bulbs.
- Plant cool-season crops such as beet, broccoli, cabbage, carrot, kohlrabi, lettuce, pea, potato, spinach, and radish. Mix small seeds like carrot and lettuce with sand before planting to get more even distribution. If you have a heavy clay soil, cover any small seeds with sand instead of soil to make it easier for the seeds to sprout.
- Encourage beneficial insects by planting alyssum and dill among the vegetables.
- Soak parsley and beet seeds in water overnight before planting.
- Sow dill and cilantro seeds in the herb garden.
- Mulch potatoes with a 6-inch-deep blanket of straw to prevent weeds, keep the soil cool, and possibly prevent an infestation of Colorado potato beetles.
- For the earliest tomato harvest, plant a quick-maturing variety such as Early Girl with a Wall-o'-Water for frost protection. Or put a sturdy tomato cage over your plant and wrap the bottom of the cage with an 18-inch-high strip of black roofing paper, then slip a clear plastic, vented bag over the cage. Keep plants protected until after the last frost.
- Provide stakes or branches for pea vines to climb. Water peas if the weather is dry, but avoid getting their leaves wet.
- If your spinach leaves often develop light-colored blotches, blame insects called leaf miners. To keep them from ruining this year's

crop, cover the plants with a lightweight cloth, such as cheesecloth or Reemay.

- Speed up the melon harvest by planting cantaloupe and watermelon seeds indoors. To avoid disrupting roots when you transplant them outdoors, plant each seed in a peat pot or paper cup.
- Keep extra mulch or a row cover handy to toss over blooming strawberries if frost threatens. As soon as the plants start to green up, prevent leather rot by spreading new mulch thick enough to keep rain from splashing from the soil onto the leaves. Postpone fertilizing June-bearing plants until after harvest.
- Mulch blueberries with pine bark chips, which help make the soil more acid as they decompose.
- When planting fruit trees, choose a north slope so flowers will open later and not be as likely to be zapped by frost.
- As soon as apple blossoms fade, put traps for coddling moths in place to prevent wormy apples. Hang one trap per apple tree.

FLOWERING PLANTS

- Fill planters with fresh potting soil, then plant frost-tolerant annuals such as nemesia, osteospermum, pansy, snapdragon, stock, and viola. If you're dividing crowded perennials such as creeping bellflowers, daylilies, foamflowers, hostas, coralbells, or lamb's ears, include some of the extra plants in mixed container plantings.
- Celebrate emerging perennials but don't give up on those that don't yet show signs of life. Some, such as balloon flower, butterfly milkweed, and hardy hibiscus, are notoriously late to appear.
- Get cool-season bedding plants off to a quick start by adding a weak dose of liquid fertilizer to their first watering; soil nutrients are often not available to plants growing in cold soil. But take it easy when fertilizing the perennial garden, since many plants react to a rich soil by growing weak and floppy.
- Prepare potted perennials for planting by first cutting off any roots that are growing outside the pots. Remove each plant, then "score" the root ball with a knife to encourage roots to grow out into the surrounding soil.
- Before planting a new flower bed, dig a 2-inch layer of compost into

the soil. In an established perennial bed, spread the compost on top of the soil around plants and top with mulch.

- For less trouble with slugs chomping on hostas, choose varieties with thick leaves.
- After nighttime temperatures stay consistently above 20 degrees, dig and divide crowded perennials such as aster, chrysanthemum, and phlox, discarding their old, woody centers. Postpone dividing perennials that bloom in spring. Also leave alone perennials that resent disturbance, including baby's breath, bleeding heart, candytuft, columbine, cushion spurge, false indigo, gas plant, goatsbeard, Japanese anemone, Lenten rose, lupine, monkshood, and Oriental poppy.
- After daffodils quit blooming, allow the foliage to die down naturally. Blame failure to bloom on one of the following: Less than half-day sun; foliage braided, bundled, or removed before it dries; or a fertilizer imbalance (too much nitrogen and too little phosphorus).
- Plant sweet peas near a chain-link fence or trellis to support the vines.
- Feed roses with a slow-release or organic fertilizer. To make your own, follow this recipe from the American Rose Society: For one mature rosebush, mix 1 cup each bone meal and cottonseed meal. Add one-half cup each blood meal, fish meal, and Epsom salts. Scratch the mixture lightly into the top 2 inches of the soil around the rose bush.
- Make notes of bare spots where spring-blooming bulbs would be welcome, such as tucked around shrubs or between slow-to-emerge perennials. Mark your calendar as a reminder to plant the bulbs in October.

AROUND THE YARD

- Top off decaying bark chips with a fresh layer of mulch to inhibit plant diseases and artillery fungi, which shoot sticky goo on house siding and automobiles.
- Prune panicle and smooth hydrangeas by cutting the shrubs back by half before new growth begins.
- Remove any winter wrap from tree trunks. If you have a staked tree, loosen the ties now and plan to remove the stake as soon as possible. Replenish mulch to maintain a 4-inch-thick blanket around all trees,

but don't allow the mulch to touch the trunk. Remove plant tags and rabbit guards that could constrict growth.

- Remove bagworms from arborvitae or other evergreens before the eggs in the bags hatch.
- Clean up established ground covers such as pachysandra or creeping myrtle quickly by using the lawnmower, with the blade set to cut as high as possible.
- If the lawn is wet, postpone mowing to avoid injury to the grass.
- When forsythia shrubs begin to bloom, spread corn gluten meal on the lawn to stop crabgrass seeds from sprouting.
- If you apply a chemical herbicide to the lawn this spring, wait four weeks before saving grass clippings for garden mulch.
- If soil is compacted from foot traffic, either rent a core aerator now, before the weather turns hot, or wait until fall to aerate the lawn.
- Fill bare spots in the lawn by sowing bluegrass or perennial rye in sunny spots or fine fescues in the shade. (If you plan to sow grass seed this spring, skip the preemergent herbicide, which keeps desirable grasses from sprouting, too.) If moss tends to crowd out grass in shady spots, improve drainage, fertilize, aerate, and test the soil to see if it's too acid.
- If you're tired of struggling to grow grass under a tree, substitute a shade-tolerant ground cover such as creeping myrtle, lungwort, or barrenwort.
- When using a fertilizer spreader, apply half the recommended amount of fertilizer. Then, to avoid striping caused by uneven fertilizer coverage, apply the second half by walking perpendicular to the first.
- If you apply a slow-release lawn fertilizer and it doesn't rain, water the lawn before using a mulching mower which might otherwise knock off the slow-release coating and release too much fertilizer at once.
- Inhibit weeds by mowing tall. Cut bluegrass and other cool-season grasses no lower than 2½ inches. Dig dandelions before they bloom.

May

- Before planting in new terra cotta pots, soak them in water for several hours. Disinfect old pots by scrubbing them in a solution of 1 part chlorine bleach to 9 parts water.

- When filling outdoor pots with soil, cover the drainage holes with scraps of weed-block fabric or coffee filters to keep out pests. Fill containers with a 4-to-1 mix of potting soil and compost to help keep the plants healthy and the soil moist. Mix pelleted fish fertilizer or other slow-release fertilizer into the soil before planting. Simplify watering chores by grouping plants in large containers that hold more soil, rather than putting individual plants in small pots.
- Refrain from moving houseplants and other tropical plants outdoors until you're assured that overnight temperatures won't dip below 50 degrees. Give the plants a sheltered spot while they gradually adjust to wind and brighter light.

VEGETABLES, FRUITS, AND HERBS

- Protect new transplants from cutworms by surrounding each plant with a cardboard collar or a bottomless paper cup.
- Just in case the weather turns out to be unfavorable for fruit-set this summer, include tomato and pepper varieties with medium-sized fruits in addition to your usual beefsteak-type tomatoes and bell peppers.
- After all danger of frost, plant seeds of borage and summer savory, and set out basil plants in the herb garden.
- Continue harvesting rhubarb by pulling, not cutting, the stalks. Pull out any flower stalks as soon as they appear.
- To catch asparagus tips in their prime, harvest spears every day or two. Snap off the spears by hand where they break naturally.
- Plant warm-season vegetables such as tomatoes, peppers, eggplants, squash, and beans. Get bean and corn seeds off to a fast start by soaking the seeds for an hour or two in warm water before planting. Also plant a second crop of lettuce for summer salads, choosing heat-tolerant varieties.
- To aid corn pollination, plant sweet corn in blocks rather than long single rows.
- When you plant cucumbers and melons, cover the row with a lightweight floating cover to thwart cucumber beetles. Make a note to remove the cover after the plants begin blooming.
- Thin beets, carrots, and lettuce seedlings.

- If you can't keep up with the harvest of leaf lettuce, shear some of the plants back to a height of 2 or 3 inches to encourage them to produce new leaves rather than go to seed.
- To make the most of space, plant "pretty" vegetables such as pepper, eggplant, leaf lettuce, and Swiss chard in flower borders.
- Remove flower buds from newly planted strawberries.
- Check apple trees every two weeks for water sprouts and twist them off. (Water sprouts are less likely to grow back if you don't have to use pruners to remove them.)

FLOWERING PLANTS

- Snip off fading flowers of spring bulbs. Refrain from braiding or bundling the yellowing foliage; allow the leaves to die down naturally before you remove them.
- When shopping for bedding plants, look for small, non-blooming plants with healthy foliage. If only blooming plants are available, shear off the flowers as soon as you get the plants home. Several hours before planting, water pots thoroughly so the plants will slip out easily. Untangle any circling roots before planting. If the roots form a solid mat, "butterfly" the root ball by slicing half way through from bottom to top. Then pull the two sections apart, like a butterfly spreading its wings.
- After the last frost, set out warm-loving annuals such as impatiens and vinca.
- Renew an established perennial bed by pulling out crowded volunteer plants and dividing overgrown clumps.
- For summerlong color under a tree, plant shade-loving annuals such as begonias, caladiums, and impatiens in containers. Sink pots into the ground and hang baskets from the tree's branches.
- Install grow-through plant supports for peonies or wrap twine a couple of times around each peony bush now to keep the plants from flopping when they bloom. Also stake dahlias.
- To keep tall varieties of asters and sedums from flopping later in the season, cut back the plants by half. Use the same trick if your Russian sage grows too big for the space you've allowed.

- Thin garden phlox to four to six shoots per plant to improve air circulation and thwart foliage disease.
- Soak seeds of morning glory, moon vine, cardinal climber and cypress vine overnight before planting.
- Plant summer bulbs such as gladioli, cannas, and calla lilies. Wait until the weather is warm and settled before planting cold-sensitive plants such as caladium and lantana.

AROUND THE YARD

- Spread mulch around lily plants and clematis vines to keep their roots cool.
- Don't bother spraying blooming dandelions, which would still produce enormous numbers of seeds before they die. Instead, dig the plants, pick off and destroy the flowers, and compost the rest.
- Dig young plants of yellow nutsedge (nutgrass) before they produce their stubborn, nut-like tubers.
- In the water garden, elevate hardy water lilies on bricks so the top of each pot is 4 to 6 inches below the water's surface. Postpone placing tropical water plants in the pool until the water's temperature rises to 70 degrees.
- After forsythia blooms fade, head back any straggly branches.
- When Vanhoutte spirea is in bud, check pines for the worm-like larvae of sawflies, which can quickly defoliate a small tree. Collect the pests by shaking any infested branch over a bucket of hot soapy water.
- If a weed tree sprouts so close to the trunk of a prized specimen that you can't dig it out or spray it, cut the top off the unwanted sapling and invert a large tin can over the remaining stub. Leave the can in place for several months.
- If necessary to prune evergreens, do it now; new growth will quickly cover your cuts. To prune pines, pinch each shoot — called a "candle" — in half. Prune junipers back any amount but leave at least a little green showing on each branch.
- Watch for web "tents" made by eastern tent caterpillars. Use a stick or broom in the evening to remove any you find, then burn or bury them.

June

- Entice butterflies to stay in your garden by adding a stone where they can bask in the sun and a pan filled with moist sand where they can sip water. Include nectar sources such as blazing star, butterfly bush, and lantana. Plant extra dill, parsley, or fennel for swallowtail larvae to munch, and butterfly or swamp milkweed for monarch larvae.
- Dump standing water from buckets, plant saucers, reservoirs in self-watering pots, toys, and any other places where mosquitoes might breed. Where you can't dump the water, add a Mosquito Dunk.
- After a rain, delay working in the garden until the foliage dries so you won't spread fungus diseases.
- Don't despair if small-to-moderate-sized hail damages your garden. Plants are often amazingly resilient, sprouting new leaves and looking much better within a few weeks.

VEGETABLES, FRUITS, AND HERBS

- Mulch the vegetable garden to conserve soil moisture, control weeds, and help prevent problems such as green potatoes, blossom-end rot of tomatoes, green-shouldered carrots, and rough beets.
- Tuck wayward tomato vines back into their cages. Remove any lower branches that have spotted foliage.
- Stop harvesting asparagus this month to help plants regain vigor for next year's crop.
- When cauliflower heads begin to form, use clothespins to clip the leaves together. Harvest as soon as the curds are fully developed. Harvest broccoli heads when well-developed but firm, before any of the tiny yellow flowers open.
- Plant Brussels sprouts, radicchio, and broccoli seeds for a fall crop. For a continuous harvest of bush beans, make a second planting of bean seeds.
- Pinch off garlic flower buds as soon as they begin to form at the top of the plants.
- Harvest new potatoes any time after the plants flower.
- Pull any seed stalks that develop on rhubarb plants.
- Don't panic at the normal "June drop" from apple trees, but do pick up and compost the dropped fruit.

- Fight gray mold in the strawberry patch by removing any rotten or moldy berries. If ants are making holes in the berries, pour boiling water over the ant hill. Protect ripening berries from birds.
- As soon as blackberry and black or purple raspberry canes are 3 feet tall, pinch a few inches off each growing tip.
- Check fruit and nut trees for signs of fall webworms; prune out any of the silky webs now, while they're still small.
- To enjoy fantastic fragrance and easy-to-pick flavoring for your iced tea, plant lemon verbena in a pot placed in a sunny spot on your patio or deck.

FLOWERING PLANTS

- If flower buds turn brown and dry up before blossoms open, pick off and destroy infested buds and any fading flowers. Spray the plant with insecticidal soap to control tiny insects called thrips, the likely culprit.
- When the flowers of baby's breath and perennial salvia fade, shear plants to encourage more blooms. Also cut back spent bloom stalks of delphiniums.
- If hosta leaves scorch in the sun, cut off damaged leaves and plan to move the plants to a shady spot in spring or fall.
- Help garden phlox stay healthy by pulling out crowded shoots.
- Plant seeds of biennials such as standing cypress and Canterbury bells for a beautiful show next summer.
- Shear tall chrysanthemums back a few inches to produce full plants with more blooms.
- Dig and divide crowded daffodils, tulips, or other spring-blooming bulbs while their dying foliage is still visible. Or use golf tees to mark the location of the bulbs so you can find them to divide in the fall.
- Dig and divide crowded magic lilies after their foliage fades.

AROUND THE YARD

- Place tropical water lilies and bog plants in the water garden as soon as the water temperature rises to 70 degrees. Fertilize water lilies by pushing one lily fertilizer tablet deep into the soil in each pot once per month, beginning now. Deprive algae of needed sunlight by adding a few drops of one of the nontoxic products that tint the water blue.

- Discourage tiny pests such as aphids or spider mites with a strong jet of water from the garden hose.
- When the weather is dry enough to water the garden, remember to water the compost pile, too.
- If weeds are clogging paths, smother the weeds with sections of damp newspapers topped with a layer of mulch.
- Help your bluegrass survive the heat by raising the height of the mower's cutting blade to 3 inches.
- Don't bother spraying a honeylocust tree if the leaves are deformed. The damaged leaves, caused by the feeding of plant bugs, will soon be replaced by new foliage.
- If ash or sycamore leaves brown and drop, rake up the fallen leaves to control anthracnose, a fungus disease.
- Remove any lilac shoots that are drooped and blackened, making your cuts several inches below any sign of the disease.
- Control bagworms on evergreens by handpicking bags before the eggs hatch, usually about the time Japanese tree lilacs begin to bloom. Spray newly hatched bagworms with *Bacillus thuringiensis* (*Bt* for short).
- Remove any suckers growing from the ground around crabapple or other trees.
- Spread bark chips or other mulch around trees to prevent "mower blight," the number one threat to trees.
- When rains fail, water this year's new trees and shrubs once a week.

July

- Rejoice if you see blossoms covered with insects that look like lightning bugs. These soldier beetles are good guys, helping control many kinds of insect pests.
- In dry weather, water container plants often, even daily. About once a week, add a low dose of liquid fertilizer to the water to replace nutrients washed away by regular watering. To keep smaller outdoor containers from drying out so quickly, set each pot inside a larger pot and pack the space between them with something that will hold moisture, such as damp leaves or moss.
- When mixing any pesticide, substitute rainwater for tap water

whenever possible. Also mix only as much as you need and avoid storing any leftovers in spray bottles.

- Don't panic if your first ripe tomato has a rotten bottom. Blossom-end rot is a problem that usually cures itself as the season progresses. Promote even soil moisture by watering in dry weather and keeping the plants mulched, steps that also help prevent cracking of the fruit.
- If tomato hornworms are devouring the foliage of your tomato plants, handpick them or spray with *Bt* (*Bacillus thuringiensis*). An exception: If you find one of the big worms with tiny, white wiggly creatures on its back, do nothing. These are the larvae of tiny parasitic wasps, already at work controlling the hornworms for you.
- If a squash vine suddenly wilts, examine the stem for what looks like a pile of sawdust surrounding a tiny hole. If you find this sure sign of vine borers, use a syringe to inject a liquid solution of *Bt* into the hole. Then mound soil over the injured part of the stem.
- Avoid bitter-tasting cucumbers by watering the plants during dry spells.
- To keep cabbage heads from splitting in wet weather, give each plant a half turn to break a few of the roots.
- Protect lettuce from baking in hot sun by suspending a piece of lightweight shade cloth over the plants.
- Plant a "second chance" vegetable garden for fall harvest, with beet, bulb-type fennel, bush bean, carrot, cucumber, kohlrabi, and zucchini seeds. (Wait until early August to plant lettuce, radish, turnip, and spinach seeds.)
- Pick beans, cucumbers and zucchinis every two or three days to keep the crops coming. Harvest eggplants as soon as each one looks glossy and is firm enough that pressing with a fingertip leaves only a slight depression.
- To prevent damage from corn earworms, use a small oil can filled with mineral oil to apply five or six drops to the tip of each ear of corn when the silks begin to brown.
- Pull mulch snug around potato plants to protect developing tubers from sunlight.
- Keep tall asparagus plants from toppling by pushing 6-foot garden

stakes into the row at 6- to 8-foot intervals, then "corral" the plants between two strands of twine tied to the stakes.

- Use a soaker or "weeper" hose to deliver water directly to the roots to help foliage stay healthy and to avoid losing water to evaporation.
- For best flavor, harvest herbs regularly, before they go to seed. If flowers form on herbs such as basil and oregano, clip them off. Harvest herbs as soon as the morning dew dries but before the hot sun cooks out the flavor.
- Renew June-bearing strawberries.
- For maximum sweetness, wait to pick fully colored blueberries until they fall easily into your hand. Keep the plants covered with bird netting until harvest ends. Pick off and destroy any mummies.
- Spray peaches with wettable sulfur at the first sign of brown rot.
- Multiply your English lavender by "layering." Bend each stem down to the soil. Hold it in place by setting a small stone or a mound of soil on the middle part of the stem to help new roots form where the stem is in contact with the soil.

FLOWERING PLANTS

- Don't hesitate to gather armloads of cosmos, lisianthus, salvia, spider flower, zinnia, and other annuals for bouquets; the more you cut, the more these plants will bloom.
- When hosta blossoms fade, cut off the flower stalks to spare the plants the extra energy needed to make seed pods.
- Remove any streaked or yellowed leaves of daylilies, both to improve the plants' appearance and to help control disease. Also remove flower stalks when blooming stops.
- Snip off faded roses to encourage new blooms and keep plants tidy.
- Keep powdery mildew at bay by watering disease-prone plants such as beebalm, garden phlox, and zinnia when the weather is dry. Water the soil, not the leaves, and thin plants to allow better air circulation.
- When the flowers of perennial geraniums fade and the plants start to look ratty, shear off old growth. Improve the appearance of annual geraniums by picking off dead flowers and any yellowed leaves.
- Use shears to speed the removal of spent blossoms from prolific bloomers such as coreopsis and dianthus.

- If Silver Mound artemisia flops open, exposing the center of the plant, cut the stems back halfway.
- If the foliage of perennials such as anise hyssop and yellow loosestrife is disfigured by the feeding of four-lined plant bugs, simply prune off the affected leaves and allow fresh new foliage to grow.
- Renew straggly looking petunias by pinching back the longest shoots, a few at a time.
- Refrain from pinching back chrysanthemum shoots after the Fourth of July.
- If tuberous begonias develop yellow patches on the leaves, dust the foliage with sulfur to control begonia mites.
- When lily blossoms fade, clip off the entire seed head. Leave the rest of the stalk and the leaves to help build a bigger bulb.
- Don't fret if flowering of cool-loving plants such as osteospermum, nemesia, or Swan River daisy temporarily stops in hot weather. Clip off any dead flowers and expect to see a new round of blooms when the weather cools.
- Don't worry if bleeding heart collapses and appears to die; it's normal for this perennial to go dormant in hot weather.
- For dried winter bouquets, gather small bunches of "everlastings" such as baby's breath, statice, and strawflowers when the blooms first open. Secure the stems with a rubber band and hang them upside-down to dry in a dark, airy place.
- Gather Japanese beetles into a pail of soapy water early in the morning, when the beetles are still sluggish.

AROUND THE YARD

- Collect rainwater from a downspout into a rain barrel equipped with a spigot, overflow fitting, and cover.
- If you don't have room for a compost pile, substitute a heavy-duty plastic bag. Fill the bag with spent plants, weeds (without seeds), and other yard and garden wastes. Add a little garden soil and sprinkle the contents with water. Hide the bag under an evergreen or shrub and give the contents several months to "cook."
- Attract insect-eating birds to the garden by keeping the birdbath filled with fresh, clean water.

- Keep the water garden looking its best by pinching off faded water lily blossoms and removing yellow leaves. Also thin out any floating plants as often as needed to keep them from taking over the water surface.
- If you have an automatic sprinkler system for your lawn, guard against killing your trees and shrubs with too much water. Avoid daily watering and, if Mother Nature delivers an inch or more of rain a week, override the automatic system to skip the watering altogether.
- Despite hot weather, don't hesitate to plant container-grown perennials, shrubs, and trees, but do water them often in dry weather the first few weeks they're in the ground.
- Mow as often as necessary to follow the one-third rule: Remove no more than one-third the height of the grass blades. In dry weather, conserve water by allowing the grass to go dormant. Know that the grass will green up again as soon as rains return.

August

- If the soil in large outdoor planters dries out enough to pull away from the sides, water slowly and repeatedly, pushing the soil back in place as it absorbs moisture. Set hanging baskets and smaller pots in a tub of warm water until the soil is evenly moist, and then push the soil back into place. Avoid adding any fertilizer when the soil is dry.
- Replace seed in birdfeeders often so it won't mold in hot, humid weather.

VEGETABLES, FRUITS, AND HERBS

- Plant a fall salad garden by sowing seeds of lettuce, radish, and spinach. For gourmet greens to harvest late in the fall, plant seeds of mache, also called lamb's lettuce or corn salad.
- Clean out any spotted or dying tomato foliage to improve air circulation. Avoid overhead watering.
- Set cans or boards under ripening melons. For best taste, hope for dry and sunny weather when watermelons and muskmelons are maturing.
- Plant turnip seeds early this month for a harvest of sweet, tender roots this fall.

- Continue to harvest herbs such as basil, savory, and oregano regularly. Clip off and discard any flower buds that form.
- Store fresh-picked tomatoes on the counter, not in the refrigerator.
- Pick corn ears when the silks are brown and dried and the ears are firm and fat. Check frequently, especially in hot weather. If the ears are poorly filled, blame lack of pollination, which often results from hot weather or rain during the critical time right after silks appear.
- Pick pears as soon as their color changes from dark to light green and the fruit releases easily with a gentle tug. Store the fruit indoors at about 70 degrees until it is fully ripe in a week or two.
- Pick peaches as soon as they soften and release easily from the tree.
- After the last of the summer-bearing raspberries is picked, cut all of the bearing canes at ground level. Save the new canes to produce next year's crop. Expect fall bearers such as Heritage to start ripening this month.
- Wait to pick grapes until the stem of each cluster turns brown. If wasps are a problem, bag grape clusters with paper bags. Before harvesting a whole cluster, taste a few grapes to be sure they're ripe.
- If you have some garden space standing idle, sow seeds of buckwheat for "green manure" to till into the soil later this fall.

FLOWERING PLANTS

- Help roses and other perennials toughen up for winter by withholding fertilizer for the rest of the garden season.
- If some plants in containers are beginning to look shabby, replace them with osteospermum, chrysanthemum, calendula, diascia, or other plants that will look nice well into the fall.
- Prevent fungal disease of large-flowered marigolds by removing blossoms as soon as they fade.
- If a purple coneflower is distorted with light-green leaves and a branching top, immediately pull and discard the plant before leafhoppers spread the disease to healthy plants.
- If the leaves of garden phlox are yellowing and dying, thin each clump, leaving only three to five of the healthiest shoots to improve air circulation.
- Expect the mother hen of your succulent hen and chicks to die after flowering, leaving the chicks to carry on.

- Plant fall-flowering crocus, colchicum, and Madonna lily bulbs. Wait until October to plant hardy spring-flowering bulbs.
- If your perennial garden has too few blooms, plan now to add more August bloomers this fall or next spring. Consider black-eyed Susan, goldenrod, Japanese anemone, plumbago, Russian sage, helenium, and tall sedum.
- Remove any spotted portions of iris leaves. Dig and divide crowded rhizomes. Discard old, woody sections as well as any that show signs of rot or borer damage.
- Plant dormant crowns of oriental poppies. If you have clumps of poppies that have grown too crowded, dig and divide them now.
- If the leaves of dahlias, marigolds, or other garden plants look pale and stippled, spray the leaves with a strong jet of water from the garden hose to thwart spider mites. Repeat every few days as long as the weather stays hot and dry. To control severe spider mite infestations, spray plants with insecticidal soap.
- Use a pair of garden scissors to turn a bedraggled midsummer border into a showpiece. Remove any yellowed or damaged leaves and dead flowers and stalks. Lightly shear straggly looking alyssum and lobelia plants. Pinch back leggy petunias and snapdragons. If leaves of lady's mantle or lungwort look ratty, shear the foliage almost to the ground.
- Stake tall gladiolus plants. Cut flower spikes for bouquets as soon as a few of their funnel-shaped blooms open. If some flowers look distorted and plants have browning leaves, remove affected parts and spray plants every three days with insecticidal soap to control thrips.

AROUND THE YARD
- In dry weather, water this year's new trees and shrubs regularly.
- Refrain from fertilizing cool-season grasses like bluegrass or fescue now because it would only serve to encourage weeds, not grass.
- Enjoy the fragrant blossoms of two unusual trees blooming this month: Japanese pagoda tree (*Sophora*) and seven-son flower (*Heptacodium*).
- To improve the appearance of butterfly bush, clip off blossoms as they brown.

September

- Bring houseplants back inside before temperatures fall below 50 degrees. Hose off the foliage, top and bottom, and check the bottoms of the pots for cocoons or other pests. If you see any small pests such as aphids or whiteflies, spray the foliage with insecticidal soap.
- If you lack enough indoor space to save large potted plants such as hibiscus, lantana, and duranta, downsize them: whack off a large portion of the roots of each plant so the remaining root system will fit in a 6-inch pot, then remove an equal portion of the stems and leaves.

VEGETABLES, FRUITS, AND HERBS

- As crops finish in the vegetable garden, remove spent plants and add them to the compost pile. Top a 6- to 8-inch layer of dead plant material with 1 to 2 inches of grass clippings or fruit and vegetable scraps, then cover with an 1-inch layer of soil. Repeat layers until the pile is about 4 feet tall.
- For more fresh salad ingredients in just thirty days, sow seeds of fast-growing arugula, or a mixture of greens (mesclun).
- Separate garlic bulbs into individual cloves and plant them pointed end up, covered with 1 or 2 inches of soil, spaced 4 inches apart.
- Pot up tender herbs such as rosemary to grow in a sunny window during the winter.
- If an early frost catches you by surprise, save tomatoes and other tender veggies by hosing off plants in the morning before sunlight hits them.
- Improve soil by sowing a cover crop of hairy vetch, winter rye or winter wheat to till into the soil in the spring.
- Pick up and destroy any dropped fruit under apple trees.

FLOWERING PLANTS

- Postpone planting spring-flowering bulbs until autumn leaves begin to fall.
- Plant peonies, placing the roots so that their pink buds, called "eyes," are covered with 2 inches of soil. Select a sunny spot with well-drained soil.

- Get outdoor containers ready for autumn by replacing struggling annuals with cold-tolerant plants such as alyssum, calendula, chrysanthemum, cup flower, dianthus, diascia, nemesia, ornamental kale, osteospermum, pansy, snapdragon, or stock.
- Dig and divide any crowded perennials that have finished blooming for the season, including astilbe, daylily, hosta, and phlox. Wait until spring to divide fall-bloomers such as aster, chrysanthemum, and sedum.
- Rejuvenate flower beds by trimming away any leaves that are ragged, yellowed, or riddled by insect holes. Remove mildewed foliage of beebalm, delphinium, or garden phlox. Cut spotted iris leaves back to healthy foliage.
- Transplant potted chrysanthemums to add color to bare spots. Consider the plants a short-term investment because fall-planted mums are less likely to survive the winter.
- To winter over annuals, take cuttings of begonia, coleus, or Joseph's coat to root in water. Root geranium cuttings in damp sand.
- For early spring color in a sunny flower bed, scatter seeds of cool-season annuals such as bachelor buttons, calendulas, larkspurs, and poppies.

AROUND THE YARD

- Plant trees and shrubs now while the cooler autumn weather will make it easy for them to adjust to their new home. Dig a hole just deep enough so that the top roots sit at soil level. Don't add fertilizer but do water deeply, then mulch with a 4-inch layer of shredded bark or wood chips. Don't allow the mulch to touch the trunk but do extend the mulch out as far as the tree limbs. Avoid staking if possible. If staking is necessary on a windy site, don't stake so tightly that the trunk doesn't have room to sway.
- Plant cool-season grasses such as bluegrass and fescue in bare spots in the lawn now that autumn weather favors grasses, not weeds. Scratch grass seed into the soil around crabgrass, which will die in the first frost. Water as often as necessary to keep the soil moist until new grasses are established.
- Spread a slow-release fertilizer on the lawn now to help the grass grow thicker and healthier.

- Expect to see some orange specks of rust disease on the lawn as temperatures cool and heavy dew forms. Mow to remove infected tips. In dry weather, water during the day so the grass blades will have a chance to dry before night.
- Don't wait until spring to dig or spot-spray dandelions and other perennial weeds. Do it now, while the plants are still small and not blooming.
- Water plants if nature doesn't, giving priority to new grass seedlings and to any perennials, shrubs, or trees planted this year. Also water the compost pile to keep the ingredients "cooking."

October

- When autumn leaves fall, begin planting spring-blooming bulbs such as daffodils, tulips, and hyacinths. For best soil drainage, plant bulbs on a berm, hillside, or raised bed.
- If deer routinely chomp on your tulips, substitute deer-resistant bulbs such as camass, daffodil, flowering onion, fritillaria, Siberian squill, snowdrop, snowflake, or star of Bethlehem.
- Tie bundles of dead blossoms, such as marigolds and zinnias, to shrubs to attract winter birds.
- Don't panic if houseplants brought back in after a summer outside drop some leaves, a natural response to lower light.

VEGETABLES, FRUITS, AND HERBS

- To keep the tomato harvest coming for a while after frost, pull up the plants and hang them upside down in your garage or basement. Or pile the plants on top of each other in the garden and cover the stack with a blanket on frosty nights, allowing the tomatoes to continue slowly ripening for several more weeks. Or store green tomatoes in a single layer in shallow boxes in a cool but frost-free spot, such as the garage or unheated basement.
- For best flavor, wait until after the first frost to harvest Brussels sprouts, Jerusalem artichokes, kale, and parsnips. To harvest Brussels sprouts, start picking from the bottom of the stalk as the small heads mature.

- Keep fresh salads coming longer by draping two layers of floating row cover over the lettuce bed.
- Leave extra beets, carrots, parsnips, and turnips in the garden. Just before the ground freezes, add a thick blanket of leaves, then harvest the roots as needed.
- For fresh chives all winter, pot up some plants now but leave the pot outside a while longer for thorough chilling.
- Harvest pumpkins and winter squash before frost, leaving about an inch of stem on each. For long-keeping, cure by spreading in a single layer in a warm spot for a week or two. Then move them to a cooler place that stays 55 to 60 degrees.
- Store potatoes in a cool, dark place.
- Clean up dropped apples, crabapples, and pears. Pick and destroy any dried fruit mummies still on the trees. Rake up fallen leaves to help control scab and leaf spot diseases.
- To protect the soil from winter erosion, spread a blanket of shredded leaves on bare ground in the vegetable garden.

FLOWERING PLANTS

- Plant lily bulbs as soon as you buy them. Also, dig and divide crowded lilies.
- After frost blackens the leaves, dig up dahlias, cannas, and gladioli to store in a cool spot indoors.
- Prepare a new flower bed for spring planting this easy way: kill grass by covering it with a layer of newspapers several sections deep, topped with a layer of bark chips or other mulch to keep the papers from blowing away.
- Transplant into the ground any roses, coralbells, or other perennials that are growing in containers. Or wait until cold weather forces the plants into dormancy, then wrap the pots with bubble wrap or other insulation and move the pots into a protected spot.
- Help perennial plants survive the winter by making sure the soil slopes away from their centers, so water won't collect there and freeze.
- Gather dried seed heads and pods from cardinal climber, globe amaranth, love-in-a-mist, purple hyacinth bean, spider flower, and other annuals whose seeds you want to save.

- When autumn leaves pile up on the lawn, forget the leaf rake. Shred leaves into fine particles with a mulching mower. Or use a bagging mower to collect shredded leaves mixed with grass clippings, perfect for mulching or adding to the compost pile.
- Postpone pruning chores until winter to avoid stimulating tender new growth this autumn.
- Empty and stack clay pots in a shed, garage, or basement. If you lack space to store large clay pots, empty them and turn them upside down outdoors.
- If the weather is dry, continue watering. Pay special attention to newly planted perennials, shrubs, trees, and grass.
- Mow any large patch of wildflowers, allowing spent flowers and foliage to remain where they fall.
- Skim autumn leaves from the surface of the water garden before they sink to the bottom. Remove hardy lilies and bog plants from their perches and set the pots on the bottom of the pond. If your pool is less than 2 feet deep, wrap the pots in a tarp and store the plants in a cool, dark place (about 40 degrees) all winter.
- Continue to mow the grass until growth stops.
- Don't panic if you see some evergreen needles yellowing and dropping, a natural autumn occurrence. Do clean out any bunch of dead needles that accumulates in a dwarf conifer or other dense evergreen.
- Enjoy fall-blooming perennials such as boltonia, monkshood, toad lily, and willow-leaved sunflower.
- Edge perennial beds.
- Create a brighter winter landscape by planting not only evergreens but also trees or shrubs that have colorful bark or persistent fruit.

November

- While the memories of this year's garden successes and failures are still fresh in your mind, make a list of plans and plants to make next year's garden the best yet.
- Put any leftover seeds in an air-tight container and store in a cool place.

- Clean and drain sprayers and loosen fittings. Move any liquid fertilizers or pesticides indoors, where they won't freeze. Store them out of children's reach.

VEGETABLES, FRUITS, AND HERBS

- Clean up plant debris in the vegetable garden to reduce problems next year with pests and diseases such as squash bugs and tomato blight. Spread a 1- to 2-inch layer of compost or manure on the bare soil and spade or till it in, leaving the surface rough. Pull up stakes and remove tomato cages. Before you store cages, remove any trace of fungus disease by cleaning with a solution of 1 part chlorine bleach to 9 parts water.
- Cut and remove the above-ground growth of rhubarb and asparagus after it's completely dead. Spread a 1- to 2-inch layer of compost around the plants.
- Combat black rot in grapes by cleaning up leaves and fruit mummies.
- Wait until the ground freezes to apply winter mulch over strawberry plants.
- Check stored green tomatoes often and throw out any that start to rot. Bring a few firm tomatoes at a time to the kitchen counter, where they can ripen at room temperature.
- Dig leeks before the ground freezes. Store them in a bucket of sand in a cool spot, such as a basement.
- Harvest horseradish and store whole roots in the refrigerator. Make small batches of sauce as needed.

FLOWERING PLANTS

- Cut peonies to the ground and remove the stems and leaves. Also remove the foliage of any disease-prone perennials, such as garden phlox, irises, and asters. If disease has not been a problem, allow the dead tops of other perennials to remain for winter interest and to attract birds to the garden to feed on seeds. Resist the urge to remove the dead tops of chrysanthemums, which are more likely to survive the winter if left in place.
- Finish planting spring-blooming bulbs such as daffodils, tulips, and hyacinths before the ground freezes. Also plant some bulbs in pots

for blooms in late winter. Water the soil, then put each pot in a bag. Refrigerate hyacinths twelve weeks (unless you buy pre-chilled bulbs), daffodils twelve to fourteen weeks, and tulips fifteen weeks.

- Start narcissus bulbs indoors for December blooms. Fill a shallow bowl two-thirds full of stones, then cover the surface with bulbs. Add more stones but leave the top halves of the bulbs exposed. Add enough water to barely touch the base of the bulbs. Set the bowl in a cool, bright spot.
- After temperatures fall below 20 degrees, protect grafted roses with a 10-inch-deep soil mound. Ignore this step if you have hardy shrub roses.

AROUND THE YARD

- Clean autumn leaves from gutters. On the lawn, use a mulching mower to "erase" the last of the leaves, or use a bagging mower to collect shredded leaves mixed with grass clippings. Use the bag's contents to mulch around strawberries or perennials, or add the contents to the compost pile.
- Stockpile autumn leaves for use as mulch or soil conditioner. Avoid walnut leaves which can harm many garden plants.
- Renew faded names on perennial plant labels and replace any brittle plastic markers with metal labels.
- Use warm autumn days to rid perennial beds of weeds such as henbit and chickweed, which bloom and set seed in early spring.
- Fill any low spots in the lawn so water won't collect and freeze. After you put your lawnmower away for the season, fertilize cool-season grasses such as bluegrass with a slow-release fertilizer. Avoid fertilizing warm-season grasses such as zoysia.
- Clean up brush piles near the garden where rabbits could hide. Protect young trees and shrubs by installing a cage of chicken-wire fence fabric around vulnerable plants. Stop winter deer damage before it starts by spraying woody plants with a repellent now.
- If the weather is dry, give perennials, shrubs, and trees an extra drink, paying particular attention to evergreens or any recently planted specimens. Also water the compost pile.
- Spread a big circle of bark chips or other mulch 2 inches deep around

any fall-planted perennials to give the roots more time to get established before the ground freezes.

- If you have a young tree with tender bark, such as a beech or maple, shade the trunk for the winter with a burlap screen or a white, spiral vinyl cover.
- Postpone spraying an anti-transpirant such as Wilt-Pruf on boxwoods, hollies, and other broadleaf evergreens until after Thanksgiving.
- Clean and remove rust from tools, then lightly coat metal parts with Jig-a-Loo or WD-40. Sand rough wood handles and give all wood surfaces a coat of linseed oil.
- Before the first hard freeze, drain the sprinkler system (unless it is a self-draining type). Unhook, drain, and put away garden hoses. Turn off the water supply to outdoor faucets if they aren't freeze-proof.
- Enjoy ornamental grasses such as feather reed grass, little bluestem, and switchgrass. Wait until March to cut ornamental grasses to the ground.
- Skim autumn leaves from the surface of the water garden before they sink to the bottom.

December

- Use evergreen trimmings to decorate window boxes and other outdoor containers. For color, gather attractive dried flowers from the garden, such as those of sedums or coneflowers. Add berried branches from shrubs such as winterberry or coralberry.
- When you eat oranges or grapefruits, save their peels in the freezer. Plan to scatter the peels in your garden beds next spring to deter digging by cats.
- If you're transporting gift plants on a cold day, do your best to protect them from chilling. Set each pot in a large plastic bag. Tie it closed, allowing plenty of room-temperature air to puff up the bag. Then hurry each plant to a warm car in its own large, roomy shopping bag. Once it's safely indoors, be sure to poke a hole in the foil wrap to allow excess water to drain out of the pot when you water.
- Store completely cooled fireplace ashes in a covered metal can outdoors to use as a source of potassium in the garden next spring.

(Use the ashes sparingly in most of the garden and not at all around acid-loving plants such as blueberries and azaleas.)

- To preserve leftover seeds to plant next spring, wrap up in tissues a half-cup of dry milk powder or silica gel. Secure the packet with a rubber band and put it with your seeds in an air-tight container.
- When selecting a Christmas tree, gently grasp a branch between your thumb and forefinger and pull it toward you. For the freshest tree, select one with the fewest needles that come off in your hand. Before bringing the tree into the house, thump it on the ground to remove dead needles and dormant insects.
- Retrieve potted amaryllis bulbs that have been resting two months or more. Water thoroughly and set the pots in a bright, cool spot. Water only sparingly at first. As soon as new growth appears, water whenever the soil feels dry to the touch.
- Try to avoid moving a Christmas cactus after it begins to bloom, since a change of location often makes buds drop. If your Christmas cactus looks shriveled and discolored, suspect over-watering. Water less frequently, and don't allow water to stand in the saucer.
- Help your houseplants make the most of the low levels of light available in winter by keeping their leaves dust-free. Reduce water and don't fertilize during winter's shortest days.
- Watch for houseplant pests, which multiply quickly indoors in a heated house. If your houseplants are infested with large numbers of pests, spray them with insecticidal soap. If you see any waxy, stationary scales on stems or leaves, wipe them off with a damp paper towel before spraying.
- Kill fungus gnat larvae by drenching the soil with a solution of 2 tablespoons insecticidal soap in a quart of warm water. Repeat in a month. To keep fungus gnats under control, allow the soil to dry out as much as possible between waterings.

VEGETABLES, FRUITS, AND HERBS

- After the soil freezes, tuck a 1- to 2-inch blanket of mulch around strawberry plants to protect their shallow roots.
- Check stored apples, potatoes, onions, and winter squash. Remove any that show signs of spoiling. Also break off and remove any potato sprouts.

FLOWERING PLANTS

- Check stored tubers, roots, and tender bulbs for decay. If the packing material surrounding dahlias feels dry, dampen it slightly.
- Select a poinsettia that has no drooping or yellowing leaves. Avoid plants that are already dropping the tiny yellow flowers in the center of the "blooms" as well as any plant still wearing its plastic shipping sleeve.
- After the soil freezes, tuck a 2-inch blanket of mulch around any shallow-rooted perennials.

AROUND THE YARD

- Reapply deer repellents, alternating among several different products so deer don't get used to a particular taste or smell.
- If you live on a busy street often treated with salt and other chemicals, erect a burlap screen or other winter barrier around your prized trees and shrubs to stop salt spray.
- Water evergreens any time the soil isn't frozen or covered with snow.
- Take your mower in for a tune-up this winter, before the professionals who sharpen mower blades and tune up engines get swamped with spring work.
- Prune any tree branches damaged in an ice or snow storm to prevent further tearing.

INDEX

calibrachoa, 17, 18, 26, 29

calla lily (fig. 42), 103, 110

Callirhoe. See poppy mallow

camass, 92, 94, 98

Campanula. See bellflower

canna, 103, 104–5

cantaloupe, 167

cape daisy (fig. 6), 11, 12

Capsicum annuum. See pepper, ornamental

cardinal climber, 137, 142

cardinal flower (fig. 33), 80–81

carex, 68

Carpathian harebell, 50

carrot, 168

caryopteris, 113

castor bean, 2, 4

Catharanthus roseus. See vinca, flowering

catmint, 37, 40, 61

cauliflower, 159–60

Ceanothus americanus. See New Jersey tea

celandine poppy, 85

celeriac, 178

celery root, 178

celosia, 26

Centaurea cyanus. See bachelor buttons

Ceratostigma. See plumbago

Chelone. See turtlehead

cherry, 187–88; controlling birds, 188; disease control, 188, 189; insect control, 188, 189; pie (sour), 187–88; sweet, 183

chervil, 204

China pinks, 10, 12, 14

Chinese artichoke, 177–78

chives, 209, 211

chokeberry, black (fig. 44), 197–98

chrysanthemum, 60

cilantro, 205, 211

Cimicifuga. See snakeroot

cinnamon vine, 137

clematis, 137–38; pruning, 141; tube (*heracleifolia*), 35–36, 38; wilt, 138

cleome, 3, 5, 6, 27

Clethra. See summersweet

climbing snapdragon, 137, 144

colchicum (fig. 40), 92, 94, 97–98

coleus, 17, 31–32

Colocasia. See elephant's ear

columbine, 36, 54

compass plant, 71

composting, 147–48

coneflower, 44, 72, 75; disease, 76

Consolida. See larkspur

container plants, 28–31, 151, 153, 204, 212–13

coralbell, 51–52, 70

coralberry, 114, 128

coreopsis (fig. 20), 37, 45–46

corn, sweet, 179–80

corn salad (fig. 58), 175, 177

Cornus. See dogwood

corydalis, yellow, 70

Corylus. See Harry Lauder's walking stick

cosmos, 2, 5, 6, 26

cotoneaster, 114, 126–27

crocus, 92, 95; fall-flowering, 97

crosnes, 177–78

cucumber, 165–66

culver's root (fig. 35), 44, 80

cup flower (fig. 10), 12, 27

cup plant (fig. 29), 44, 72–73

currant, alpine, 113

cushion spurge, 37, 91

cypress vine (fig. 51), 142

daffodil, 92–93, 94

dahlberg daisy (fig. 7), 2, 5, 6, 27

dahlia, 101–2, 103

daisy, African. *See* osteospermum
daisy, cape (fig. 6), 11, 12
daisy, dahlberg (fig. 7), 2, 5, 6, 27
daisy, Swan River, 10
Dalea purpurea. See purple prairie clover
daphne, 114, 125–26
Datura metel. See angel's trumpet
daylily, 37, 41, 47–48
deer, plants favored by, 93, 99,
deer-resistant plants, 5, 65, 77, 92, 112, 118, 124, 130, 212
delphinium, 61
Dianthus chinensis. See China pinks
diascia, 10–11
Dicentra cucullaria. See Dutchman's breeches
Dicentra spectabilis. See bleeding heart
diervilla, 114, 118
dill, 207–8, 211, 212
diseases, of annuals: aster yellows, 23; botrytis, 22; downy mildew, 16; gray mold, 22; powdery mildew, 8, 19
———, of berries, 194
———, of bulbs: canna virus, 105; lily virus, 99
———, of fruit trees: apple scab, 185; bacterial canker, 188; black knot, 188–89; brown rot, 189; cedar/apple rust, 189; fire blight, 184, 185, 187; leaf spot, 189
———, of grapes, 190–91
———, of herbs: downy mildew, 203; fusarium wilt, 203; powdery mildew, 203
———, of perennials, 62–63; aster yellows in coneflower, 76; daylily rust, 63; hosta crown rot, 64; leaf streak, 63; mildew, 53, 57
———, of shrubs: bacterial blight,

125; crown gall, 133–34; powdery mildew, 120, 125; stem canker, 129
———, of vegetables: bacterial wilt, 166; corn smut, 148; early blight, 148; late blight, 148, 156–57; septoria leaf spot, 148
———, of vines: clematis wilt, 138
———, of wildflowers: aster yellows, 76; mildew, 72, 82
dividing perennials, 61–62
dog-tooth violet, 92, 95
dogwood, 114, 129
Dryopteris. See ferns, wood
Dutchman's breeches, 83–84
Dutchman's pipe, 137, 141
Dyer's greenwood, 113, 114, 130

Echinacea: *pallida*, 72; *purpurea*, 44, 72, 75, 76
edamame, 162
eggplant, 154–55
Egyptian star-flower, 6, 27
elderberry, 133
elephant's ear, 103, 108
Eleutherococcus. See aralia
endive, 175
English ivy, 137, 141
epimedium (fig. 17), 36, 44, 57, 70
Eranthis. See winter aconite
Eryngium amethystinum. See sea holly
Eryngium yuccifolium. See rattlesnake master
Erythronium. See dog-tooth violet
Eucomis. See pineapple lily
Eupatorium. See Joe-Pye weed
euphorbia, 6, 9, 37, 91
Eurybia divaricata. See aster, white wood
Eustoma grandiflorum. See lisianthus
evergreen shrubs: broadleaf, 130–31; pruning, 132

Fallopia, 141
false indigo (fig. 26), 75, 78–79;
    dwarf, 78
fan flower, 29
feather reed grass, 66–67
fennel, 207–8; bulbing (Florence),
    178–79
ferns, 59; Christmas, 59; Japanese
    painted, 59; maidenhair (fig. 21),
    59; wood, 59
fescue, blue, 67
Filipendula rubra. See queen-of-the-
    prairie
firecracker vine, 137, 143
five-leaf aralia (fig. 48), 113, 117
flax, perennial, 40
floating row cover, 153, 169, 175
floss flower, 2, 10, 27
foamflower, 36, 38–39, 65, 70, 85
foamy bells, 70
forsythia, 111–12, 115
four o'clock, 2, 27
French tarragon, 207
fritillaria, 92, 94, 96
fruit trees, 183–89; cross-pollination,
    183; dwarf, 183–85; organic
    disease control, 189; suckers, 184;
    winter trunk protection, 188
fungicides, 63; baking soda, 63;
    GreenCure, 63; sulfur, 63, 189

Gaillardia. See blanket flower
Galanthus. See snowdrop
garden cleanup, 147–48, 165, 181
garlic, 171–72
gas plant, 65
gayfeather. *See* blazing star
gazania, 6, 27
Genista. See Dyer's greenwood
Gentiana. See bottle gentian
geranium, annual, 20–21

geranium, perennial, 37, 70; bigroot,
    66; wild, 85
Geranium macrorrhizum, 66
Geranium maculatum, 85
Geum triflorum. See prairie smoke
ginger, wild, 70, 84
gladioli. *See* gladiolus
gladiolus, 103, 106–7
globe amaranth (fig. 9), 2, 27
glory-of-the-snow, 92, 94
goatsbeard (fig. 22), 37, 53; dwarf, 42
golden Alexander, 44, 84
goldenrod, 45
gomphrena (fig. 9), 2, 27
gophers, 99
grape, 190–91; diseases, 190–91; har-
    vesting, 190; pruning, 190
grape hyacinth, 92, 94, 96
grasses, ornamental, 66–68, 75, 87;
    blue fescue, 67; blue oatgrass,
    66; bottle brush, 68; care of, 67;
    cool-season, 67; feather reed,
    66–67; Japanese forest, 68; little
    bluestem, 75, 87; northern sea
    oats, 68; prairie dropseed, 75,
    87; purple moor, 67; for shade,
    67–68; switch grass, 66, 87; tufted
    hair, 67; warm-season, 67
grasses, prairie, 75, 87; little blue-
    stem, 75, 87; prairie dropseed, 75,
    87; switch grass, 66, 87
Grecian windflower, 92, 96–97
ground covers, 68–70; for large
    areas, 70
guinea-hen flower, 96

Hakonechloa. See Japanese forest
    grass
Harry Lauder's walking stick (fig.
    43), 130
Helenium. See Helen's flower

kale, 160; ornamental, 12, 13
kerria. *See* Japanese kerria
kiss-me-over-the-garden-gate, 3, 27
Kochia scoparia. See summer cypress
kohlrabi (fig. 57), 160–61
Koreanspice viburnum, 116, 123

lady's mantle, 43, 70
lamb's ear, 40, 66
lamb's lettuce, 177
Lamiastrum. See Herman's Pride yellow archangel
lamium (fig. 15), 43–44, 66
Lamprocapnos. See bleeding heart
lantana, 27, 28
larkspur, 3, 27
Lathyrus. See perennial pea
lavender, 211–12
leadplant, 40
leek (fig. 60), 172
legume inoculant, 162
lemon balm (fig. 63), 205–6, 212
lemon grass, 206
lemon verbena, 206
Lenten rose (fig. 13), 36, 38
lespedeza. *See* bushclover
lettuce, 174–75; summer crisp (Batavian), 175
Liatris. See blazing star
licorice mint. *See* anise hyssop
licorice plant, 30
lilac, 115, 124–25; Korean, 115, 124; Manchurian, 115, 124
lily, 98–100; Orienpets, 100
Linum. See flax
lisianthus, 6, 24–25
little bluestem, 75, 87
lobelia, 9
Lobelia cardinalis. See cardinal flower
Lobularia maritime. See sweet alyssum

Lonicera. See honeysuckle vine
loosestrife, purple, substitutes for, 81
love-in-a-mist (fig. 1), 3, 27, 32
love-lies-bleeding (fig. 5), 32
lungwort, 37, 58, 70
Lycoris. See magic lily

mache. *See* corn salad
magic lily (fig. 41), 100–101
Malabar spinach, 144, 176
malva, 4
mandevilla, 137, 143–44
marigold, 6, 22–23, 27
Matthiola incana. See stocks
Maurandella. See climbing snapdragon
mayapple, 83
meadow rue (fig. 19), 52–53
melampodium (fig. 3), 3, 6, 27
melon, 166–67
Mertensia. See Virginia bluebell
mesclun, 174
Mexican hat, 73
Mexican shell flower. *See* tiger flower
Mexican sunflower, 4, 27
mignonette, 33
milkweed, 40, 73, 81; butterfly, 40, 73; swamp, 81
mint, 204
Mirabilis. See four o'clock
Missouri primrose, 40
mockorange, 115, 126
monarda, 45. *See also* beebalm
monkshood, azure (fig. 11), 36, 38
moonflower (fig. 55), 137, 142
morning glory, 137, 141–42
moss rose, 3, 5, 6, 9–10, 27
mulching, 146, 152

naked ladies. *See* magic lily
nemesia, 11, 12